T0280172

Indigenous DC

Indigenous DC

▲

NATIVE
PEOPLES
AND THE
NATION'S
CAPITAL

ELIZABETH RULE

▼

Georgetown University Press / Washington, DC

The publisher is not responsible for third-party websites or their content. URL links were active at time of publication.

Library of Congress Cataloging-in-Publication Data

Names: Rule, Elizabeth, author.
Title: Indigenous DC : native peoples and the nation's capital / Elizabeth Rule.
Other titles: Indigenous District of Columbia
Description: Washington, DC : Georgetown University Press, [2023] | Includes bibliographical references and index.
Identifiers: LCCN 2022014036 (print) | LCCN 2022014037 (ebook) | ISBN 9781647123208 (hardcover) | ISBN 9781647123222 (ebook)
Subjects: LCSH: Indians of North America—Washington (D.C.) | Indian activists—Washington (D.C.) | Indians of North America—Museums. | Indians of North America—Material culture. | Monuments—Washington (D.C.) | Indian art—Washington (D.C.)
Classification: LCC E78.D6 R85 2023 (print) | LCC E78.D6 (ebook) | DDC 975.300497—dc23/eng/20220726
LC record available at https://lccn.loc.gov/2022014036
LC ebook record available at https://lccn.loc.gov/2022014037

♾ This paper meets the requirements of ANSI/NISO Z39.48-1992 (Permanence of Paper).

24 23   9 8 7 6 5 4 3 2   First printing

Printed in the United States of America

Cover design by Erin Kirk
Interior design by Matthew Williams

For my family.

CONTENTS

ILLUSTRATIONS

ACKNOWLEDGMENTS

This book originated from my work with dozens of incredible, up-and-coming Indigenous students participating in the Native American Political Leadership Program; these relationships exemplified the age-old adage of teachers learning equally—if not more—from their students, and for this I am grateful. Similarly, the mentors in my life—Matthew Guterl, Françoise Hamlin, Tom Brooks, and Eileen Findlay, to name a few—have supported my development as a writer, researcher, and thinker, especially in the creation of this first book project. I was able to carry out this work with the essential support from the MIT Solve Indigenous Communities Fellowship as well as the Library Company of Philadelphia's Innovation Award. I owe many thanks, also, to Al Bertrand and his guidance as editor of this work. It has been a pleasure and privilege to write this text in Washington, DC, and I am thankful to the Indigenous and scholarly communities in the area for welcoming me into this space and showing me reflections of our people throughout the city. I first came to our nation's capital as a young Native intern myself, through the support of the Chickasaw Nation, which has bolstered my educational and professional pursuits in a variety of ways for over ten years. I'm proud to say, "Chikashsha saya!"

This book is dedicated to my family, without whom this project would not be possible. To Mom, who taught me how to write and always entertained my intellectual curiosity. To Dad, who inspired me to serve our community and fearlessly advocate for Indian Country. To Katy, who has been by me through it all, including relocating to Washington together. To Ricardo, my greatest support, favorite person, and the best conversation partner.

Introduction

Washington, DC, Is Indian Land

The Washington Monument. The National Mall. The White House. Capitol Hill. These are the iconic images most people call to mind when visualizing the capital of the United States. Lesser known are the sites of Indigenous importance found throughout the city testifying to the historic tribal nations that have lived on this land since time immemorial as well as the contemporary Indigenous communities that call the District of Columbia home to this day. While imposing government buildings, striking national monuments, and a cosmopolitan urban culture aptly characterize the District, these elements are a far cry from society's stereotypical Native American imagery of the Wild West. Make no mistake, however: Washington, DC, is Indian land.

Although Indigenous peoples lived upon the lands now known as the District of Columbia for thousands of years prior to European settlement, Native Americans represent the least populous racial demographic in the District today. DC Health Matters Collaborative reports that out of DC's more than 717,000 residents in 2021, a total of 2,573 identify as American Indian / Alaska Native, and 513 identify as Native Hawaiian / Pacific Islander, composing 0.36 percent and 0.07 percent of the population, respectively.[1] One can reasonably assume that these numbers are low and that additional Indigenous individuals are not captured in this data but rather fall under the nonspecified "2 or more races" category.[2] These local racial demographics also fall below the national average, where the American Indian and Alaska Native communities reach 9.7 million, or 2.3 percent of the total United States population.[3] Of those included in this count, 3.7 million, or approximately 1 percent, reported American Indian or Alaska Native as their single racial identifier and 5.9 million, or roughly 1.8 percent, identified being American Indian or Alaska Native in combination with one or more other races; those who identify as Native Hawaiians alone or in combination with other races compose just under one-half of a percentage point of the nation's population.[4]

While this community may be relatively small, especially in Washington, DC, we remain mighty and proud. Well over a dozen organizations and advocacy groups in the DC area—including the Native American Rights Fund, the Native American Contractors Association, the National Congress of American Indians, the National Indian Education Association, the Bureau of Indian Affairs, the National Council of Urban Indian Health, the National American Indian Housing Council, the National Museum of the American Indian, the National Indian Gaming Association, the Indian Law Resource Center, the American Indian Society of Washington DC, the National Association of Tribal Historic Preservation Officers, the Association on American Indian Affairs, the Native American Financial Services Association, and more—serve the Indigenous community across all sectors of business and life. Nearly all of these offices operate on a national scale and perform the essential task of furthering Indigenous issues in the United States' capital city. They are staffed by Native people representing tribal nations headquartered throughout the country, and many intentionally come to DC precisely to affect positive change through these positions. Cohorts of Indigenous students similarly flock to the halls of Congress each summer, joining the ranks of DC's well-known intern cadres in order to grow professionally and become the next generation of tribal leaders. Visiting delegations of tribal government officials regularly make their way to DC for business negotiations, professional conferences, and agency meetings. Ho-Chunk anthropologist Reyna K. Ramirez identifies such urban places frequented by intertribal Native communities as "hubs" imbued with the "power to strengthen Native identity and provide a sense of belonging, as well as to increase the political power of Native peoples."[5] Nowhere in the world is the essence of the nation-to-nation, government-to-government relationship shared between sovereign tribal nations and the US federal government more readily apparent. In this way, too, Washington, DC, exists as the political capital of Indian Country as a whole.

In addition to the diaspora of Native people who call this city home, these lands remain the traditional ancestral homelands of Indigenous groups whose lives here predated the very existence of Washington and even the United States. Fifteen miles south of the District, present-day Accokeek, Maryland, hosts the site of the historic Piscataway capital, Moyaone, situated at the meeting of the Potomac River and Piscataway Creek.[6] Capt. John Smith mapped this location and its Piscataway residents in 1608, but scholars and traditional teachers have indicated that Indigenous peoples inhabited Moyaone for thousands of years.[7] The Piscataway, an Algonkian people, migrated to this western Chesapeake territory after splitting from the Lenni Lenape and Nanticoke further north.[8] Governed by a *tayac*, or chief, the Piscataway confederacy included multiple subtribes, allying Anacostan, Portobac, Mattawoman, Nanjemoy, and potentially more, all centered around Moyaone.[9] The Anacostan, also known as Nacotchtank or Nacotchanke, established their primary village in present-day Southeast DC near Joint Base Anacostia–Bolling, along the eastern shore of the Potomac and Anacostia Rivers.[10] Additional Nacotchtank villages spanned from today's Palisades neighborhood in the northwestern corner of Washington to Arlington, Virginia, demonstrating their territorial expanse across the entirety of what is now the nation's capital.[11]

Beginning in 1564, disease brought by European settlers devastated Indigenous populations in Maryland and the surrounding areas; by the mid–seventeenth century, only approximately 10 percent of these communities remained.[12] This period additionally saw dramatic land loss for the Piscataway. King Charles officially deeded their homelands to Lord Baltimore in 1632, and within two years' time, European settlers had flooded the territory.[13] By the turn of the century, the Piscataway sought refuge from encroachment by allying with their northern Seneca neighbors and resettled first on Harrison Island, approximately forty miles northwest of Washington, and then on Heater's Island, fifteen miles further up the Potomac River.[14] The few remaining Piscataway eventually established a presence in Pennsylvania alongside their Nanticoke relatives, where they lived for approximately half of the eighteenth century.[15] A faction of this group fully integrated into Nanticoke society and are recounted in this historical record as one and the same from this period forward, while another subset of the Piscataway population permanently established themselves among the Iroquois, identifying today as Wolf Clan of the Cayuga at Six Nations Reserve in Canada.[16] By the onset of the War of 1812, historian Gabrielle Tayac (Piscataway) recounts, a mere twenty-five Piscataway individuals existed as an independent entity.[17]

This Piscataway band journeyed back to their traditional lands in Maryland in the early nineteenth century.[18] The few remaining families made their homes in Prince George's and Charles Counties and, faced with a segregationist society, "suffered an attrition of ethnic consciousness."[19] The national, pan-Indian American Indian Movement of the 1960s and 1970s ushered in a cultural revitalization and political reawakening of the Piscataway.[20] Community leaders Billy Tayac, Turkey Tayac, and Avery Wind Rider chartered the Piscataway Conoy Indians, Incorporated, in 1974 as a tribal service organization that welcomed Piscataway descendants, Indigenous peoples affiliated with other tribes, and non-Native allies alike into its ranks.[21] During this time,

Chief Turkey Tayac led the campaign to legally protect the Piscataway sacred site of Moyaone by placing twenty acres of land into federal trust to create Piscataway National Park, thereby securing Piscataway cultural and ceremonial access to this vital land plot.[22] With the backing of tribal leaders around the nation, an act of Congress in 1979 ensured that Chief Turkey Tayac would be interred at this traditional burial ground for Piscataway chiefs alongside generations of ancestors before him.[23]

The Piscataway community remains active in the twenty-first century. On January 9, 2012, Maryland governor Martin O'Malley issued an executive order extending state recognition to both the Piscataway Indian Nation and the Piscataway Conoy Tribe, the latter of which is divided into the Piscataway Conoy Confederacy and Subtribes and the Cedarville Band of Piscataway Indians.[24] They are the first and only state-recognized tribes in Maryland; the state has no federally recognized tribes.[25] This status supports the Indigenous communities by making available new resources in the areas of public health, education, cultural preservation, and more. For Billy Redwing Tayac, late chief of the Piscataway Indian Nation, state recognition carries weight because "it says we're still here. We're not invisible people. That's very important."[26]

Neighboring the Piscataway, the Powhatan Paramountcy once dominated a huge swath of what we now recognize as Virginia, known then as Tsenacommacah or Tsenacomoco.[27] This territory—which in the early seventeenth century ranged from present-day Tysons, Virginia, down and along the western Potomac riverbank all the way to the mouth of the Chesapeake Bay and across to the Eastern Shore peninsula—made up the traditional ancestral homelands of the chiefdom's more than thirty distinct communities.[28] Powhatan, or Wahunsonacock, led this alliance and grew it to become the largest and most powerful paramount chiefdom in the region.[29] Historians estimate that fifteen thousand individuals lived under Powhatan's rule at its peak and that, in terms of military power, the chiefdom commanded between ten and twenty times the might wielded by the Jamestown colonists.[30] Iconic figures of American history such as Pocahontas, John Rolfe, and Capt. John Smith hailed from and interacted with, respectively, the Powhatan Paramountcy.

Of particular relevance to this history of Washington, DC, the Doeg, also known as the Dogue or Tauxenent, established themselves as the northernmost Powhatan tribe. Living throughout what are now Fairfax and Prince William Counties, Doeg territory extended approximately thirty-five miles from Tysons to Prince William Forest Park. Like many of their neighbors in the Powhatan Paramountcy and Piscataway Confederacy, the Doeg suffered greatly from the disease, violence, and land loss wrought by settler colonialism. Members of this group responded to the rapidly changing environment of the mid–seventeenth century by moving their villages east of the Potomac River to join with other tribal groups or by relocating south to the Rappahannock River.[31] Nevertheless, some descendants of the Doeg community continue to identify Tysons, Virginia, as well as Washington, DC, and the surrounding areas as home to this day.[32]

Although the historic Doeg—and, by extension, Powhatan Paramountcy—land base is now incorporated into the state of Virginia, in the late eighteenth century these upper reaches of Powhatan's domain fell within the original boundaries of the District of Columbia. Forty original "boundary stones" erected in 1791 and 1792 outlined the hundred-square-mile District following an agreement between Alexander Hamilton, a representative of the northern states, and Thomas Jefferson, a voice for the southern states, that authorized the establishment of the capital in July 1790.[33] These stones, installed at one-mile intervals, formed a near-perfect square with its corners aligned to the cardinal directions.[34] The Washington of today maintains its original border with Maryland and three of its vertex boundary stones, the northern of which is set just west of downtown Silver Spring, the eastern of which stands at the intersection of Eastern and Southern Avenues Northwest, and the southern of which remains in Jones Point Park in Alexandria. On July 9, 1846, Congress voted to retrocede the thirty-one square miles originally given by Virginia to create the District of Columbia, returning historic Doeg lands once again to the jurisdiction of the commonwealth.[35]

Today the state is home to seven federally recognized Indigenous nations: the Chickahominy Indian Tribe, Chickahominy Indians Eastern Division, Monacan Indian Nation, Nansemond Indian Nation, Pamunkey Indian Tribe, Rappahannock Tribe, and the Upper Mattaponi Indian Tribe. These tribes—along with the state-recognized Cheroenhaka (Nottoway), Mattaponi, Nottoway, and Patawomeck—are headquartered within the southern portion of the state. Most but not all of these identify with the historic Powhatan Paramountcy, although today they operate independently as distinct sovereign nations. The US Department of the Interior granted federal recognition to the Pamunkey Indian Tribe in 2015, making it the state's first federally recognized tribe effective January 28, 2016.[36] Landmark legislation passed through Congress approved the federal recognition of the six other tribal nations through the Thomasina E. Jordan Indian Tribes of Virginia Federal Recognition Act, which was signed into law by President Donald Trump in January 2018.

Amid centuries of evolving land occupancy and relationality, the fact that Washington has been an Indigenous place since ancient times remains indisputable. Archaeological evidence points to the presence of Indigenous peoples in the Washington, DC, area stretching back between eleven thousand and twenty thousand years.[37] Ancient tools unearthed in the District, such as stone axes and projectile points, date back to between 8,000 and 500 BC; such tools are thought to have been fashioned out of materials taken from quarries in present-day Rock Creek Park.[38] In 1975, when President Gerald Ford installed a swimming pool on White House grounds, the excavated White House lands were found to include a number of Indigenous artifacts, including seventeen pieces of quartz/quartzite, two quartz projectile points, a piece of broken pottery, and a fragment of biface originating from the Archaic to Late Woodlands periods.[39] William Henry Holmes, a noted city archaeologist, observed that such remnants of Native life in the nation's capital are so prevalent in the area that "the laborer who sits by the wayside breaking boulders for our streets passes them by the thousands beneath his hammer; it is literally true that in this city, the capital of a civilized nation is paved with the art remains of a [Native] race who occupied its site in the shadowy past."[40]

While such ancient artifacts largely remain out of view of the public eye, additional remnants of precontact Indigenous cultures testify to a Native presence in the DC area: place names. From the neighborhood to the river, and from schools to parks, the word "Anacostia" appears throughout Washington. "Anacostia" is a variant of "Nacotchtank" as used by seventeenth-century English Jesuits who settled in the area, and, thus, the Nacotchtank became known as Anacostans.[41] Like the Anacostia, the Potomac River's name harkens back to the original inhabitants of the land. "Potomac" is an Algonquian word whose meaning relayed the river's significance as a trading hub; it has also been spelled "Patowmack," "Parawomeke," "Patawomek," and "Patawomeck" throughout the historical record.[42] "For Powhatan, Nanticoke, and Piscataway people," reads the Return to a Native Place exhibit on the Algonquian peoples of the Chesapeake on permanent view at the National Museum of the American Indian, "the power of these words links us to our ancestors."[43]

Far too often Native peoples, when discussed at all, are relegated to bygone history by our national narrative rather than discussed as modern nations and people. Indigenous historian Philip J. Deloria's *Indians in Unexpected Places* and *Playing Indian* offer sustained analyses into how popular notions of Indianness have informed American identity and modernity. Building on Deloria's work, this book shines a light on the often overlooked sites of Indigenous importance in Washington, DC, in hopes of redressing this plague of invisibility and erasure afflicting our nation's first Americans. In keeping with political theorist Kevin Bruyneel's *Settler Memory*, this text also confronts "the simultaneous absence and presence of Indigeneity . . . inherent to . . . U.S. political life" by examining Indigenous peoples within the settler-colonial seat of power: Washington, DC.[44] This way "the aim is not to tell a completely different story" about the nation's capital "but to tell the same story differently," such that settler colonialism and Indigenous resistance to it is made visible in a space broadly conceived of as synonymous with the settler state.[45] I also draw inspiration from gender studies scholar Mishuana Goeman's writings on Indigenous geographies with the intention of "understanding the processes that have defined our current spatialities in order to sustain vibrant Native futures."[46]

By encouraging readers to recognize Indigenous influences on the capital city, the purpose of this text is to show the ways in which Native peoples have lived in relationship with this land and have traveled, worked, and rallied here to advance Indigenous issues. Indigenous populations are embedded into the fabric of Washington's history, remain active in this space, and will thrive into the future of this city. It is not the intention of this text to weigh in on various contested claims to identity, land, and political power involving any of the groups mentioned herein or to provide an authoritative history of these groups. In contrast, this book contributes to the essential body of literature dedicated to contemporary Indigenous topics, with history used as a touchpoint from which we understand ourselves today and as the root from which we build our future.

Chapter 1 emphasizes the government-to-government relationship between tribes and the United States by discussing the long history of Indigenous leaders who have traveled to Washington in order to represent tribal interests in the capital city. These individuals include historic delegates as well as present-day politicians, and the chapter additionally takes up reflections of these individuals in physical sites across the District. In chapter 2 I analyze public commemorations of Indigenous figures, cultures, and histories, with specific attention granted to the operations of memory as it presents in museums, monuments, and statues. The third chapter focuses on Indigenous activism in DC, revealing how activists have brought intertribal issues to an international stage by organizing in this prominent place. Chapter 4 then turns to Native arts—murals, sculpture, and more—on view throughout the District of Columbia in order to highlight the various Indigenous cultural imprints upon the capital and the ways in which they complement the political action for which the city is known. I conclude by positing that Washington, DC, serves as the political capital of Indian Country and reflect on my work to shine a light on this Indigenous space through a digital humanities and public history mapping project, the Guide to Indigenous DC. From delegates to monuments, activism to arts, visitors and residents of the United States' capital city alike can conclude: Washington, DC, is Indian land.

NOTES

1. "American Indian / Alaskan Native Population," DC Health Matters, accessed October 18, 2021, https://www.dchealthmatters.org/demographicdata/index/view?id=1503&localeId=130951.

2. "American Indian / Alaskan Native Population."

3. "2020 Census: Native Population Increased by 86.5 Percent," *Indian Country Today*, August 13, 2021, https://indiancountrytoday.com/news/2020-census-native-population-increased-by-86-5-percent.

4. "Hawaiian/ Pacific Islander Population in US Grew Nearly 28% in 2020 Census," *KITV*, August 12, 2021, https://www.kitv.com/story/44514564/hawaiian-pacific-islander-population-in-us-grew-nearly-28-in-2020-census; and "2020 Census: Native Population Increased."

5. Renya K. Ramirez, *Native Hubs: Culture, Community, and Belonging in Silicon Valley and Beyond* (Durham, NC: Duke University Press, 2007), 3.

6. Gabrielle A. Tayac, *Spirits in the River: A Report on the Piscataway People* (Washington, DC: Smithsonian Institution, National Museum of the American Indian, 1999), 6.

7. Tayac, 7.

8. Tayac, 10.

9. Tayac, 6; and DC Women Eco-Leaders, "Interview Piscataway Indians," Youtube video, 11:04, October 7, 2014, https://www.youtube.com/watch?v=KjQ1ggMGsOU.

10. Tayac, *Spirits in the River*, 18; and Cecily Hilleary, "Native Americans Were Original Residents of Nation's Capital," *Voice of America*, January 16, 2020, https://www.voanews.com/a/usa_native-americans-were-original-residents-nations-capital/6182622.html.

11. Hilleary, "Native Americans Were Original Residents"; and "Native Peoples of Washington, DC," National Park Service, accessed October 19, 2021, https://www.nps.gov/articles/native-peoples-of-washington-dc.htm.

12. Tayac, *Spirits in the River*, 28.

13. Tayac, 7.

14. Tayac, 41.

15. Tayac, 47.

16. Tayac, 54, 55.

17. Tayac, 48.

18. Tayac, 62.

19. Tayac, 65; and Gabrielle Tayac, interview with author, October 8, 2020.

20. Tayac, *Spirits in the River*, 68; and Gabrielle Tayac, interview with author, October 8, 2020.

21. Tayac, *Spirits in the River*, 73.

22. Tayac, 77.

23. Tayac, 78.

24. Mark Miller, "Maryland Recognition in Hand, Piscataway Leaders Split on Seeking Federal Status," *Capital News Service*, January 13, 2012, https://cnsmaryland.org/2012/01/13/maryland-recognition-in-hand-piscataway-leaders-split-on-seeking-federal-status/.

25. Michael Dresser, "O'Malley Formally Recognizes Piscataway Tribe," *Baltimore Sun*, January 9, 2012, https://www.baltimoresun.com/maryland/bs-xpm-2012-01-09-bs-md-omalley-tribes-20120109-story.html.

26. Miller, "Maryland Recognition in Hand."

27. James D. Rice, "War and Politics: Powhatan Expansionism and the Problem of Native American Warfare," *William and Mary Quarterly* 77, vol. 1 (January 2020): 11; and "History," Nansemond Indian Nation, accessed October 19, 2021, https://nansemond.org/history/.

28. "New Signs, New Stories Unveiled at Freedom Hill Park," Fairfax County Virginia, accessed October 19, 2021, https://www.fairfaxcounty.gov/parks/park-news/2021/z-ir132; "Family Strength," Fairfax County Virginia, accessed October 19, 2021, https://www.fairfaxcounty.gov/parks/sites/parks/files/Assets/images/Nature%20and%20History/History/IR-132a.jpg; and James Mooney, "The Powhatan Confederacy, Past and Present," *American Anthropologist* 9, no. 1 (January–March 1907): 130; and Rice, "War and Politics," 11.

29. Rice, "War and Politics," 11.

30. Rice, 24.

31. "Native American Heritage."

32. FFXParks, "Freedom Hill Park Land Ceremony and Sign Dedication," Youtube video, 32:16, August 3, 2021, https://www.youtube.com/watch?v=X5Tlb3ZQB_Q; and "Powhatan Tribes," Powhatan Museum of Indigenous Arts and Culture, accessed October 21, 2021, http://www.powhatanmuseum.com/Powhatan_Tribes.html.

33. Marcus Baker, "The Boundary Monuments of the District of Columbia," *Records of the Columbia Historical Society* 1 (May 1897): 251; and Edwin Darby Nye, "Revisiting Washington's Forty Boundary Stones, 1972," *Records of the Columbia Historical Society* 48 (1973): 741.

34. Baker, "The Boundary Monuments of the District of Columbia," 216.

35. Tim St. Onge, "Modest Monuments: The District of Columbia Boundary Stones," *Worlds Revealed: Geography and Maps* (blog), Library of Congress, May 17, 2017, https://blogs.loc.gov/maps/2017/05/modest-monuments-the-district-of-columbia-boundary-stones/; and Richard Brownell, "The Alexandria Retrocession of 1846," *Boundary Stones*, July 8, 2016, https://boundarystones.weta.org/2016/07/08/alexandria-retrocession-1846.

36. "About the Tribe," Pamunkey Indian Tribe, accessed October 21, 2021, https://pamunkey.org/.

37. "Why A Local American Indian Tribe Doesn't Want Official Recognition," *Kojo Nnamdi Show*, February 6, 2018, https://wamu.org/story/18/02/06/why-a-local-native-american-tribe-doesnt-want-official-recognition/; "Return to a Native Place," exhibit, National Museum of the American Indian, Washington, DC; and Hilleary, "Native Americans Were Original Residents."

38. Hilleary, "Native Americans Were Original Residents"; and "Return to a Native Place."

39. Paul Chaat Smith, *Everything You Know about Indians Is Wrong* (Minneapolis: University of Minnesota Press, 2009), 60; and Robert L. Humphrey and Mary Elizabeth

Chambers, *Ancient Washington: American Indian Cultures of the Potomac Valley* (Washington, DC: George Washington University, 1977).

40. Smith, *Everything You Know about Indians Is Wrong*, 60.

41. Doug Herman, "American Indians of Washington, D.C., and the Chesapeake," American Association of Geographers, July 3, 2018, https://www.aag.org/author/doug-herman/.

42. "Indigenous Peoples, Virginia Indians, and Alexandria," City of Alexandria Virginia, August 26, 2021, https://www.alexandriava.gov/historic/info/default.aspx?id=118419.

43. "Return to a Native Place."

44. Kevin Bruyneel, *Settler Memory: The Disavowal of Indigeneity and the Politics of Race in the United States* (Chapel Hill: University of North Carolina Press, 2021), 2.

45. Bruyneel, 31.

46. Mishuana Goeman, *Mark My Words: Native Women Mapping Our Nations* (Minneapolis: University of Minnesota Press, 2013), 3.

1 Tribal Delegates in DC

The people of the Piscataway Confederacy and Powhatan Paramountcy with traditional, ancestral ties to the greater Washington area, and whose presence in the region far outdated the settler establishment of the city, are not the only Indigenous peoples to have left their mark on the nation's capital. Since 1789 scores of Native American delegates representing a variety of tribal nations have traveled to the District of Columbia.[1] For more than two centuries these distinguished tribal leaders advocated on behalf of their people for treaty rights, entered into negotiations with the federal government, established peace agreements, and sought to resolve conflict with local officials and agents.

Indian delegations peaked in the mid-1800s as the United States consolidated its power and embarked upon a campaign of western expansion—a period most notably marked by events such as the War of 1812; the Indian Removal Act of 1830, which resulted in the infamous Trail of Tears; the Mexican-American War (1846–48); and the American Civil War (1861–65). These national developments prompted increased diplomatic meetings between tribal nations and the federal government. During this same time US Supreme Court Chief Justice John Marshall defined the relationship between American Indian tribes and the United States through his rulings in a trio of cases, now referred to as the Marshall Trilogy. The Marshall Trilogy has gone on to become a cornerstone of federal Indian law, laying the groundwork for the legal concept of tribes' inherent sovereignty, their status as "domestic dependent nations," and the federal government's trust responsibility to them.

During their time in Washington, tribal delegates regularly met with the president of the United States, secretary of the Department of the Interior, commissioner of Indian Affairs, members of Congress, and other high-ranking government officials. One itinerary for an 1857–58 delegation of ninety representatives from across thirteen tribal nations included a slew of government meetings and treaty signings, alongside events ranging from balls and theater performances to tours of the Smithsonian Institution.[2] Dakota delegate Little Crow offers insight into the experiences of the delegations in the new environment by remarking to Acting Commissioner Charles E. Mix, "I have come a long way and intend, while in your village, to walk your streets as a proud man."[3] The delegates' striking presence in the capital served as the impetus for the Smithsonian Institution's first photography collection, a project heralded by the first secretary of the Smithsonian, which grew to include thousands of delegate portraits by the turn of the century.[4]

While some of these delegations resulted in strong diplomatic relations, others proved more confrontational. Attorneys began accompanying the trips to Washington and representing their tribal clients in dealing with the federal government in 1824. The first to do so was Georgetown-trained Choctaw lawyer James L. McDonald, a key figure in safeguarding the Choctaw's Mississippian territory from land encroachment and securing adequate compensation for lands ceded in Arkansas.[5] In another instance, four Kānaka Maoli (Native Hawaiian) delegates delivered petitions to President William McKinley and Congress in 1897 demonstrating that a full 95 percent of the Kānaka Maoli population did not support the US annexation of Hawaii.[6] Despite these protests, McKinley annexed Hawaii one year later; in 1959, it became the fiftieth state admitted into the Union.

Historian of the American West Herman J. Viola has also pointed out the mixed legacy of these tribal delegations. He notes that for the Indigenous nations, delegate meetings provided opportunities to act out their inherent sovereignty and deal with the United States on a government-to-government basis. The federal government, however, often approached these gatherings as efforts to subsume tribes under federal power and encourage assimilation into Euro-American culture.

Many tribal delegates completed multiple diplomatic trips between the capital and their homelands, while some established new homes in their workplace. Others would pass on before completing their journey home, making Washington their final resting place. The proud legacy of these tribal leaders lives on today in the built environment of Washington, DC, and in the spirit of Indigenous advocacy flowing through the town.

Dumbarton Bridge

Decades before Washington developed as the nation's capital, Georgetown existed autonomously. These neighboring areas merged in 1871, and

Dumbarton Bridge was erected to increase accessibility between the two.[7] Today Dumbarton Bridge, also known colloquially as Buffalo Bridge, remains a distinctive and celebrated landmark in the nation's capital.

Lining the bridge's sides are fifty-six busts of Oglala Lakota leader Mathó Wanáȟtake, also known as Kicking Bear (1846–1904). Kicking Bear was a long-time advocate for his people and a respected cultural leader. He became a distinguished warrior for having fought in the 1876 Battle of Little Bighorn, a victory for the Plains Indians over Lt. Col. George Armstrong Custer. Kicking Bear rose to prominence among the Lakota, in particular, for growing the popularity of the Ghost Dance, a spiritual practice believed to reunite Indigenous peoples with their ancestors in order to rid the Americas of colonists and restore peace in unity with the land.[8] In an 1890 speech, Kicking Bear described the promises the Ghost Dance offered to Native peoples: "My brothers, I bring to you the promise of a day in which there will be no white man to lay his hand on the bridle of the Indian's horse. When the red men of the prairie will rule the world and not be turned from the hunting grounds by any man."[9] This pan-Indian movement sparked a unity among tribes that posed a threat to encroaching colonial power over tribal nations and, in the eyes of white America, demonstrated a move away from the assimilationist goals of the time.

The United States responded to this spiritual revitalization with violent intervention. Thus, the press regularly referred to ghost dancers, including Kicking Bear, as "Indian hostiles" and incarcerated practitioners.[10] On December 29, 1890, under orders from President Benjamin Harrison to suppress the Ghost Dance, the US 7th Cavalry slaughtered between 270 and 300 Lakota.[11] More than half—between 170 and 200—were unarmed women and children attempting to flee the carnage.[12]

Kicking Bear and twenty-six fellow ghost dancers who survived the massacre were subsequently jailed at Fort Sheridan, Illinois.[13] After a brief period of imprisonment, he was released into the custody of Col. William F. Cody, the namesake of Buffalo Bill Cody's Wild West Show. Kicking Bear, along with a cadre of Lakota prisoners, performed in the traveling Buffalo Bill Show, including an 1891–92 European tour.[14] For proponents of westward expansion, "show Indians" served the dual purposes of showcasing American Indian culture to the world while also seeking to demonstrate the superiority of Western ways of life to Native peoples; for Ghost Dance leaders like Kicking Bear, performance and global travel offered a compelling alternative to incarceration.[15]

Four years after crossing back over the Atlantic, Kicking Bear was elected by his community to represent Lakota interests in Washington, DC, as a tribal delegate.[16] The five-member delegation was the first to be chosen by the community members themselves, rather than appointed by the Indian agent.[17] Traveling by way of the Pennsylvania Railroad, they arrived in the capital on February 27, 1896. While in town the delegates found lodging at the Hotel La Fétra, located at 11th and G Street NW. They departed more than two weeks later, on March 14.[18]

Agenda points for their negotiations included land claims to former reservation lands in northern Nebraska, the lifting of the reservation's "licensed-trader" system in order to allow for business competition on the reservation, and the ability for Native community members to appoint their own chief cattle herder.[19] Within their first day of business, the delegation met with Commissioner of Indian Affairs Daniel M. Browning, Acting Secretary of the Interior Judge Simms, and General Stanton at the War Department, as well as completed a sight-seeing tour of the city.[20] In the following days they would meet with President Grover Cleveland and with House and Senate members of the "Indian committees."[21] One DC newspaper reported of the delegation, "Those who have had to do with Little Wound, Kicking Bear, Capt. Thunder Bear, George Fire Thunder and the interpreter, Philip Wells, are unanimous in declaring that no body of Indians or white men ever behaved more circumspectly in this city than have these representatives of the Pine Ridge Sioux."[22]

During his time in Washington, Kicking Bear also met regularly with ethnographer James Mooney, who persuaded Kicking Bear to allow Smithsonian anthropologists to create a "life mask" replica of his face.[23] This process included covering the model's face in gelatin before applying plaster strips to create the mold. To breathe during this hours-long ordeal, Kicking Bear relied on straws inserted into his nostrils.[24] The cast went on to appear in the Smithsonian Museum of Natural History for decades. It originally sat atop a staged replica of Kicking Bear, donning his own donated shirt, leggings, feathers, and tobacco pouch.[25] When curators retired these fragile objects in the 1950s, however, Kicking Bear's life mask remained on a new figure labeled only as a "Sioux Warrior."[26] The life mask was also incorporated into the decorative element design of Dumbarton Bridge.

Six years after Kicking Bear's death in 1904, father-son architect team Glen Brown and Bedford Brown IV, along with sculptor Alexander Phimister Proctor, began construction on Dumbarton Bridge. The bridge was created to connect the Georgetown and Kalorama neighborhoods after Georgetown's incorporation into Washington in 1871. Not only would this bridge provide a practical pathway between two points, but the popular City Beautiful design

FIGURE 1.1. Detail of Dumbarton Bridge
Historic American Buildings Survey / Historic American Engineering Record / Historic American Landscapes Survey collection, Prints & Photographs Division, Library of Congress, HAER DC,WASH,594-7.

theory ensured stylistic elements of grandeur with the purpose of uplifting local residents' spirits and benefiting urban life.[27] The City Beautiful influence manifested in the bridge's massive scale, neoclassical foundation, Roman features, and painstakingly hand-dimpled surface.[28]

Nostalgia for the American frontier also permeated City Beautiful design and is made evident at Dumbarton Bridge through the incorporation of Native American motifs. A striking fifty-six hand-carved sculptures of Kicking Bear, derived from the life mask held by the Smithsonian, decorate the bridge arches. At each end of the bridge Alexander Phimister Proctor's giant bronze bison further bring the American western character to the capital. The eight-foot-tall and fourteen-foot-long sculptures weigh in at a whopping 5,800 pounds each.[29]

The bridge was completed in 1915, but Kicking Bear didn't live to see his likeness replicated in a permanent architectural feature in the District of Columbia. Reflecting on the significance of the bridge, historian Joseph Genetin-Pilawa notes the paradox of the architect's intentions to address American nostalgia for the "vanishing" Indian but how, in doing so, he forever enshrined the portrait of an anticolonial warrior on the city's built environment. The very fact that the life mask was created during Kicking Bear's trip to Washington—a journey dedicated to advocating for Indigenous rights, sovereignty, and self-determination—speaks to the irony of Proctor and Brown's intention to honor what they viewed as a bygone past. Today Dumbarton Bridge reminds passersby that Native people have been and always will be in Washington, DC, fighting for their people.

Embassy of Tribal Nations

People from around the world travel to Washington, DC, to view and work at the stunning foreign embassies and diplomatic headquarters. What many may not realize, however, is that, in addition to foreign nations, a number of American Indian tribal nations have established these governmental outposts in the capital as well. Located in the Dupont Circle neighborhood at 1516 P Street NW, the Embassy of Tribal Nations is housed in one of Washington's iconic row houses. The embassy's relatively modest structure is such that pedestrians could easily pass by without recognizing its significance as the capital city's landing ground for hundreds of tribal nations, their leadership, and their advocacy work.

The National Congress of American Indians (NCAI) unveiled the Embassy of Tribal Nations in late 2009, but the organization itself first took shape in 1944 in response to the emerging threat of termination.[30] Commencing with

House Concurrent Resolution 108 in 1953, the United States adopted "termination" as its official policy stance toward Native Americans, where termination signified the end of the federal-tribal trust relationship and concluded the federal government's responsibility to tribal nations as outlined in various treaties. Essentially, termination sought to destroy tribes' very existence as tribes. For the roughly twenty years of the termination era, in the words of prominent Standing Rock Sioux theorist Vine Deloria Jr., "termination [was] used as a weapon against the Indian people in a modern war of conquest."[31] The thinking behind such policy followed that former members of terminated tribes would dissolve into Euro-American culture and exist simply as racial minorities, devoid of all the rights and privileges of citizenship in a sovereign Indigenous nation. An estimated 13,263 individual Native Americans were disenfranchised in this manner.[32] The federal government also stood to benefit from such a ploy as tribes collectively lost 1,365,801 acres of land.[33] At the time of writing his famous *Custer Died for Your Sins: An Indian Manifesto* in 1969, Deloria characterized termination as "the single most important problem of the American Indian people at the present time."[34]

In response to this federal attack on tribal sovereignty, treaty rights, and Indigenous ways of life, the NCAI was formed. The organization's goals, which continue to drive its actions today, are fourfold.[35] First and foremost, the NCAI seeks to "protect and enhance treaty and sovereign rights." This mission strikes at the very foundation of tribal nations as sovereign and self-governing entities. Critically, it also speaks to the need to protect that status amid centuries of political attacks, ranging from the 1940s termination era to more recent events such as drilling for the Keystone XL Pipeline, challenges to the constitutionality of the Indian Child Welfare Act, and revocation of land-into-trust decisions from previous administrations.

The NCAI lists the security of traditional laws, cultures, and ways of life "for our descendants" as the second component of its mission statement.[36] Such an aspiration stems directly from historical attempts by the United States to assimilate American Indians into the Euro-American mainstream, many of which involved direct physical violence and inflicted intergenerational trauma. Gen. Richard Henry Pratt, founder of the first boarding school for Native American children, summarized the lengths to which the assimilation project would go in his infamous mantra, "Kill the Indian, save the man."[37]

The NCAI's third aim is to "promote a common understanding of the rightful place of tribes in the family of American governments."[38] This educational component of the organization's mission confronts the myth of the vanishing

Indian and the resulting misconception that Native peoples no longer exist in the United States. On the contrary, tribal nations compose a central form of government in the United States, regularly engage in negotiations and agreements with state and local governments, and enjoy a government-to-government relationship with the federal United States. Despite the ill-conceived notion of tribal law and governance as a niche area of interest, the workings and decisions of tribal governments yield major outcomes relevant to the lives of all Americans.

Finally, the NCAI is dedicated to improving the quality of life for Native communities and peoples.[39] This overarching commitment to the well-being of Indigenous America signals the organization's work in a variety of inter-connected areas. These include physical and mental health, economic develop-ment, spiritual strength, environmental harmony, youth advancement, elder protections, political empowerment, and more.

During their first meeting, sixty-seven delegates from nearly forty tribes came together behind this mission. They convened at the Cosmopolitan Hotel in Denver, Colorado, on November 15, 1944, to charter the NCAI.[40] The following day the group adopted the original NCAI Constitution, and on November 18 NCAI passed its first resolutions—dedicated to voting rights and land claims—and thus laid the groundwork for that year's policy agenda and set the stage for decades of advocacy to follow.[41] Tribes represented in the 1944 NCAI included Arapaho, Blackfeet, Caddo, Cherokee, Cheyenne, Chick-asaw, Chippewa, Choctaw, Comanche, Creek, Delaware, Flathead, Fox, Gros Ventre, Jicarilla Apache, Kiowa, Menominee, Mohegan, Nez Percé, Northern Cheyenne, Osage, Papago, Potawatomi, Santa Clara Pueblo, San Juan Pueblo, Sauk, Shoshone-Bannock, Sioux, Southern Ute, Stockbridge-Munsee, Ute, Walapai, Western Shoshone, and Winnebago.

The original NCAI participants represented a strong cross section of the American Indian population, with mixed educational, professional, and regional backgrounds. Many individuals had already established themselves in Indian Country through their election or appointment to tribal councils or employment with the Bureau of Indian Affairs. A number of these char-tering members were also college graduates and had trained as anthropolo-gists, attorneys, business owners, community leaders, or even professional athletes.[42] Thus, the formation of the NCAI marked one of the largest and most diverse displays of intertribal unity in the early twentieth century.

In its first year of existence, the NCAI grew to incorporate three hundred members and ensured representation from nearly all tribes at the time.[43]

President Richard Nixon called for an end to the termination policy approach to Native peoples in 1970 and committed to a path forward through newfound belief in tribal self-determination.[44] The Indian Self-Determination and Education Assistance Act of 1975, passed during the Gerald Ford administration, solidified the federal government's support for Native governments' abilities to chart their own futures. The organization remained active through this challenging time and for decades beyond, weighing in on some of the most high-profile issues affecting Indian Country. Such widely publicized policy issues—the 1978 American Indian Religious Freedom Act, the 1988 Indian Gaming Regulatory Act, the 1996 Native American Housing Assistance and Self-Determination Act, President Bill Clinton's 1996 Executive Order on Sacred Sites Protection—were all touched by the NCAI.

In all of this advocacy, the NCAI depends upon the baseline principles of tribal sovereignty and Indigenous nationhood. The combination of treaty history, legal precedent, and the United States' own fundamental documents makes clear that tribes occupy a distinct governmental position as sovereign Native nations.[45] As such, the decision to establish an embassy—an embodiment of tribal nationhood and the government-to-government relationships they enjoy with the United States—followed naturally.[46]

The vision for a national tribal embassy received far-reaching support from tribal governments and Indigenous individuals whose collective giving made the building purchase possible. Within the approximately first five years after kicking off the capital-raising campaign, hundreds of donors had raised $2.7 million for the cause.[47] The NCAI purchased the $8.5 million building that would house the Embassy of Tribal Nations in May 2009.[48]

The facilities include 17,000 square feet of office space, workstations for tribal leaders visiting DC, and numerous art features throughout the space.[49] Additionally, as the NCAI envisions, "an Embassy of Tribal Nations is more than just bricks and mortar. . . . It's about enhancing our image and standing as governments within the family of governments."[50] The embassy's location a mere handful of blocks away from DC's iconic Embassy Row further drives home this point.

A project nearly thirty years in the making, the Embassy of Tribal Nations opened its doors on November 3, 2009. Opening day brought seventy tribal leaders and hundreds of members of the public to share in traditional foods, enjoy powwow dance, and offer a ceremonial blessing. "It's a new time, it's a new era," said Ernie Stevens Jr. (Oneida Nation of Wisconsin), chair of the National Indian Gaming Association. "We call this Indian country in

Washington, DC—right here, right now. I think it's going to make a difference. This is our home."[51]

In 2013 alone, thirty-one groups totaling more than three hundred individuals visited the Embassy of Tribal Nations. International visitors from more than fifteen countries, spanning the Middle East, South America, Oceania, the Caribbean, North America, and Africa, conducted business and engaged in educational opportunities at the embassy. Dozens of high-level officials—tribal leaders, senior members of the US Cabinet, Indigenous leaders from outside the United States, senior UN personnel, ambassadors, and foreign ministers—have found their way to the Embassy of Tribal Nations.[52]

The Embassy of Tribal Nations represents a constituency of member tribes in their work with Washington and does so in the capacity of a nonprofit organization. In addition to this advocacy for Indian Country collectively, individual Indigenous nations have also erected governmental outposts in Washington. These establishments fundamentally differ from the work of the NCAI due to their governmental status as sovereign Indigenous nations. The Chickasaw Nation and Navajo Nation are two of a small handful of tribes with a permanent DC presence.

Establishing a Chickasaw Nation embassy became a priority for Chickasaw Nation governor Bill Anoatubby in the mid-1990s, a goal that coincided with the appointment of Charles Blackwell as the first tribal ambassador to the United States. Governor Anoatubby envisioned the creation of both the embassy and the ambassadorship as steps to reemphasize the formal government-to-government relationship enjoyed between the Chickasaw Nation and the United States.[53] Listed in the Yellow Pages as the Chickasaw Embassy, the red brick, corner unit townhouse office on Capitol Hill is officially named the Piominko House as an homage to the great eighteenth-century Chickasaw leader Piominko.

Founded in 1984 and located less than a mile away from the US Capitol, the Navajo Nation Washington Office does not officially brand itself as an embassy. Much of the work conducted at this location—analyzing congressional legislation, interpreting the impact of federal decision-making on the Navajo Nation, and advocating for the tribe on a national level—is consistent with the work of embassies.[54] Navajo Nation President Jonathan Nez reflects, "If the federal government allows countries, nations, to do that [establish embassies], why can't the Navajo Nation do that in Washington, DC?"[55]

On a practical level for the NCAI, "This town [Washington, DC] is the town that has the most impact on Indian Country," notes Ron Allen, Jamestown

FIGURE 1.2. Embassy of Tribal Nations
Embassy of Tribal Nations, 2016, Washington, DC.

S'Klallam Tribe of Washington chair and former NCAI president.[56] Symbolically, the Embassy of Tribal Nations represents the "vision and dream of our
old tribal warriors of the past" made manifest.[57] Embassy of Tribal Nations
board member and citizen of the Nisqually Tribe of Washington Billy Frank Jr.
said the following about the future of the embassy: "We are here to stay.

We are long-timers. We aren't moving through here just today and tomorrow. We're here from now on."[58] Indeed, through the presence of the Embassy of Tribal Nations and other Indigenous embassies, tribal governments from across America are establishing permanent diplomatic outposts on the ancestral homeland of the Piscataway people.

Congressional Cemetery

The Congressional Cemetery stands out as one of the few substantial green areas in downtown Washington, along with such distinguished sites as the National Mall, the US Capitol property, and monument grounds. Originally founded as the Washington Parish Burial Ground, decades of congressional appropriations and the purchase of plots by a number of members of Congress throughout the early nineteenth century inspired its colloquial name, Congressional Cemetery.[59] While many associate this National Historic Landmark with the US senators and representatives memorialized there, few realize that the Congressional Cemetery also serves as the final resting place for thirty-six Native American delegates, dignitaries, advocates, and their families, who passed on while working on behalf of their people in the nation's capital.

Founded in 1807, the Congressional Cemetery is the first national burial ground in the United States.[60] The thirty-five-acre Capitol Hill property predated Arlington Cemetery by seventy years. Bordering southeast DC's Anacostia River, it remains the largest private landholding, owned by Christ Church, Washington Parish. More than fifty-five thousand individuals—many members of Congress, diplomats, members of the military, and acclaimed artists—are interred at the Congressional Cemetery. Fourteen thousand headstones and thirty thousand burial sites punctuate the property. Eight hundred of those plots belong to the federal government, along with 165 cenotaphs erected to honor members of Congress.[61] This historic cemetery remains active today, more than two hundred years after its first burial in 1807.[62]

At the Congressional Cemetery, the built environment testifies to the visibility of Native peoples in Washington, both past and present, and highlights the interwoven relationship between the United States and tribal nations. The tribal leaders whose remains rest here hailed from eleven tribal nations, which speaks to the diversity of tribes who have left their imprint on the capital city. The Congressional Cemetery, however, also serves as an important reminder of the strained—and, at times, fatal—nature of Indigenous presence, advocacy, and work in Washington, DC.

Many tribal leaders and families of the deceased return to this hallowed ground to honor those who went before them. In May 2010, for instance, representatives from five nations—the Cherokee, Choctaw, Muscogee (Creek), Sisseton Wahpeton Oyate, and Pawnee—hosted a multiday remembrance event.[63] This included a day of service dedicated to beautification and restoration of tribal delegates' gravesites, a day of storytelling recounting the lives and feats of these tribal leaders, and a public reading by Kansas senator Sam Brownback and Washington representative Jim McDermott of the Resolution of Apology to Native Peoples, a bill signed by President Barack Obama to apologize to Native nations for the United States' "long history of official depredations and ill-conceived policies."[64] Furthermore, the American Indian Society of Washington DC gathers each Memorial Day to pay tribute to these fallen leaders by decorating their gravesites. This practice originated with Choctaw chief and delegate Peter Pitchlynn in 1874 and continues nearly 150 years later.[65]

In alphabetical order of tribal affiliation, the tribal leaders and some of their stories are as follows.

ARAPAHO

Chief Taza of the Chiricahua peoples inherited his position from his father, the famed leader Cochise. While on his deathbed in 1874, Cochise urged his eldest son to maintain peace with American settlers and to carry on his legacy of protecting their Apache community from white encroachment.[66] Taza took up this command, declaring, "Heretofore it has been universally known through the country that my father has taken care of this tribe. I have not been known to the people, but I will endeavor to show the world I can take care of them as well as my father."[67]

Taza assumed this leadership position at thirty-one years of age and spent the subsequent years shielding his people from hardship and defending their lands from exploitation. In 1875, for instance, ranching and mining lobbyists succeeded in pushing forward legislation that dissolved the Chiricahua reservation in Arizona Territory, a land base that Cochise had secured a mere four years before. This development not only displaced the Chiricahua people but also reduced their rations, leaving the community destitute and impoverished.[68]

Taza assembled a tribal delegation to seek recourse in Washington. To financially support the journey to the capital, the Apache leader made the sacrifice of subjecting himself to performing in Western sideshow acts along the way.[69] Shortly after arriving in the District of Columbia, however, Taza suddenly passed on September 26, 1876.[70] The official cause of death was declared to be pneumonia.[71] A number of his tribesmen doubted the pneumonia narrative put forward and instead grew suspicious of foul play—namely, that their leader had been poisoned.[72]

Hastily departing Washington in order to marry his fiancée in Ohio, the Indian agent who had coordinated Taza's DC negotiations neglected to make funerary arrangements for the fallen leader.[73] Taza's body was placed into an unmarked grave. Not until 1971, when the American Indian Society of Washington DC organized to redress this travesty, did the burial site gain a headstone.[74] Visitors should note that the grave marker displays a carved image of what the organizers envisioned as Taza's likeness. There are no known photographs of the chief.

CHEROKEE

The Congressional Cemetery is the final resting place of more descendants of the Cherokee than any other tribal nation. Totaling fourteen graves, these Cherokee individuals represent the single largest tribal group in the cemetery by a factor of two. The deceased include students and professionals, elders and children.

Three members of the Coodey family passed in Washington in 1849. The patriarch, William Shorey Coodey, had established himself as a prominent Cherokee politician with a regular hand in official tribal business. Coodey first took up the post of secretary for the Cherokee delegation to Washington, DC, in 1830.[75] In this role, as illustrated by his appointment to the December 1831 delegation, Coodey and his fellow delegates petitioned the US secretary of war for relief from the state of Georgia's acts of aggression, including the seizure of gold mines, armed removal of Cherokee citizens from their property, surveys of Cherokee lands for purposes of distribution to white settlers, and land claims that ran counter to treaty history.[76] Coodey confronted many challenges to this agenda, as his advocacy unfolded amid President Andrew Jackson's Indian removal campaign, codified under the Indian Removal Act of 1830. Embodying the anti-Indian sentiment of the moment, for instance, the secretary of war declined to meet with the Cherokee delegation altogether, prompting Coodey and the others to remain in the District for an extended period throughout that winter of 1831.[77]

Coodey bore witness to the atrocities of the Trail of Tears. In a letter to a friend he recounted, "In all the bustle of preparation there was a silence and stillness of the voice that betrayed the sadness of the heart. At length the word was given to go on. . . . At that very moment a low sound of distant thunder fell upon my ear—in almost an exact westerly direction a dark spiral cloud was rising above the horizon and sent forth a murmur I almost thought a voice of divine indignation for the wrongs of my poor and unhappy country-men, driven by brutal power from all they loved and cherished in the land of their fathers to gratify the craving of avarice."[78] Observing this dark stain on American history likely inspired his advocacy for the Cherokee people moving forward.

In addition to representing his community in negotiations with the United States, William S. Coodey also served as a delegate in intertribal affairs. In June 1835 the Cherokee National Council selected Coodey and three others to approach the Eastern Cherokees in talks regarding tribal unity.[79] This del-egation resulted in Coodey's authorship of the 1839 Act of the Union. This fundamental document consolidated governmental power for the separated Cherokees, some of whom had been forcibly relocated to Indian Territory through the Trail of Tears, while other factions had either remained in their eastern lands or relocated out west in the early nineteenth century.[80] Through this legislation the eastern and western groups united as "one body politic, under the style and title of 'The Cherokee Nation.'"

That same year Coodey achieved perhaps his most well-known success: writing the Cherokee Nation Constitution. The constitution was adopted on September 6, 1839, in present-day Tahlequah, Oklahoma, and offered a symbol of Cherokee survival and strength after removal.[81] The Cherokee Nation of Oklahoma governed under this constitution for more than seventy years.[82] Not until June 6, 1976, did the Cherokee Nation of Oklahoma enact the Con-stitution of the Cherokee Nation of Oklahoma.[83]

Coodey maintained his political involvement with the tribe for the remain-der of his life. Highlights included running for principal chief in 1847, serving as acting principal chief of the Cherokee Nation, holding the position of presi-dent of the first National Committee to organize under the 1839 constitution, being selected as speaker of the Cherokee National Council the same year, and joining a delegation to the Comanche Nation.[84] His diplomatic work regularly brought him to Washington, where he could be seen strolling Pennsylvania Avenue with his close friend Massachusetts senator and the US secretary of state Daniel Webster; onlookers noted that "the two distinguished men . . . made a striking pair, and people turned to look at them."[85] Beginning his career in advocacy at the young age of twenty-four, William Shorey Coodey served his Cherokee people for nineteen years until his untimely death in 1849 at age forty-three.

Coodey was preceded in death by his seventeen-year-old daughter, Henrietta Jane Coodey. She received her education from the Patapsco Female Institute in Ellicott City, Maryland, and had begun working there as a music instructor. Conflicting records suggest that she succumbed to a fever on January 28, 1849, while her headstone indicates that she passed two months later, in March.[86]

William Shorey Coodey passed at 6:30 in the morning on April 16, 1849, while in Washington, DC. Coodey's death and funeral proved to be a high-profile affair, especially when compared to those of other Native Americans who had lived and worked in Washington. The US Marine Band led his funeral procession down Pennsylvania Avenue to the Congressional Cemetery.[87] The details of his passing and funeral proceedings received media coverage in outlets such as the *Baltimore Sun*, the *National Intelligencer*, and the *Washington Union*, which fondly referred to him as a "citizen of the Cherokee Nation, long and favorably known to the government and to the citizens of Washington as an able and faithful representative of the Cherokee people."[88]

Coodey was interred next to his daughter, Henrietta Jane, who had passed shortly before. The Coodey family plot in the Congressional Cemetery also includes William Coodey's infant daughter, Charlotte Jane Coodey. Each of their headstones proudly proclaims their Cherokee tribal affiliation and are engraved with the Cherokee seven-point star, or sacred fire, symbol.[89]

Other Cherokee leaders resting at the Congressional Cemetery include

- Judge Richard Fields (1808–73), an attorney and Cherokee Nation administrator. Fields served as the chief justice of the Cherokee Supreme Court from 1855 to 1857.[90] Washington's *Evening Star* newspaper reported that Fields's funeral took place on Friday, April 30, with attendance from close friends and a number of representatives from the Cherokee Nation.[91]
- Capt. John Looney (ca. 1776–1846), chief of the Western Cherokees, also known as the "Old Settlers," during the time of the signing of the Act of Union.[92] Earlier in life, Looney served in the 1813–14 Creek War under Gen. Andrew Jackson, wherein he was severely wounded and received a lifetime pension from the US government for his service.[93] He died on May 15, 1846, while serving on a Cherokee delegation in Washington, DC, and was buried the following day.[94]

- Capt. James McDaniel (1823–68), a Civil War veteran who served in the 2nd Indian Regiment, US Volunteers.[95] McDaniel served as president of the Cherokee Senate and on December 11, 1867, was appointed to serve as a Cherokee delegate to Washington.[96] He succumbed to pneumonia in February 1868.[97]
- Capt. Thomas Pegg (1804–66), noted Cherokee politician. Pegg served in the Cherokee senate from 1853 to 1855 and became president of the Cherokee National Council in 1861. First commissioned as a major in the First Cherokee Mounted Rifles, a Confederate army regiment, he then joined the Union army's Third Indian Home Guard Regiment as a captain one year later. From 1862 to 1863, Pegg served as acting principal chief of the Cherokee Nation and spent later years advocating for the Cherokee people during Reconstruction.[98] As part of these efforts Pegg served as one of the associate justices of the Supreme Court of the Cherokee Nation and joined a delegation to Washington, where he perished on April 22, 1866.[99] Reporting on the death of Captain Pegg and other leaders, the Cherokee National Council penned, "[Pegg and others] have been called from earth, and now sleep with our fathers, who were their associates amid scenes of trial that have rarely befallen any people. But they will continue to live in example. Let their virtues be cherished among a grateful and afflicted people."[100]
- Capt. John Rogers (ca. 1776–1846), principal chief of the Western Cherokee.[101] Rogers, the nephew of two Western Cherokee principal chiefs, John Jolly and Tahlonteeskee, rose to prominence first due to his service under Andrew Jackson in the Creek War (1812–13) and later as the leader of the Western Cherokee effort to resist the 1839 unification effort to bring the western and eastern bands together as one Cherokee Nation.[102] Rogers was the last elected chief of the Western Cherokee, taking his post on October 11, 1839.[103] As a member of the Cherokee National Council, he was involved in sending delegations to the capital city.[104] Rogers is interred at the Congressional Cemetery next to his infant child, who passed in 1841.[105] The burial sites of Johnson K. Rogers, 1808–69, son of John Rogers and Cherokee citizen Sarah Cordery Rogers, and of his infant child (1841), are located only a short distance away.[106]
- Johnson K. Rogers (1808–69) relocated to Washington, DC, in 1838, a city he called home for more than thirty years until his death.[107]

In Washington, Johnson Rogers worked as an attorney for the Cherokees, as an assistant in the Department of the Interior's Indian Office, and as the secretary of the House of Representatives Committee on Indian Affairs.[108] In 1934 his grandnephew recalled of his move to Washington, DC, "When the Cherokees began their departure [on the Trail of Tears], Uncle Johnson Rogers, a brilliant, swashbuckling, hard fighting fellow exclaimed with a violent oath, 'My people are going West, but I'm going to headquarters.'"[109]

- Ezekiel Starr (ca. 1802–46), Cherokee Nation politician. Starr, a member of the controversial Treaty Party that supported Indian Removal to the west, ventured to Washington in the winter of 1843–44, and again the following winter, to seek federal support of the Treaty Party.[110] He also served as a delegate to Washington, DC, in 1846. The purpose of this trip was to seek support from President James K. Polk to end the violence between the Treaty Party and Ross Party—two Cherokee factions—as a result of the signing of the Treaty of New Echota in 1835 and the string of hundreds of revenge killings following in its aftermath.[111] Starr passed on four weeks into this trip, and the cause of death was identified as erysipelas.[112] His efforts to secure peace proved victorious, as both sides of the dispute signed a peace treaty in August 1846 under the leadership of Principal Chief John Ross.[113]

- Bluford West (ca. 1808–46), an "Old Setter," or Western Cherokee, and judge of the Cherokee Nation. West had traveled to Washington in order to resolve a dispute between the Eastern and Western Cherokees over ownership of his salt mine and died during this trip.[114]

CHIPPEWA/OJIBWE

Waub-O-Jeag (d. 1863), chief of the Gull Lake Band of Ojibwe, is also referenced in scholarship as Wawbojeeg, Waubojeeg, Wa-boo-jig, Waabojiig, Waub-o-jeeg, Wa-bo-jeek, Waub Ogeeg, or, most commonly, White Fisher.[115] Before becoming a chief and in his status as a warrior, White Fisher was among the signatories of the 1837 Treaty of St. Peters, which ceded Ojibwe lands to the United States for purposes of lumber production, and which upheld the tribes' hunting, fishing, and gathering rights on this land.[116] In 1863 he joined a delegation invited to Washington, DC, to negotiate the cession of Ojibwe lands in the Michigan peninsula.[117] This March 28, 1863, treaty resulted in the loss of thirteen million acres of tribal lands and the set-aside of fourteen reservations within the ceded territory.[118] Shortly after the signing, Congress exerted pressure on the Ojibwe to move westward by unilaterally amending the treaty such that the reservations were only secured for a period of five years rather than as permanent homes, as originally negotiated.[119] White Fisher passed on in Washington, DC, from smallpox.[120]

Other Ojibwe leaders resting at the Congressional Cemetery include:

- A-Mouse (d. 1866), chief of the Lac de Flambeau and Chippewa River divisions of the Chippewa.[121] Also known as Little Bee, A-Moose or Ah-mous, this tribal leader resisted the removal of his people from their traditional lands and the starvation that followed. He participated in an 1852 delegation to Washington in order to fight the impending removal orders westward, to Wisconsin, and again in 1862 to advocate for an increased reservation land base and the security of annuity payments promised via treaties.[122]
- Osk Kaw Bu Wis (d. 1866), a tribal delegate to Washington.[123] He can also be found in historical records under the names and spellings Shau-ba-wis, Shaw-bo-Wis, Oak-Caw-Bu-Wis, or Shawbowis.[124] Reports on the cause of death vary from the "black measles," known today as Rocky Mountain spotted fever, to smallpox.[125] Osk Kaw Bu Wis had been staying at the delegate headquarters at Third Street SW and Independence Avenue SW (formerly B Street) and was buried in the Congressional Cemetery on March 20, 1866.[126]
- St. Germain (d. 1866), chief and delegate to the District of Columbia.[127] He was buried on March 20, 1866, along with Osk Kaw Bu Wis.[128]

CHOCTAW

Pushmataha (1764–1824) is widely regarded as the "greatest of all Choctaw chiefs."[129] His early life was marked by his accomplishments as a warrior, a virtue that later thrust Pushmataha into leadership roles within his tribe, beginning as a representative of his Six Towns Division of the Choctaw Confederacy.[130] In his mid-thirties, Pushmataha became a chief and used his power to advocate for Choctaw land rights and to resist removal. In 1824 he traveled to Washington, DC, as part of a delegation seeking to secure federal payment as negotiated in the Treaty of Doak's Stand in 1820. Although Pushmataha had won the affection of then-senator Andrew Jackson as a result of his lending Choctaw military support in the Creek War of 1813, the mission of the delegation went unfulfilled for more than sixty years.[131] Pushmataha died of croup during this delegation visit, passing in late December 1824.[132]

FIGURE 1.3. Flowers being placed on Pushmataha's grave in the Congressional
Cemetery
Harris & Ewing photograph collection, Prints & Photographs Division, Library of Congress,
LC-DIG-hec-44676.

Pushmataha was the first Native American delegate to be buried at the
Congressional Cemetery.[133] Under presidential orders, the US federal government purchased his burial plot.[134] Historian Herman Viola characterized the
December 26 proceedings as Washington's "most impressive funeral for an
Indian delegate."[135] Jackson led a mile-long procession of two thousand politicians, officials, and locals, accompanied by "several military companies . . .
the marines from the navy yard and two bands of music."[136] Following his final
wishes, addressed to Jackson and requesting that "the big guns be fired over
me," Pushmataha received a twenty-one gun salute.[137]

In the summer of 2011 Chief Gregory E. Pyle, Assistant Chief Gary Batton,
and members of the Tribal Council visited past Choctaw leaders buried at the
Congressional Cemetery.[138] Among them were Peter Perkins Pitchlynn. Born
in 1806, Pitchlynn made his work with the US federal government the focus
of his career, starting in the 1850s and continuing to his death in 1881.[139]
At the start of the Civil War, Pitchlynn met with President Abraham Lincoln to

discuss the Choctaw position in the war.[140] Although the majority of Choctaw citizens supported the Confederacy, and Pitchlynn himself was a slave owner, the two agreed that the official Choctaw position would remain neutral.[141] Pitchlynn served as chief from 1864 to 1866 before relocating to Washington, DC, in 1867 for the remainder of his life.[142] In 1876 Pitchlynn was listed as one of only nine tribal "resident delegates" in DC and the only representative from the Choctaw Nation.[143] In Washington, he advanced Choctaw interests by pursuing the claims to compensation for lands lost or sold and by opposing allotment under the impending Dawes Act of 1887.[144] His work as a tribal representative in dealings with the US government was inspired by his father, John Pitchlynn, who had served as the Choctaw interpreter for George Washington.[145] This legacy remained, as Pitchlynn's children made their lives in DC as well. Along with Chief Pitchlynn, the Congressional Cemetery is the final resting place of Pitchlynn's children, Lee Pitchlynn (ca. 1866–1936), Sophia Pitchlynn (1864–1942), Thomas Pitchlynn (1856–93), and Samson Pitchlynn, 1857–58) and grandson Emmett Kennedy (1876–90).[146]

CREEK

Efar Emarthlar (d. 1888), Creek delegate.[147] In the Census of the Creek Nation, East, taken following the March 24, 1832, Treaty of Cusseta, which ceded Creek lands east of the Mississippi to the United States, Emarthlar is listed as a principal chief. The census states that Emarthlar, along with the other nine chiefs of the Cussetaw Towns, was appointed to this position by the General Council on November 29, 1832.[148] Emarthlar is also found in historical records under the name David Thompson.[149]

Other Creek leaders resting at the Congressional Cemetery include Daniel S. Aspberry (d. 1856), Creek delegate.[150]

DAKOTA / SISSETON WAHPETON OYATE

Kan Ya Tu Duta, also known as Kangiduta or Scarlet Crow, began his work with the United States in 1862 by serving as a US Army scout during the Dakota Uprising. In the following years he further built his relationship with the United States by becoming a tribal delegate to Washington, DC, and by advocating against the removal of his people from their homelands in Minnesota westward to South Dakota.[151] This political stance marked him as a vocal opponent to the treaty his tribe intended to sign while in Washington—a position that many believe led to his untimely death.[152] The Sisseton Wahpeton Treaty, an agreement establishing the Sisseton Reservation, was signed on February 19, 1867, and included the "X" mark of Scarlet Crow.[153] Five days later, on February 24, the delegate was discovered missing from his lodgings at New York and 19th Street.[154] The investigation, prompted by Scarlet Crow's fellow delegates, lasted two weeks before the discovery of his remains in Arlington, Virginia, near the present-day Key Bridge.[155] Indian Agent Joseph Brown suspected foul play. Examining the evidence, including the knot-tying technique used and the flimsiness of the tree branch, Brown indicated that he thought that the scene was staged by reward- or ransom-seeking killers to appear as a suicide by hanging.[156] Despite these misgivings, the official cause of Scarlet Crow's death remains suicide.

Scarlet Crow was buried in the Congressional Cemetery on March 13, 1867.[157] For forty-nine years, the "small grave" in the "corner of the cemetery" remained unmarked.[158] In 1916 Congress installed a headstone in his honor, only after his son, Sam Crow, had petitioned them to do so four years earlier.[159] Nearly one hundred years later, in late 2001, North Dakota senator Byron Dorgan ventured to the Congressional Cemetery in search of Scarlet Crow's resting place. He granted $1.25 million toward restoration of the cemetery following the state of disarray he discovered. On this effort, Senator Dorgan offered, "It is my hope that this funding will honor the memory of Scarlet Crow by restoring dignity to his final resting place. This funding is a tribute to this dedicated Native American, Scarlet Crow, whose life came to such a tragic and untimely end in our nation's capital."[160]

KIOWA

In the spring of 1863, the height of the Civil War, President Lincoln invited a cohort of fourteen Apache, Arapaho, Caddo, Cheyenne, Comanche, and Kiowa delegates to Washington, DC.[161] The fifty-nine-year-old Kiowa leader O Com O Cost, more often referred to as Yellow Wolf, joined this delegation.[162] The purpose of this meeting was to ensure tribes' support for the Union, and during this time they negotiated a treaty, although never ratified, allowing Kiowas and Comanches to sell cattle captured in Texas to US Army contractors in New Mexico and Indian Territory (present-day Oklahoma).[163] The afternoon of March 27, 1863, after meeting with Lincoln, the delegates posed for a now-famous photograph in the White House conservatory in which Yellow Wolf proudly donned the large silver Peace Medal given by Thomas Jefferson to Yellow Wolf's family.[164] Eight short days after the photographer captured this moment, Yellow Wolf succumbed to pneumonia in his Washington, DC, hotel.[165] His fellow delegates honored Yellow Wolf while on his deathbed, marking his face, hands, and feet with red paint and dressing him in new clothing and blankets. They also broke his bow and arrows at the time of passing, and then compiled the pieces into a package of effects to be kept alongside the leader.[166] Yellow Wolf was buried in a government-provided coffin on April 5, 1863, his silver Peace Medal with him forever.[167]

NEZ PERCÉ

Ut Sin Malikan was deeply involved in the treaty negotiations that shaped the outcome of the Nez Percé in the mid-nineteenth century. Under the alternate spelling U-ute-sin-male-cun, he signed the first treaty between the tribe and the United States in 1855, an agreement that ceded 7.5 million acres to the federal government but retained land usage rights for the tribe.[168] He is also the first Nez Percé signatory, identified as "Ut-sin-male-e-cum" and signed by his "X" mark, on the June 9, 1863, treaty between the tribe and the United States.[169] This treaty, colloquially known as the "Steal Treaty" or "Sell Out Treaty," shrunk the preexisting Nez Percé treaty territory by five million acres—approximately 90 percent of the land—and set the stage for the Nez Percé Flight, a war between the tribe and the US Army that lasted from June 17 to October 5, 1877.[170] Although an eventual signatory, the tribal leader opposed the terms of the treaty and its further division of Nez Percé homelands.[171]

Ut Sin Malikan, then seventy-five years old, joined a four-member delegation to Washington in 1863 in an effort to renegotiate. The journey took the tribal leaders by steamboat over to Portland, through San Francisco, and down to Central America; the group boarded a train to cross the Isthmus of Panama before heading to New York City and then on to Washington.[172] His agenda additionally involved petitioning the government for overdue payment for lands previously ceded. The tensions surrounding such negotiations frame the conflicting stated causes of Ut Sin Malikan's death ten days after his arrival in the capital. Reports cite typhoid or general "illness" as the cause of death, but many in the tribe maintain that he fell to his death after an unknown white assailant pushed him out of his hotel window.[173]

In 2018 five of Ut Sin Malikan's family traveled from Arizona, Idaho, and Washington to the Congressional Cemetery to honor their ancestor. The group assembled on Indigenous Peoples' Day to replace his headstone, which, after 155 years, had sunk into the earth and worn so that it was barely legible. The new marker dignifies Ut Sin Malikan as a "respected leader" and "visionary" who "spoke truth, sought justice for all Nez Percé." The original headstone remains on-site and now sits at the foot of the grave. Speaking to the family's decision not to repatriate their ancestor to his homelands, Ut Sin Malikan's great-great-granddaughter Dr. Roberta Paul reflected, "He's a warrior. In our tradition, where a warrior dies, that's where he's buried."[174]

PAWNEE

Tuk A Lix Tah, also known as Tuckalixtah or Owner of Many Horses, served as a member of a fourteen-person Pawnee delegation to Washington, DC, in 1858. This delegation began its journey to the capital on November 10, 1857, embarking on a four-week trek east to negotiate land ownership as settlers following the gold rush passed en masse through their plains territory in present-day Nebraska. Given the tribe's location on the California and Utah trails, as well as previous skirmishes with Mormon groups, the Pawnee entered into a treaty with the United States that ceded 12 million acres and set aside an additional 200,000 acres for their reservation. The trip to Washington furthermore served the federal government's goal of intimidating the tribe with military strength.[175]

After some four months in DC, Tuk A Lix Tah died of pneumonia in late March 1858.[176] In recognition of his status as a warrior in his community, he was buried with his tomahawk and knife. His body was dressed in a black suit and white gloves and was placed into a mahogany coffin with silver detailing.[177] The funeral drew thousands.[178] The procession included twenty-seven carriages, and all tribal delegates in Washington attended to pay their respects.[179] At the gravesite the Pawnee delegation leader reflected that Tuk A Lix Tah was buried like a great chief.[180] Yet, despite the grandeur of these proceedings, the tribal leader was left in an unmarked grave. Not until November 1994, as part of Native American Heritage Month, did employees of the Bureau of Indian Affairs organize to mark his resting place.[181] To this day his tombstone remains incorrectly placed approximately ten plots north of the burial site.[182]

SAC AND FOX

QuahQuahMahPeQuah (d. 1873), tribal delegate.

WINNEBAGO/HO-CHUNK

Prophet joined his tribe's 1859 delegation to Washington, DC, where he perished. While in the capital, this delegation signed the Treaty with the Winnebago on April 15, 1859, which sold the western portion of their Blue Earth reservation in Minnesota. Mounting financial pressures incurred after removal to this reservation and the taking up of farming practices prompted the cession. In this treaty, one sees that Prophet is noted as "being sick" and, thus, his representative, Big Bear, signed by proxy.[183]

Tribal Delegates Today

From Dumbarton Bridge to the Embassy of Tribal Nations, and from the Capitol Building to the Congressional Cemetery, the legacies of tribal delegates are inscribed on the District's built environment. Some of these Native American leaders returned from Washington to their communities with stories of having achieved treaty negotiations, mingled with politicians, and shaken hands with the president. Others made Washington their home and established families here. Still, some tribal delegates perished in pursuit of a better life for their tribal nations, making the capital city their final resting place.

In all cases, the examples set by these historical figures continue to inspire the contemporary work of tribal leaders, attorneys, businesspeople, politicians, historians, activists, and more. As modern peoples with a government-to-government relationship with the United States, Native nations maintain a constant presence in the capital. This diaspora, made up of representatives from 574 Indigenous governments, exists in relationship with the original inhabitants of this land.

Although tribal delegates operated in Washington throughout the nineteenth century, the notion of tribal representation to the United States federal government has also emerged as an innovative arena for tribal advocacy more recently. In 1995, for instance, the Chickasaw Nation appointed the first-ever ambassador from a tribal nation to the United States. This position broke new ground both symbolically and politically, as the ambassador served as an embodied representation of one sovereign government, the tribe, and its dealings with another, the United States.

Chickasaw governor Bill Anoatubby appointed Charles Blackwell as the Chickasaw Nation's ambassador to the United States in March 1995.[184] Blackwell, born July 30, 1942, in El Reno, Oklahoma, achieved prominence throughout his career of service to Native American people. He received his bachelor of arts from East Central State College in Ada, Oklahoma, in 1964 and graduated from the University of New Mexico School of Law in 1972. Blackwell worked as an attorney for the American Indian Law Center until 1974, when he became the associate director of the Special Scholarship Program in Law for American Indians. From 1974 to 1977, Blackwell simultaneously served as the assistant dean and as a professor at the University of New Mexico School of Law.

He went on to found the First American Business Center, where he advanced tribal economic development; championed environmental causes by sitting on the Environmental Protection Agency Director's National Clean Air Action Advisory Committee; and, in 1997, was the only Native American appointed by President Bill Clinton to the Presidential Advisory Council on HIV/AIDS.[185] Blackwell was a conversational speaker of the Chickasaw language.[186] Prior to his appointment as ambassador, Blackwell served as delegate from the Chickasaw Nation to the United States. He held this position for five years, from 1990 through 1995.[187] Reflecting on the creation of the delegate position, and later the ambassadorship, Governor Anoatubby noted, "Appointment of an official ambassador helped to reinforce the formal government-to-government relationship the Chickasaw Nation had with the federal government."[188] In 1995 Governor Anoatubby and the ten-member Chickasaw legislature confirmed Blackwell as ambassador to the United States. The ceremony took place in Washington, DC, and coincided with the two hundredth anniversary of the first official meeting between Chickasaw tribal representatives and President George Washington.[189]

In his role as ambassador, Blackwell was instrumental in establishing the Chickasaw Nation's embassy in Washington. Now known as Piominko House, the embassy originated as Pushmataha House, named for the Choctaw Nation leader and tribal delegate Pushmataha, who died while on official business in Washington, DC, in 1824.[190] Pushmataha House additionally offered diplomatic headquarters to the Mohegan Tribe and Picuris Pueblo, and it functioned as the office of the Native Affairs and Development Group, headed by Blackwell.[191] He held this position for eighteen years, until his death. Ambassador Charles Blackwell passed on January 2, 2013, in Rockville, Maryland, at seventy years of age.[192]

The development of a tribal ambassadorship to the United States—a reality made possible by Blackwell's service—furthered the strategic goals of formalizing the nation-to-nation relations between tribal nations and the US federal government, enacting tribal sovereignty, and representing tribal nationhood. Governor Anoatubby recalled early conversations with Blackwell: "We agreed that there was a need for the tribes to revive a tradition of diplomatic relations with other governments."[193] Ultimately, the Chickasaw Nation's creation of an ambassadorship from the tribe to the United States advanced not only the tribe's individual interest but also those of all of Indian Country by expanding the limits of the government-to-government relationship near the turn of the twenty-first century.

Nearly twenty-five years after Ambassador Blackwell's appointment, the Cherokee Nation has similarly embarked on an innovative path to tribal representation in Washington, DC. In 2019 the Cherokee Nation began its fight for a tribal post in the House of Representatives. "A Cherokee Nation delegate to Congress is a negotiated right that our ancestors advocated for," Kim Teehee, the nominee for the position asserts, "And today, our tribal nation is stronger than ever and ready to defend all our constitutional and treaty rights."[194]

Although the Cherokee Nation only recently began the process of establishing this role, the precedent for the development extends back nearly two hundred years. In 1835, amid mounting pressure from the federal government to push Native peoples west of the Mississippi, a minority faction of the Cherokee Nation signed the highly contested Treaty of New Echota. The provisions of the treaty ceded the Cherokee homelands to the United States and initiated the Trail of Tears, a forced 1,200-mile walk during which five thousand Cherokees perished. The treaty also stipulated, however, that the tribe would always have a voice in federal politics. The Treaty of New Echota guaranteed that a Cherokee delegate would have a seat in the House of Representatives.[195]

Indeed, this treaty right to Cherokee representation in the US Congress is also found in treaties signed both before and after the Treaty of New Echota. Fifty years prior, the 1785 Treaty of Hopewell similarly included this provision, as did the Treaty of 1866, ratified almost a century later.[196] The Cherokee Nation has upheld their side of these legally binding agreements and have even incorporated this particular right into the Cherokee Nation Constitution.[197] Cherokee Nation principal chief Chuck Hoskin Jr. notes that the year of the treaty negotiations have no bearing on their validity and applicability today: "[The treaties] are still in full force and effect. The rights outlined for us have no expiration date."[198] He further emphasized that "Americans ought to know that just because it's been 180 years doesn't mean we've sat back for 180 years. It means we have been suppressed and ripped apart during most of that time."[199] Now it has come time for the federal government to live up to its word.[200]

Thus, when Chief Hoskin took office in August 2019, the appointment of a delegate to the House of Representatives was a priority action item, and Cherokee Nation citizen and DC attorney Kim Teehee emerged as a natural fit for this historic position.[201] Teehee was born on March 2, 1966, and spent her formative years in Claremore, Oklahoma. She attended Northeastern State University in Tahlequah, Oklahoma, and received her juris doctorate from the University of Iowa.[202] Under the mentorship of Wilma Mankiller, the first woman to serve as principal chief of the Cherokee Nation, Teehee followed Mankiller's advice to cut her chops as a young professional by working in Washington.[203] Once there she spent a decade in service to the House of Representatives Native American Caucus as a Hill staffer before joining the Obama administration's White House Domestic Policy Council as the first senior policy adviser for Native American affairs. In this capacity Teehee advanced such important developments as the UN Declaration on the Rights of Indigenous Peoples, the Violence Against Women Act, the 2009 Presidential Memorandum on Tribal Consultation, Executive Order 13592: Improving American Indian and Alaska Native Educational Opportunities and Strengthening Tribal Colleges and Universities, and three White House Tribal Nations Conferences. Teehee then returned to the Cherokee Nation to take up posts as the vice president of governmental relations for Cherokee Nation businesses and as the director of government relations for the Cherokee Nation.[204]

In the fall of 2019 Chief Hoskin nominated Kim Teehee as the Cherokee Nation delegate to the US House of Representatives. The tribal council unanimously approved the nomination, and President Barack Obama penned a personal letter of congratulations: "I could not be prouder of your new job representing the Cherokee Nation in Congress!"[205] As part of her responsibilities, Teehee can introduce federal legislation, vote with committees, and debate on the House floor. The position is in many ways, such as the nonvoting status, akin to those of representatives of US territories and the District of Columbia.[206]

Teehee continues to wait for congressional approval before the role becomes official. The path to this congressional action could take shape in a more permanent form, as legislation that would create a seat for the Cherokee Nation delegate, of which Teehee would be the first. Alternatively, the Speaker of the House could seat the delegate directly, although this action could be reversed by future Speakers.[207] In any case, members of Congress on both sides of the aisle are largely in agreement that the treaty provisions should be enacted. Oklahoma representative and Chickasaw Nation citizen Tom Cole agreed that "there is no question that the Cherokee Nation has a legitimate case to make."[208]

As the Cherokee Nation continues to advance this spearheading development, Chief Hoskin reflects, "We owe it [to] our ancestors, who wisely negotiated this guaranteed right not once or twice but three times in treaty negotiations with the US government."[209] Indeed, the presence of a Cherokee tribal representative in the US Congress would signal a victory not only for the tribe but for all who seek a greater voice for Native peoples in federal affairs and champion the cause of ensuring that the federal government upholds its obligations to the first Americans. As the largest Native American tribe in the United States, the Cherokee Nation, Chief Hoskin believes, is well-positioned to champion this cause.[210]

Together, Kim Teehee and Charles Blackwell provide two twenty-first-century examples of how the legacy of historic tribal delegates lives on in Washington, DC. Like the ancestors who charted this path hundreds of years prior, Teehee, Blackwell, and thousands of contemporary Native Americans like them continue to advocate for Indigenous peoples in the nation's capital city. Their contributions remain visible in the built environment of the District, their critical work impacts the lives of Natives peoples throughout the United States, and their stories continue to inspire Indian Country.

NOTES

1. Herman J. Viola, *Diplomats in Buckskin: A History of Indian Delegations in Washington City* (Bluffton, SC: Rivilo, 1995), 22.

2. "Itinerary of Delegates in Washington, 1857–1858," Peabody Museum of Archaeology and Ethnology at Harvard University, accessed July 24, 2020, https://www.peabody.harvard.edu/node/2258.

3. "Itinerary of Delegates in Washington, 1857–1858."

4. Heather A. Shannon and Sky Campbell, "Prominent Americans: Photographs of Treaty Delegates at the Smithsonian," *American Indian Magazine*, Summer/Fall 2014, https://www.americanindianmagazine.org/story/prominent-americans-photographs-treaty-delegates-smithsonian.

5. Viola, *Diplomats in Buckskin*, 31.

6. Noenoe K. Silva, *Aloha Betrayed: Native Hawaiian Resistance to American Colonialism* (Durham, NC: Duke University Press, 2004), 157.

7. Topher Mathews, "The Interesting Story of the Dumbarton Bridge," Greater Greater Washington, August 18, 2010, https://ggwash.org/view/6132/the-interesting-story-of-the-dumbarton-bridge.

8. John G. Neihardt, *Black Elk Speaks* (Lincoln: University of Nebraska Press, 1932), 182.

9. James McLaughlin, *My Friend the Indian* (Cambridge, MA: Riverside, 1910), 185.

10. Sam A. Maddra, *Hostiles? The Lakota Ghost Dance and Buffalo Bill's Wild West* (Norman: University of Oklahoma Press, 2006).

11. Alyssa Mt. Pleasant and David A. Chang, "The Horror of Trump's Wounded Knee Tweet," *Politico Magazine*, January 17, 2019, https://www.politico.com/magazine/story/2019/01/17/the-horror-of-trumps-wounded-knee-tweet-224024.

12. Mt. Pleasant and Chang.

13. Maddra, *Hostiles?*, 3.

14. Callum Cleary, "A Forgotten Fight? Kicking Bear and the Dumbarton Bridge," *Boundary Stones* (blog), December 12, 2017, https://blogs.weta.org/boundarystones/2017/12/12/forgotten-fight-kicking-bear-and-dumbarton-bridge#footnote-1.

15. Cynthia L. Landrum, "Kicking Bear, John Trudell, and Anthony Kiedis (of the Red Hot Chili Peppers): Show Indians" and Pop-Cultural Colonialism," *American Indian Quarterly* 36, no. 2 (Spring 2012): 190; and Philip J. Deloria, *Indians in Unexpected Places* (Lawrence: University of Kansas Press, 2004), 69.

16. "Selected the Indian Delegates," *Omaha Daily Bee*, February 15, 1896, https://chroniclingamerica.loc.gov/data/batches/nbu_emerson_vero1/data/sn99021999/00206539501/1896021501/0908.pdf.

17. "Big Sioux Here," *Evening Star*, February 28, 1896, https://chroniclingamerica.loc.gov/data/batches/dlc_havanese_vero1/data/sn83045462/00280655053/1896022801/0141.pdf.

18. "Big Sioux Here."

19. "Big Sioux Here."

20. "Big Sioux Here."

21. "Chiefs at the Navy Yard," *Evening Star*, February 29, 1896, https://chroniclingamerica.loc.gov/lccn/sn83045462/1896-02-29/ed-1/seq-1/#date1=1896&index=2&rows=20&words=Bear+Kicking&searchType=basic&sequence=0&state=District+of+Columbia&date2=1896&proxtext=%22kicking+bear%22&y=19&x=14&dateFilterType=yearRange&page=1.

22. "The Sioux Delegation," *Evening Star*, March 13, 1896, https://chroniclingamerica.loc.gov/lccn/sn83045462/1896-03-13/ed-1/seq-12/#date1=1896&index=3&rows=20&words=Bear+Kicking&searchType=basic&sequence=0&state=District+of+Columbia&date2=1896&proxtext=%22kicking+bear%22&y=19&x=14&dateFilterType=yearRange&page=1.

23. "With an Indian Warrior," *Evening Star,* May 30, 1896, https://chroniclingamerica.loc.gov/lccn/sn83045462/1896-05-30/ed-1/seq-15/#date1=1896&index=1&rows=20&words=Bear+Kick+Kicking&searchType=basic&sequence=0&state=District+of+Columbia&date2=1896&proxtext=%22kicking+bear%22&y=19&x=14&dateFilterType=yearRange&page=1.

24. Landrum, "Kicking Bear, John Trudell, and Anthony Kiedis," 191.

25. David Ewing Duncan, "The Object at Hand," *Smithsonian* 22, no. 6 (September 1991): 22.

26. Duncan, "The Object at Hand," 22.

27. Mathews, "The Interesting Story of the Dumbarton Bridge."

28. Frank Ahrens, "A Bridge Too Far," *Washington Post*, July 6, 2000, https://www.washingtonpost.com/archive/lifestyle/magazine/2000/07/16/a-bridge-too-far/ab40030a-e66e-40b8-a6cd-5ade494dcfb8/.

29. Ahrens.

30. "Mission and History," National Congress of American Indians, accessed August 6, 2020, http://www.ncai.org/about-ncai/mission-history.

31. Vine Deloria Jr. *Custer Died for Your Sins: An Indian Manifesto* (Norman: University of Oklahoma Press, 1988), 76.

32. Thomas W. Cowger, *The National Congress of American Indians: The Founding Years* (Lincoln: University of Nebraska Press, 1999), 100.

33. Francis Paul Prucha, *The Great Father: The United States Government and the American Indians* (Lincoln: University of Nebraska Press, 1984), 1058.

34. Deloria, *Custer Died for Your Sins*, 75.

35. "Mission and History."

36. "Mission and History."

37. Quoted in K. Tsianina Lomawaima, *They Called It Prairie Light: The Story of Chilocco Indian School* (Lincoln: University of Nebraska Press, 1994), 145.

38. "Mission and History."

39. "Mission and History."

40. "The Founding Meeting of NCAI," National Congress of American Indians, accessed August 6, 2020, http://www.ncai.org/about-ncai/mission-history/the-founding -meeting-of-ncai.

41. "The Founding Meeting of NCAI."

42. Cowger, *The National Congress of American Indians*, 40; and "The Founding Meeting of NCAI."

43. "The Founding Meeting of NCAI."

44. "Seventy Years of NCAI," National Congress of American Indians, accessed August 6, 2020, http://www.ncai.org/about-ncai/mission-history/seventy-years-of-ncai.

45. See, for instance, *Cherokee Nation v. Georgia* (1832) and the US Constitution's Indian Commerce Clause.

46. "Embassy of Tribal Nations," National Congress of American Indians, accessed August 6, 2020, http://www.ncai.org/about-ncai/embassy-of-tribal-nations.

47. *National Congress of American Indians Annual Report* (Washington, DC: National Congress of American Indians, 2008), 4.

48. "NCAI Purchases Building for Tribal Embassy in DC," *Indianz.com*, May 7, 2009, https://www.indianz.com/News/2009/014426.asp.

49. Nikole Hannah-Jones, "Tribal Embassy Opens in Washington, DC," *Oregonian*, November 2, 2009, https://www.oregonlive.com/race/2009/11/tribal_embassy_opens_in _washin.html.

50. *National Congress of American Indians Annual Report* (Washington, DC: National Congress of American Indians, 2009), 7.

51. Hannah-Jones, "Tribal Embassy Opens in Washington, DC."

52. *National Congress of American Indians Annual Report* (Washington, DC: National Congress of American Indians, 2014), 48.

53. "Chickasaws Name U.S. Ambassador," *Oklahoman*, March 2, 1995, https:// oklahoman.com/article/2494136/chickasaws-name-us-ambassador.

54. "About the Navajo Nation," Navajo Nation Washington Office, accessed August 15, 2020, https://www.nnwo.org/About-the-Navajo-Nation.

55. Pauly Denetclaw, "A Native Embassy Row? Navajo Nation Is Looking for a DC Home," *Indian Country Today*, March 18, 2019, https://indiancountrytoday .com/news/a-native-embassy-row-navajo-nation-is-looking-for-a-dc-home -mYTKMERKCUeHnWFnmrnx9A.

56. "Indian Country Shows Support for Washington Embassy," Indianz.com, March 3, 2015, https://www.indianz.com/News/2005/006804.asp.

57. *National Congress of American Indians Annual Report* (2008), 4.

58. "Indian Country Shows Support for Washington Embassy."

59. *Walking Tour: American Indians* (Washington, DC: Association for the Preservation of the Historic Congressional Cemetery, 2007), https://congressionalcemetery.org/wp -content/uploads/2022/03/American-Indian-Walking-Tour-rev.-03.2022_compressed.pdf.

60. "Rules and Regulations," Congressional Cemetery, accessed August 15, 2020, https://congressionalcemetery.org/rules-regulations/.

61. *Walking Tour: American Indians*.

62. "Rules and Regulations."

63. "Native Nations Honor Ancestors Interred at Congressional Cemetery," *Cherokee Phoenix*, May 20, 2010, https://www.cherokeephoenix.org/Article/index/3854.

64. "Native Nations Honor Ancestors Interred at Congressional Cemetery."

65. Viola, *Diplomats in Buckskin*, 167.

66. Edwin R. Sweeney, ed., *Cochise: Firsthand Accounts of the Chiricahua Apache Chief* (Norman: University of Oklahoma Press 2014), 268.

67. Sweeney, *Cochise*, 290.

68. Rachel Cassidy, "'Hear Me, My Chiefs,'" *Buried History* (blog), National Museum of the American Indian, April 8, 2013, https://blog.nmai.si.edu/main/2013/04/buried -history-hear-me-my-chiefs.html.

69. Cassidy.

70. "Pushmataha, Famous Indian Buried in Congressional Cemetery," *Congressional Record—Senate*, May 19, 1976, 14575.

71. Viola, *Diplomats in Buckskin*, 159.

72. Cassidy, "'Hear Me, My Chiefs.'"

73. Viola, *Diplomats in Buckskin*, 165.

74. Cassidy, "'Hear Me, My Chiefs.'"

75. Carolyn Thomas Foreman, "The Coodey Family of the Indian Territory," *Chronicles of Oklahoma* 25, no. 4 (Winter 1947–48): 325.

76. Foreman, 326.

77. Foreman, 326.

78. Quoted in Foreman, 331.

79. Foreman, 328.

80. Foreman, 332.

81. "History," Cherokee Nation, accessed August 17, 2020, https://www.cherokee.org /about-the-nation/history/.

82. "Cherokee Nation Constitution," Cherokee Nation, accessed August 17, 2020, https://www.cherokee.org/our-government/cherokee-nation-constitution/.

83. The Cherokee Nation ratified a new constitution once again, most recently in 2003.

84. Foreman, "The Coodey Family of the Indian Territory," 323, 332, 338, 339.

85. Foreman, 339.

86. Carolyn Thomas Foreman, "A Cherokee Pioneer, Ella Floora Coodey Robinson," *Chronicles of Oklahoma* 7, no. 4 (1929): 366.

87. Foreman, "The Coodey Family of the Indian Territory," 340.

88. Foreman, 340; and Foreman, "A Cherokee Pioneer, Ella Floora Coodey Robinson," 368.

89. "CN Desecrating Sacred Symbol," *Cherokee Phoenix*, October 27, 2008, https://www .cherokeephoenix.org/Article/index/2365.

90. "Capt Richard George Fields," Find A Grave, last modified September 9, 2004, https://www.findagrave.com/memorial/9440562/richard-george-fields.

91. *Evening Star*, March 1, 1873, https://chroniclingamerica.loc.gov/lccn/sn83045462 /1873-03-01/ed-1/seq-8/.

92. Robert J. Conley, *A Cherokee Encyclopedia* (Albuquerque: University of New Mexico Press, 2007), 141.

93. *Walking Tour: American Indians*.

94. Conley, *A Cherokee Encyclopedia*, 141; and "Other Famous Indians Buried in the Congressional Cemetery," *Congressional Record–Senate*, May 19, 1976, 14575.

95. *Walking Tour: American Indians*.

96. William Penn Boudinot, ed., *Laws of the Cherokee Nation, Passed during the Years 1839–1867* (St. Louis: Missouri Democrat Print, 1868), 167, 195.

97. Viola, *Diplomats in Buckskin*, 159.

98. Trevor M. Jones, "Pegg, Thomas," *The Encyclopedia of Oklahoma History and Culture*, accessed September 1, 2020, https://www.okhistory.org/publications/enc/entry.php?entry=PE008.

99. Jones; and Boudinot, *Laws of the Cherokee Nation*, 140.

100. Boudinot, *Laws of the Cherokee Nation*, 141.

101. *Walking Tour: American Indians*.

102. Doyne Cantrell, *Western Cherokee Nation of Arkansas and Missouri: A History, a Heritage* (Morrisville, NC: Lulu, 2009), 12; and Robert A. Myers, "Cherokee Pioneers in Arkansas: The St. Francis Years, 1785–1813," *Arkansas Historical Quarterly* 56, no. 2 (Summer 1997), 131.

103. Cantrell, *Western Cherokee Nation of Arkansas and Missouri*, 12.

104. Appointment of and Instructions to Delegates from Western Cherokee Sent to Washington City, January 11, 1838, John Ross Papers, 4026.513-.1, Gilcrease Museum, Tulsa, OK.

105. *Walking Tour: American Indians*.

106. John Downing Benedict, *Muskogee and Northeastern Oklahoma: Including the Counties of Muskogee, McIntosh, Wagoner, Cherokee, Sequoyah, Adair, Delaware, Mayes, Rogers, Washington, Nowata, Craig, and Ottawa* (Chicago: S. J. Clarke, 1922).

107. Donald Ricky, *Indians of Louisiana* (St. Clair Shores, MI: Somerset, 1999), 231.

108. Ricky, 231; and John R. Finger, *The Eastern Band of Cherokees, 1819–1900* (Knoxville: University of Tennessee Press, 1984), 52.

109. Ricky, *Indians of Louisiana*, 231.

110. "Death," *Daily National Intelligencer*, April 8, 1846, https://images.findagrave.com/photos/2012/107/9452172_133466603978.jpg.

111. OsiyoTV, "Cherokee Almanac: Ezekiel Starr and the Cherokee Civil War," YouTube video, 4:07, April 8, 2019, https://www.youtube.com/watch?v=1W1Wl_Sg-e8.

112. "Death," *Daily National Intelligencer*.

113. OsiyoTV, "Cherokee Almanac: Ezekiel Starr and the Cherokee Civil War."

114. U.S. Congress, House, *Estate of Bluford West*, 52nd Cong., 1st sess., 1892, H. Rep. 182, 1, https://digitalcommons.law.ou.edu/cgi/viewcontent.cgi?article=6867&context=indianserialset.

115. *Walking Tour: American Indians*; Charles E. Cleland, *Rites of Conquest: The History and Culture of Michigan's Native Americans* (Ann Arbor: University of Michigan Press, 1992), 227; Charles E. Cleland, *The Place of the Pike (Gnoozhekaaning): A History of the Bay Mills Indian Community* (Ann Arbor: University of Michigan Press, 2001), 21; Charles Joseph Kappler, ed., "Treaty with the Chippewa, 1837," in *Indian Affairs: Laws and Treaties*, vol. 2 *Treaties* (Washington, DC: Government Printing Office, 1904), 492; Ben Cahoon, "Native American Nations," *World Statesman*, n.d., accessed September 18, 2020, https://www.worldstatesmen.org/US_NativeAM.html; Minnesota Historical Society, *The Fox and Ojibwa War* (St. Paul: Minnesota Historical Society, 1872), 346; Joel E. Whitney, *Portrait of Wa-Bo-Jeek, (White Fisher) Chief of Gull Lake Band 1860*, 1860, Photo, National Anthropological Archives, Smithsonian Institution, Suitland, Maryland, https://americanhistory.si.edu/old-collections/search?edan_q=*:*&edan_fq[]=date:%221860s%22&edan_fq[]=culture:%22Indians+of+North+America+Northeast%22&edan_fq[]=set_name:%22James+E.+Taylor+scrapbook+of+the+American+West+1863-1900%22; and Miléna Santoro and

Erick Detlef Langer, *Hemispheric Indigeneities: Native Identity and Agency in Mesoamerica, the Andes, and Canada* (Lincoln: University of Nebraska Press, 2018), 197.

116. Kappler, ed., "Treaty with the Chippewa, 1837," 492.

117. Cleland, *Rites of Conquest*, 226.

118. Cleland, 227; Santoro and Detlef Langer, *Hemispheric Indigeneities*, 197.

119. Santoro and Erick Detlef Langer, *Hemispheric Indigeneities*, 198.

120. *The Spirit of Missions* (Burlington: J. L. Powell, 1837), 377.

121. William W. Warren, ed. *History of the Ojibway People* (St. Paul: Minnesota Historical Society Press, 1984), 226.

122. Gail Guthrie Valaskakis, *Indian Country: Essays on Contemporary Native Culture* (Waterloo, ONT: Wilfrid Laurier University Press, 2005), 14.

123. *Walking Tour: American Indians.*

124. "Obituaries Surname O," *Congressional Cemetery*, accessed August 6, 2020, https://congressionalcemetery.org/wp-content/uploads/2019/09/obit-surname-O.pdf; and *Walking Tour: American Indians.*

125. "Other Famous Indians Buried in the Congressional Cemetery," 14575; and "Obituaries Surname O."

126. "Obituaries Surname O"; and Robert Pohl, "Lost Capitol Hill: B Street House (Pt. 1)," *The Hill Is Home* (blog), December 28, 2009, https://thehillishome.com/2009/12/lost-capitol-hill-b-street-south-pt-1-2/.

127. *Walking Tour: American Indians.*

128. "Other Famous Indians Buried in the Congressional Cemetery," 14575.

129. John Swanton, *Source Material for the Social and Ceremonial Life of the Choctaw Indians* (Washington, DC: Government Printing Office, 1931), 4.

130. Greg O'Brien, "Pushmataha: Choctaw Warrior, Diplomat, and Chief," *Mississippi History Now*, July 2001, http://www.mshistorynow.mdah.ms.gov/articles/14/pushmataha-choctaw-warrior-diplomat-and-chief.

131. Gideon Lincecum, *Pushmataha: A Choctaw Leader and His People* (Tuscaloosa: University of Alabama Press, 2004), 98.

132. Lincecum, *Pushmataha*, 89.

133. Viola, *Diplomats in Buckskin*, 167.

134. Batton, "Congressional Cemetery Final Resting Place."

135. Viola, *Diplomats in Buckskin*, 165.

136. Lincecum, *Pushmataha*, 99; and Viola, *Diplomats in Buckskin*, 165.

137. Lincecum, *Pushmataha*, 99.

138. Batton, "Congressional Cemetery Final Resting Place."

139. W. David Baird, *Peter Pitchlynn: Chief of the Choctaws* (Norman: University of Oklahoma Press, 1986).

140. Peter Pitchlynn, "A Man between Nations: The Diary of Peter Pitchlynn," *Missouri Review* 14, no. 3 (1991): 61.

141. Pitchlynn, 61.

142. James P. Pate, "Pitchlynn, Peter Perkins," in *The Encyclopedia of Oklahoma History and Culture*, https://www.okhistory.org/publications/enc/entry.php?entry=PI013; Gary Batton, "Congressional Cemetery Final Resting Place for Two Honored Choctaw Chiefs," *Biskinik*, July 2011, 3.

143. Viola, *Diplomats in Buckskin,* 88.

144. Pate, "Pitchlynn, Peter Perkins."

145. Batton, "Congressional Cemetery Final Resting Place."

146. *Walking Tour: American Indians.*

147. *Walking Tour: American Indians.*

148. U.S. Congress, Senate, *Correspondence on the Subject of the Emmigration of Indians between the 30th November 1831, and 27th December 1833, with Abstracts of Expenditures by Disbursing Agents,* 14th Cong., 1st sess. to 48th Cong., 2nd sess., 1835, S. Doc. 512, 335.

149. *Walking Tour: American Indians.*

150. *Walking Tour: American Indians.*

151. Rebecca Boggs Roberts and Sandra K. Schmidt, *Historic Congressional Cemetery* (Charleston, SC: Arcadia, 2012), 111.

152. Rachel Cassidy, "Dangerous Missions: Indian Diplomats and Foul Play in the Nation's Capitol," *American Indian Magazine,* Summer 2013, 42.

153. "Treaty Timeline," Relationships: Dakota and Ojibwe Treaties, accessed July 3, 2020, http://treatiesmatter.org/treaties/timeline; Treaty with the Sioux–Sisseton and Wahpeton Bands, February 19, 1867, Indian Treaties, 1789–1869, 60693882, National Archives and Records Administration, College Park, MD; and Kangiduta (Scarlet Crow) (1867), The Church of the Epiphany, accessed July 7, 2020, http://epiphanydc.org/2017/03/13/march-15-kangiduta-scarlet-crow-1867/.

154. Cassidy, "Dangerous Missions."

155. Rachel Cassidy, "Foul Play," *Buried History* (blog), National Museum of the American Indian, January 4, 2013, https://blog.nmai.si.edu/main/2013/01/introducing-buried-history-edition-1-foul-play.html.

156. *Walking Tour: American Indians*; and Cassidy, "Dangerous Missions."

157. "Other Famous Indians Buried in the Congressional Cemetery," 14575.

158. U.S. Congress, Senate, Committee on Indian Affairs, Oversight Hearing on Amendment to the Native American Graves Protection and Repatriation Act, 109th Cong., 1st sess., 2005, 20–21.

159. Cassidy, "Dangerous Missions," 44.

160. "Inside the Beltway," *Washington Times,* November 8, 2001, https://www.washingtontimes.com/news/2001/nov/8/20011108-030943-1967r/.

161. Clifford Krainik and Michele Krainik, "Photographs of Indian Delegates in the President's 'Summer House,'" White House Historical Association, Spring 2009, https://www.whitehousehistory.org/photographs-of-indian-delegates-in-the-presidents-summer-house.

162. *Walking Tour: American Indians.*

163. Mary Jane Warde, *When the Wolf Came: The Civil War and the Indian Territory* (Fayetteville: University of Arkansas Press, 2013), 226.

164. Krainik and Krainik, "Photographs of Indian Delegates"; and Viola, *Diplomats in Buckskin,* 101.

165. Krainik and Krainik, "Photographs of Indian Delegates."

166. "Death of an Indian Chief," *Evening Star,* April 6, 1863, https://chroniclingamerica.loc.gov/data/batches/dlc_alf_ver01/data/sn83045462/00280654206/1863040601/0065.pdf.

167. "Indian Delegation, 1863," White House Historical Association, accessed July 7, 2020, https://www.whitehousehistory.org/photos/indian-delegation-1863; and "Death of an Indian Chief."

168. "The Treaty Period," National Park Service, accessed July 11, 2020, https://www.nps.gov/nepe/learn/historyculture/the-treaty-era.htm#:~:text=After%20more%20than%20a%20week,the%20US%20Senate%20in%201859.

169. Treaty with the Nez Perces, June 9, 1863, University of Tulsa, http://resources
.utulsa.edu/law/classes/rice/Treaties/14_Stat_0647_Nez_Perces.htm.

170. "The Flight of 1877," National Park Service, accessed July 11, 2020, https://www
.nps.gov/nepe/learn/historyculture/1877.htm.

171. Cassidy, "Dangerous Missions," 44.

172. Jourdan Bennett-Begaye, "'Most Prominent' Headstone of Nez Percé Leader
Replaced," *Indian Country Today*, October 15, 2018, https://indiancountrytoday.com/news
/most-prominent-headstone-of-nez-perce-leader-replaced-yOwHXpKG4ku5A-D1TeqF4g.

173. Cassidy, "Dangerous Missions," 44.

174. Bennett-Begaye, "'Most Prominent' Headstone."

175. J. Sterling Morton, ed., "Pawnee Indians in the City," *Conservative*, December 26,
1901, 9.

176. Conflicting reports show Tuckalixtah's death occurred on March 24, 28, 29, or 30,
1858. Viola, *Diplomats in Buckskin*, 159; Diana Loren and Desireé Martinez, "Itinerary of
Delegates in Washington, 1857–1858," *Breaking the Silence: Nineteenth-Century Indian Del-
egations in Washington, D.C.*, Peabody Museum of Archaeology and Ethnology at Harvard
University, 2005, https://www.peabody.harvard.edu/node/2258; and Morton, "Pawnee
Indians in the City."

177. Viola, *Diplomats in Buckskin*, 165.

178. Morton, "Pawnee Indians in the City."

179. Viola, *Diplomats in Buckskin*, 165; and Loren and Martinez, "Itinerary of Delegates
in Washington, 1857–1858."

180. Viola, *Diplomats in Buckskin*, 165.

181. Ben Nighthorse Campbell, foreword to *Diplomats in Buckskin: A History of Indian
Delegations in Washington City*, by Herman J. Viola (Bluffton, SC: Rivilo, 1995), 8.

182. *Walking Tour: American Indians.*

183. Charles Joseph Kappler, ed., "Treaty with the Winnebago, 1859," in *Indian Affairs:
Laws and Treaties*, vol. 2, *Treaties* (Washington, DC: Government Printing Office, 1904),
792.

184. "Chickasaws Name U.S. Ambassador."

185. Tony Choate, "Chickasaw Nation Ambassador Charles W. Blackwell—A Man
of Vision," *Chickasaw Nation*, January 4, 2013, https://www.chickasaw.net/News/Press
-Releases/Release/Chickasaw-Nation-Ambassador-Charles-W-Blackwell-%E2%80%93
-1305.aspx; and "Charles W. Blackwell," Chickasaw Hall of Fame, Chickasaw Nation,
accessed July 22, 2020, https://hof.chickasaw.net/Members/2014/Charles-Blackwell.aspx.

186. "Charles W. Blackwell."

187. Choate, "Chickasaw Nation Ambassador."

188. Choate.

189. "Chickasaws Name U.S. Ambassador."

190. "Five to Be Inducted into Chickasaw Hall of Fame," *Chickasaw Times*, November
2020, http://www.chickasawtimes.net/Web-Exclusives/Archive/2014/March/Five-to-be
-inducted-into-Chickasaw-Hall-of-Fame.aspx.

191. "Five to Be Inducted"; and Presidential Advisory Council on HIV/AIDS, *AIDS:
No Time to Spare: The Final Report to the President of the United States* (Washington, DC:
Presidential Advisory Council on HIV/AIDS, 2000, 72.

192. "Five to Be Inducted."

193. Choate, "Chickasaw Nation Ambassador."

194. Brigit Katz, "Kimberly Teehee Will Be the Cherokee Nation's First Delegate to Congress," *Smithsonian Magazine*, September 4, 2019, https://www.smithsonianmag.com/smart-news/kimberly-teehee-cherokee-nations-first-delegate-congress-180973046/.

195. Katz.

196. Chuck Hoskin Jr., "The 184-Year-Old Promise to the Cherokee Congress Must Keep," *New York Times*, September 17, 2019, https://www.nytimes.com/2019/09/17/opinion/cherokee-house-of-representatives.html?auth=login-email&login=email.

197. Chuck Hoskin Jr., "Cherokee Nation's Historic Delegate to Congress," *Indianz.com*, September 30, 2019, https://www.indianz.com/News/2019/09/30/cherokee-nations-historic-delegate-to-co.asp.

198. Hoskin, "Cherokee Nation's Historic Delegate to Congress."

199. "A Treacherous Choice and a Treaty Right," *NPR*, April 8, 2020, https://www.npr.org/transcripts/824647676.

200. Hoskin, "Cherokee Nation's Historic Delegate to Congress."

201. "A Treacherous Choice."

202. Kerri Lee Alexander, "Kimberly Teehee," National Women's History Museum, accessed December 3, 2020, https://www.womenshistory.org/education-resources/biographies/kimberly-teehee.

203. Jourdan Bennett-Begaye, "Kim Teehee Is the 'One Woman Show,'" *Indian Country Today*, November 3, 2019, https://indiancountrytoday.com/news/video-kim-teehee-is-the-one-woman-show-X-8w-TghZUywSsg9KjM1Wg.

204. Alexander, "Kimberly Teehee."

205. Bennett-Begaye, "Kim Teehee Is the 'One Woman Show.'"

206. Katz, "Kimberly Teehee Will Be the Cherokee Nation's First Delegate to Congress."

207. Hoskin, "The 184-Year-Old Promise."

208. Caroline Halter, "Cherokee Nation Lays Out Two Paths for Sending Delegate to Congress," *KOSU*, November 5, 2019, https://www.kosu.org/post/cherokee-nation-lays-out-two-paths-sending-delegate-congress.

209. Hoskin, "Cherokee Nation's Historic Delegate to Congress."

210. Hoskin.

2 First Peoples in Monuments, Museums, and Military Service

Native Americans in the US Armed Forces have served in every major US military engagement of the last 245 years.[1] In fact, Native peoples enlist at the highest per capita rate of any ethnic group—4.6 percentage points higher, to be exact.[2] At present, approximately 31,000 active duty servicemen and -women hail from Indigenous communities, and another 140,000 Native veterans continue to tell their stories of service and inspire the upcoming generations.[3] At Native American powwows and social gatherings, attendees will often note the extensive honors placed upon veterans, as evidenced by the opening of events with a Color Guard procession, the playing of a veterans' song, and more.

Much, but not all, of the widespread call to military service so prevalent in Indian Country stems from a culture-based warrior tradition, which began well before European contact, that merged with American military efforts beginning with the Revolutionary War and continuing into the present.[4] "I am American and I am Indian and I am a vet," reflected Air Force veteran senator Ben Nighthorse Campbell (Northern Cheyenne), "I believe I was compelled to serve to honor the warrior tradition, which is inherent to most Native American societies—the pillars of strength, honor, pride, devotion, and wisdom."[5] American Indian studies scholar Tom Holm (Cherokee/Muskogee [Creek]), himself a Marine Corps veteran of the Vietnam War, similarly points to the long history of warrior societies, cultural ceremonies, and distinct meanings of war among tribal communities as elements that frame contemporary Native military service and make it unique.[6] Holm thus identifies "cultural values as opposed to political views" as the driving force behind Native enlistment.[7] Veteran counselor Harold Barse (Kiowa) reflected on his own experience: "You can't confuse Indian patriotism with your regular American-type patriotism (mom, apple pie, and things like this); the American Indian doesn't view it that way. When they serve, they are serving for their people."[8]

In his work on Lakota and Dakota service in the Vietnam War, historian John Little (Standing Rock Sioux Tribe) points to ways in which military service for Native peoples in more recent times has provided the ability to "find meaning for Native values in the white world" and assist in the construction of a personal Indigenous identity.[9] Simultaneously, however, Little's study reveals the racism that Native service members faced, from name-calling and racial epithets to being selected to walk point, leading troops into combat as the first and most exposed soldier.[10] The story of John Raymond Rice illuminates precisely this difficult tension between non-Native society, the First Americans, and the tradition of service to one's country, and it shines a light on the role of Washington, DC, in this complex narrative.

Sgt. 1st Class John Raymond Rice (Ho-Chunk) was born in 1914 on the Winnebago Indian Reservation in Nebraska.[11] As a child he attended government-run Indian schools before enlisting in the Army in 1940.[12] In World War II Rice was deployed to the Pacific Theater, where he distinguished himself as a lead scout and earned a Purple Heart.[13] His comrades described him fondly as a "real soldier," and his wife, Evelyn, spoke of his "love" for the Army. Despite overcoming malaria and the infamous "jungle rot" during his first tour, the dedicated serviceman reenlisted in 1946.[14]

Rice again saw combat during the Korean War.[15] Along with the Eighth Regiment of the First Cavalry Division, he fought in the Battle of the Pusan Perimeter, an effort to maintain control of the remaining portion of the Korean peninsula under South Korean rule.[16] Rice also served off the field in the role of accompanying fallen soldiers to their homes for burial rites.[17] On September 6, 1950, Rice perished while holding the Naktong River line in the Second Battle of Naktong Bulge.[18]

The sergeant's widow, Evelyn Rice, secured plots in the Sioux City Memorial Park Cemetery as her and her husband's final resting place. However, Evelyn Rice, herself a white woman, was not provided notice of the cemetery's "whites only" policy. Thus, the August 28, 1951 funerary proceedings unfolded as outlined until cemetery officials intervened right before the moment of internment.[19] Refusing to bury a Native American in the Memorial Park Cemetery, the staff notified Evelyn Rice of the interruption hours after the mourners had left the scene.[20] They encouraged Evelyn Rice to complete the burial by signing a document verifying that her late husband was a white man.[21] To this, she rebuffed: "When these men are in the Army, they are all equal and the same. I certainly thought they would be the same after death."[22] Evelyn did not consent.

The family moved his body to Ho-Chunk lands as word of the botched burial made its way up the chain from the soldier who had escorted his remains, to his commanding officer, to the Army's quartermaster general, and all the way to Washington.[23] When news that a Ho-Chunk veteran, killed in combat, had been denied the dignity of a burial because he was "not a member of the Caucasian race" reached the White House, President Harry Truman resolved that "the National appreciation of patriotic service should not be limited by race, color or creed."[24] The president then made arrangements for Rice to be interred in Arlington National Cemetery—a gesture to both honor Rice's service and to humiliate the Memorial Park Cemetery as propagators of racism against the nation's fallen heroes.

On September 5, 1951, Sgt. 1st Class John Raymond Rice was buried at Arlington National Cemetery with full military honors.[25] Servicemen escorted Rice's family to Washington for the "simple, beautiful, and moving" service.[26] A parade—including an American Legion Honor Guard, three infantry accompaniments, a platoon of eighteen, and members of the Veterans of Foreign Wars—marched to the US Army Band, paying their respects alongside Ho-Chunk tribal representatives who performed a traditional flag song.[27] Seven horses brought Rice's casket to the gravesite. The president himself sent a wreath to be presented and ensured that a military representative relayed his condolences.[28]

While this grand display certainly offered a public condemnation of racism against Native American service members, the gesture did not solve the problem of prejudice itself. In fact, Rice's widow brought a $180,000 discrimination suit against the Memorial Park Cemetery and lost in a 4–4 United States Supreme Court decision issued in November 1954. Evelyn Rice's ashes were laid to rest next to her husband in Arlington National Cemetery on May 12, 2006.[29]

The John Rice incident lays bare the uneasy realities of anti-Native racism, even as directed against those who paid the ultimate sacrifice for their country.[30] His gravesite at Arlington National Cemetery—a visible retaliation against this discrimination—bears witness to an ugly history that must not be forgotten, and it pushes viewers to apply these lessons to the injustices of today. The remainder of this chapter shines a light on similar sites of testimony: the memorials, monuments, and museums around Washington, DC, dedicated to honoring outstanding Native American contributions to the nation.

US Marine Corps War Memorial

Adjacent to Arlington National Cemetery, the US Marine Corps War Memorial remains among the most visited sites in the Washington, DC, area by tourists and locals alike. The memorial, raised by President Dwight D. Eisenhower on November 10, 1954, is dedicated "in honor and memory of the men of the United States Marine Corps who have given their lives to the country since November 10, 1775."[31] Over 1.5 million visitors come to the memorial each year.[32]

Also known colloquially as the Iwo Jima Memorial, the structure gained this nickname as a reference to its subject matter. The memorial showcases thirty-two-foot statues of six Marines raising an even taller US flag at Iwo Jima, a volcanic island in the Ogasawara Archipelago of Japan, during World War II.[33] As one of the few remaining islands under Japanese control by 1945, the capture of Iwo Jima became a primary target in the Pacific campaign.[34]

On February 23, 1945, men from the 4th and 5th Marine Division completed their five-day mission to secure Iwo Jima. Marines of Company E, 2nd Battalion, scaled Mount Suribachi and raised an American flag atop the peak for others to see across the island.[35] Ultimately, the raising of the flag on Mount Suribachi became not only a symbol of the Allies' success at Iwo Jima but of their victory in World War II as a whole.

Joe Rosenthal of the Associated Press captured the afternoon raising of a second, larger American flag in a now-iconic photograph.[36] That year he received a Pulitzer Prize for this work.[37] The US Marine Corps War Memorial offers a 3D replication of Rosenthal's photo.[38]

Artist Felix W. de Weldon transformed the image into a larger-than-life sculpture. He worked with the (then believed to be) three surviving men from the photo, including Ira Hayes (Akimel O'odham), to construct their likenesses. The plaster mold was then taken to New York City to be cast in bronze, a process that took approximately three years. A three-truck caravan transported the dozen pieces—the largest weighing more than twenty tons—down to Washington, DC, for assembly atop a Swedish granite base. The $850,000 project was funded exclusively through the private giving of Marines, naval servicemembers, and their friends and family.[39]

President Eisenhower presided over the memorial's dedication ceremony, held on the 179th anniversary of the US Marine Corps founding. At its base, the names and dates of every major Marine Corps engagement since 1775 appear in a gold ring. The sculpture itself features the six thirty-two-feet-tall Marines in bronze, raising a flagpole measuring sixty feet long. The piece stands approximately seventy-eight feet high. A real American flag waives atop the pole; by presidential proclamation, the flag flies at all times.[40]

The six Marines featured in the memorial are Pvt. 1st Class Ira Hayes, Corp. Harlon Block, Corp. Harold "Pie" Keller, Pvt. 1st Class Harold Schultz,

FIGURE 2.1. US Marine Corps War Memorial
Historic American Buildings Survey / Historic American Engineering Record / Historic American Landscapes Survey collection, Prints & Photographs Division, Library of Congress, HALS VA-9-5.

Pvt. 1st Class Franklin Sousley, and Sgt. Michael Strank. Even in the age of photography, the identification of these individuals proved a rocky task. Not until 2019 did the Marine Corps accurately identify the proper men in their correct positions, as detailed in Rosenthal's photograph.[41]

Harlon Block lunges at the base of the pole, driving it into the ground. When creating the sculpture and for years after, the figure behind Block and to his right was believed to be John Bradley, who, in fact, posed for de Weldon during the molding process. Archival research revealed, however, that the soldier in this position in Rosenthal's photograph is actually Franklin Sousley.[42]

Sousley did appear in the original sculpture, albeit in the wrong position. He was portrayed in the memorial standing behind Bradley, two spots—rather than one—behind the front man. The man in Sousley's inaccurate position was later discovered to be Harold Schultz.[43]

Michael Strank stands shoulder-to-shoulder with the Sousley/Schultz figure. Only in late 2019 did a team of historians uncover that the man in front of Strank had been inaccurately identified as Rene Gagnon for seventy-four years.[44] In fact, Gagnon did not appear in the photograph at all.

Ira Hayes appears at the far left, both hands outstretched toward the flag-pole. Born on the Gila River Reservation on January 12, 1923, Ira Hamilton Hayes was the eldest of six siblings.[45] He grew up among his Pima community near Sacaton, Arizona, and his family made their living in subsistence farming and cotton production.[46] At age nineteen, Hayes followed his father's path by joining the Marine Corps Reserve on August 26, 1942, amid World War II; his father had served in World War I.[47] Recruit training took young Hayes to San Diego and then to Camp Gillespie, where he completed paratrooper training and earned his silver wings.[48]

As a private first class and automatic rifleman, Hayes served in the Company B, 3rd Parachute Battalion, Divisional Special Troops, 3rd Marine Division at Camp Elliott, California, beginning December 2, 1942.[49] Three months later Hayes set sail for the Pacific Theater.[50] There he went on to see battle throughout 1943 in the Battle of Vella Lavella Island and in the Bougainville Island campaign. Hayes returned to San Diego in early 1944, joined the 5th Marine Division at Camp Pendleton, and expanded his career by attending additional training in Hawaii.[51]

In January 1945 Ira Hayes was among seventy thousand Marines sent to Iwo Jima. He was one of only forty-seven thousand who survived, and one of a mere five survivors from his forty-five-man platoon. After the now-iconic raising of the flag to signal American victory, Hayes continued in combat for more than a month.[52] He and Harold "Pie" Keller became national heroes as the only flag raisers to make it back to the United States.[53]

Hayes was honored with the Navy and Marine Corps Commendation Medal, along with a Combat "V" and Combat Action Ribbon. His story made its way into popular culture through the 1949 John Wayne film *The Sands of Iwo Jima*, in which Hayes plays himself.[54] Hayes's transition to the spotlight, however, did not come easily. He passed on January 24, 1955, due to a tragic accident a mere ten weeks after the unveiling of the US Marine Corps War Memorial.[55] Hayes was only thirty-three.[56]

Today Hayes is remembered as a hero in his Pima community. Native youth look up to Hayes and other veterans as role models, and Pima youth like Brian Alphus Jr., a prospective Marine himself, says that Hayes's legacy has in many ways fulfilled the positive modeling of a father figure. Valerie Fagerberg, a resource navigator for the Pima veteran community, celebrates Hayes's resilience in navigating survivor's guilt and posttraumatic stress disorder. "For him to go through what he was put through and for this community to come together and honor him, as a tribal member, makes me very proud," she says.[57] Two thousand miles away, near the capital, the fallen Marine is forever commemorated through the US Marine Corps War Memorial and through his internment in Arlington National Cemetery.

National Museum of the American Indian

For many members of the public, the National Museum of the American Indian (NMAI) functions as the singular representation of Indigenous peoples in the nation's capital. It is certainly the largest, most well-known, and most widely celebrated institution in Washington, DC, dedicated to Native Americans. But as this text sets out to reveal, the NMAI is far from being the District's only resource for learning about Native peoples, nor is it the only visible marker of their presence.

What sets the NMAI apart from any other site of Indigenous importance in Washington is its immense institutional backing. The 800,000-item collection that forms the foundation of the NMAI's current 825,000 holdings, however, originated from an entirely different source.[58] As a personal venture of George Gustav Heye, the avid collector's early acquisitions of southwestern material started in 1898 but quickly expanded to the purchase of entire international archaeological portfolios in five years' time. By 1908 Heye had filled his apartment and a warehouse with artifacts and collaborated with the University of Pennsylvania to exhibit the items. This installation foreshadowed the creation of Heye's own independent institution, the Museum of the American Indian, in 1916. As the museum's director for life, Heye deeded his entire collection to it. The Museum of the American Indian opened its New York City venue—located at 155th and Broadway—to the public in 1922. With the construction and unveiling delayed by World War I, the collection numbered 58,000 objects by the time it welcomed its first visitor. This number jumped to 163,000 items in 1929 and again to 700,000 by Heye's death in 1957.[59]

The Museum of the American Indian struggled for thirty years after Heye's passing, but a relationship with the Smithsonian breathed new life into the collections. On November 28, 1989, President George H. W. Bush established the NMAI as a bureau of the Smithsonian Institution and, under the Smithsonian's guidance, the Museum of the American Indian was rebirthed as the National Museum of the American Indian.[60] Director W. Richard West (Southern Cheyenne) led the NMAI away from Heye's anthropological "preservation" mission and steered the museum toward new relationships with tribal nations, consultations with Indigenous communities, and reciprocal community-based work.[61] The Smithsonian also established the NMAI as a three-part institution composed of the George Gustav Heye Center, also known as the NMAI-New York, which opened in Manhattan in 1994; the research-oriented Cultural Resources Center, opened in 2003 in Suitland, Maryland; and the flagship NMAI in Washington, DC.[62] Now, with support from the Smithsonian Institution, the NMAI receives official government endorsement. This backing enables public programming, research initiatives, and educational exhibits as well as maintenance of the physical buildings themselves.

The NMAI opened its doors on September 21, 2004.[63] At the time of its creation, it was the eighteenth Smithsonian museum. A 25,000-person procession featuring representatives from five hundred Indigenous communities marched on the National Mall to celebrate its launch. Approximately 92,300 visitors from around the world took part in the week-long festival commemorating the opening.[64] The opening proved to be the largest Native American gathering in history.[65] During its first full year of operation, it welcomed 2.2 million visitors. Today the NMAI is the second-most-recently created Smithsonian museum, trailing only the National Museum of African American History and Culture, which opened in 2016. The Smithsonian reports that 960,933 individuals toured the NMAI in 2019.[66]

Indeed, the very presence of the NMAI represents an enormous "win" for Indian Country. The inclusion of an institution dedicated to the First Americans—alongside such reputable DC icons as the National Air and Space Museum, the National Museum of Natural History, the American Art Museum, and the National Portrait Gallery—immediately imbues the NMAI with a sense of national importance and recognizable excellence. Furthermore, its home on the National Mall positions the museum as highly visible, ready to capture the attention of those previously unaware of its existence and draw public audiences into educational conversations about Native American issues.

In addition to its premier location, the NMAI structure stands out on the National Mall through its architectural and landscaping features that emphasize Native North American, rather than European, styles.[67] This difference enhances visitors' experiences and opens the door for a greater sense of engagement with the building itself, and its surroundings and land, as opposed to merely the contents it contains. The architectural design emerged through close collaboration between lead architect Douglas Cardinal (Blackfoot) and Indigenous consultants, featuring elements both tribal-specific and relevant to a broad Native community.[68] In particular, Cardinal's signature curvilinear concept of stacked bands that form the distinctive structure of the limestone

FIGURE 2.2. National Museum of the American Indian
Photograph in the Carol M. Highsmith Archive, Prints & Photographs Division, Library of Congress, LC-DIG-highsm-12698.

museum pays homage to geology, nature, and landscape.[69] The building is also perfectly aligned with the cardinal directions and features an east-facing entrance—both reflections of Native spirituality and worldview.[70]

The NMAI extends to its exterior features its dedication to connecting with the land and existing in harmony with the natural environment. Taken as a whole, the 4.25-acre plot houses 27,000 trees, shrubs, and herbaceous plants from 150 species. With a creek running through the property, a wetlands area of birch, milkweed, lilies, willow, and wild rice reflects the natural environment of the local Chesapeake region.[71] Another croplands environment showcases Indigenous agricultural traditions, such as natural pest control through ladybugs, and farming techniques of complementary crops like corn, beans, and squash, also known as the "Three Sisters."[72] On the northern side of the campus, a hardwood forest mirrors the Blue Ridge Mountains, while a separate meadow area features medicinal plants.[73]

As this strategic landscaping demonstrates, no feature of the NMAI exists without purpose. Such is also the case with what may appear at first glance to be nondescript stones placed around the exterior. These forty Grandfather Rocks punctuate the landscape to welcome visitors and signify the relationship between Indigenous peoples and the land. These boulders were blessed by the Montagnais First Nation in Canada before journeying to Washington, again receiving a ceremonial welcome upon their arrival. Another four stones serve as cardinal direction markers, honoring the four directions and the Indigenous communities from each area. The north stone originated from the Northwest Territories of Canada, the east stone comes from the Monocacy Valley in Maryland, the south stone hails from Puerto Williams, Chile, and the west stone arrived from Hawai'i.[74]

Tributes to Piscataway culture can also be found throughout the museum. The Indigenous foods café's name, Mitsitam, translates to "let's eat" in the Piscataway and Delaware languages.[75] The dome covering the main gathering area and entrance/exit space of the museum has also been named to honor the Piscataway Conoy community. The dome's name, Potomac, comes from the Piscataway language and denotes "a place where rivers and people come together and where the goods are brought in."[76] While noting the success of the intentional contrast between the NMAI's aesthetic features and the neoclassical style of many surrounding buildings, museum studies scholar Mario A. Caro still challenges the underwhelming lack of local influence: "Lost is the visual index that locates this place as the traditional home of the original inhabitants of the area, the Piscataway and the Delaware nations."[77]

Inside, the NMAI functions as a "living" museum, designed to be "neither formal nor quiet."[78] Permanent installations at the time of its opening included *Our Universes: Traditional Knowledge Shapes Our World* (retired in 2021), *Our Peoples: Giving Voice to Our Histories* (retired in 2014), and *Our Lives: Contemporary Lives and Identities* (retired in 2015). These exhibits emerged out of a new method of "community-curation," which defied the silos created by discipline-specific approaches to Native peoples.[79] Exhibits are complimented by a range of multimedia experiences offered by a theater, shop, food court, galleries, lectures, performances, and more. Native studies scholar Amanda J. Cobb-Greetham (Chickasaw) speaks to the irony—and power—of the fact that through the NMAI, as a museum, the very institutions that she proposes as "the fourth major force of colonization after guns, God, and government, . . . Native Americans have turned an instrument of colonization and dispossession into something else—in this case, into an instrument of self-definition and cultural continuance."[80]

The innovative approaches of the NMAI did elicit some criticism from the museum community. Reviewers Edward Rothstein of the *New York Times* and Paul Richard and Marc Fisher of the *Washington Post*, for instance, charged the museum with a lack of cohesion.[81] In response to feedback like Fisher's, which charges that the museum adopted the "trendy faux-selflessness of today's historians and let the Indians present themselves as they wish to be seen," Cobb-Greetham retorts that "the critics judged the NMAI based on the purpose *they* wanted it to serve rather than the purpose *it* serves."[82] Many Native Studies scholars even add that "curators should regard the criticism as a compliment," as the diversion away from colonial museological methods and creation of a new approach to Native peoples in museums clearly succeeded, even if it was misunderstood by select audiences.[83] Some critics from the Native American audience, however, also find that the very federal endorsement that allows for the NMAI's work is inherently a downfall.[84] "As a federal institution," some suggest, "[the NMAI] merely offers state-sanctioned presentations that serve the United States' own interests as a colonizing state, rather than the interests of the indigenous peoples it purports to serve."[85]

As exhibitions change and new programming emerges, the NMAI continually offers fresh avenues for learning about the Indigenous peoples of the Americas. Indeed, the NMAI "exists not to give specific Native Americans a voice"; rather, "it exists to argue that history itself is subjective and that the Native American experience of colonization cannot be understood until the nature of the varied histories themselves is understood."[86] The institution's prominence also serves the purpose of acting as an entry point for those learning for the first time about Native peoples—from their histories to contemporary worlds, from arts to artifacts, from politics to ceremony. For these reasons, the NMAI is a fitting and necessary institution, deserving of its spotlight on the National Mall.

Native Leader Statues in the US Capitol

Since the early nineteenth century, twenty-two senators and representatives of Native American descent have served in the US Congress. These elected politicians reflected the true diversity in Indian Country by hailing from various tribal nations and serving several different states. Their legacy also highlights the truly bipartisan nature of Indian affairs, with both sides of the political aisle reflected in their leadership.

The brief, one-year term of Mississippi senator Hiram Revels (1827–1901), of Black and Lumbee ancestry and Republic persuasion, marked the first Native American—and first African American—to serve in the US Senate.[87] Ben Nighthorse Campbell (1933–), a member of the Northern Cheyenne Tribe of Montana, represents the full gambit of federal political service, having held office in both the Senate and House of Representatives and having run on both Democratic and Republican tickets; he is the most recent Native American Senator.[88] Since 2000, five tribal members have held seats in the US House of Representatives, including Oklahoma Democrat Brad Carson (Cherokee), Oklahoma Republican Tom Cole (Chickasaw), Oklahoma Republican Markwayne Mullin (Cherokee), Kansas Democrat Sharice Davids (Ho-Chunk), and New Mexico Democrat Deborah Haaland (Laguna Pueblo).[89]

In addition to housing the offices of these Native politicians, the US Capitol Building also holds statues of a number of notable Native historical leaders. These statues pay homage to the contributions the individuals made to their Indigenous communities and the nation as a whole. Visitors can see most of these statues on display in Emancipation Hall, with others located in the National Statuary Hall and on the second floor of the House connecting corridor. The collection also contains dozens of paintings, sculptures, and murals featuring various scenes of Indian history, a reminder that one cannot divorce US history and development from the First Americans—the original occupants of this land.[90]

SEQUOYAH

Sequoyah's service to his people through the creation of the first written Cherokee syllabary has earned him the affection of Cherokees and admiration of all nearly two hundred years after his death. His legacy lives on through every word of the Cherokee language spoken by elders and youth alike. Indeed, Indigenous language is one of the four cornerstones of peoplehood—along

SE-QUO-YAH

PUBLISHED BY F.W. GREENOUGH PHILAD.ᵃ

FIGURE 2.3. Portrait of Sequoyah holding Cherokee syllabary
Popular Graphic Arts collection, Prints & Photographs Division, Library of Congress,
LC-DIG-pga-07569.

with sacred histories, ceremonies and religions, and connection to land—and offers a backbone to Cherokee cultural perseverance today.[91]

The son of a Cherokee mother and white father, historians estimate that Sequoyah was born in 1770 in the Cherokee town outside Fort Loudon, now located in present-day Tennessee.[92] The young hunter, fur trader, and silversmith was raised primarily by his mother and immersed in Cherokee culture.[93] His great-uncle, in fact, had been a leader in the community through his position as a Cherokee chief. By contrast, Sequoyah's father is thought to have been a trader captured by the Cherokee who was released after a period of six years and later began a second family in Kentucky.[94]

Official work on the syllabary began in 1809. Sequoyah sought out to develop the written Cherokee language in solitude, taking up residence in Wills Valley between Cherokee communities in Arkansas, Tennessee, and Georgia.[95] He lived here for the decade between 1810 and 1820.[96] At first Sequoyah began his process by attempting to create a character to convey a full sentence. He later initiated a system that associated symbols with individual words and then transitioned to a pictographic method in which images reflected the literal meaning behind the words.[97] In the end each of these efforts proved overwhelming and unclear. This dilemma led Sequoyah to focus his efforts on the finite number of sounds that make up the spoken Cherokee language and to translate those sounds into characters.[98]

Sequoyah completed the syllabary in approximately 1819.[99] The end product consists of a table of eighty-six sounds and their associated symbols.[100] Literary scholar Ellen Cushman (Cherokee) emphasizes that this writing system was "uniquely Cherokee" and pushes back against the common understanding of Sequoyah's invention as merely an alphabet.[101] She criticizes this conceptualization: "The Cherokee syllabary has always been interpreted through an alphabetic bias, a bias that not only obscures the instrumental workings of this writing system but also forces its creation and maintenance into Western ideologies of noble, civilized Cherokees who are brothers and sisters because they use a writing system."[102] Indeed, the writing system reflects a morphographic system where each sound and the affiliated script is imbued with layers of meaning and "provides markers of and keys to Cherokee worldview."[103] The complexity demonstrated here suggests that Sequoyah himself intentionally rejected the English alphabet as an influence behind his creation.[104]

Sequoyah's Cherokee government embraced the written language in 1821, making it available to Cherokee citizens and others interacting with the tribe.[105] In 1824 the Cherokee Nation Legislative Council awarded Sequoyah a medal for this innovation.[106] The writings of Cherokee chief John Ross further credit Sequoyah for setting an example for other tribal nations, applaud him for creating a system accessible to youth and elders alike, and emphasize the role the syllabary had in the creation of a Cherokee literary canon.[107] The first tribal language newspaper published in the United States—the *Cherokee Phoenix*—deployed Sequoyah's writing system and opened new doors of tribal empowerment with its first edition released in 1828.

Sequoyah's investment in the politics of his tribal nation complimented his efforts around the Cherokee language. Shortly after beginning his main endeavor, Sequoyah also enlisted in the US military as part of the War of 1812 against the British and their Creek tribal allies; he saw conflict under Gen. Andrew Jackson at the Battle of Horseshoe Bend in 1813.[108] Three years later, in 1816, Sequoyah joined a controversial group of Cherokees in signing a treaty that ceded Cherokee lands in Tennessee to the United States.[109] Here he signed under his English name, George Guess.[110] In 1828 Sequoyah traveled to Washington, DC, as a representative of his tribe to advocate on behalf of Cherokees displaced by land loss. Continuing his dedication to uniting the dispersed Cherokee community, he passed while searching for a band of his tribesmen who had relocated to Mexico.[111]

Today Sequoyah's contribution continues to impact the culture and well-being of the Cherokee people. At a time when nearly 64 percent of Cherokee citizens neither speak nor understand the Cherokee language, the tribe's Education Services emphasizes language-learning immersion schools that use Sequoyah's syllabary over the Roman alphabet.[112] Such efforts prove particularly important as a service to the younger generations, when, as of 2002, the Cherokee Nation could not claim a single fluent speaker under the age of forty. Despite this dearth, the fact that a full 95 percent of Cherokee citizens indicate that language is a critical component of Cherokee identity and culture further speaks to the critical necessity of such initiatives.[113] In this way, "every single use of [the Cherokee syllabary] helps the tribe's language survive and is a political act that traces its legacy to Sequoyah."[114]

The state of Oklahoma gave the Sequoyah statue to the United States Capitol in 1917.[115] He was the first Native American to be honored by inclusion in the National Statuary Hall Collection.[116] Like Will Rogers, also a Cherokee Nation citizen and the second statue contributed by Oklahoma twenty-two years later, Sequoyah is one of the few individuals to receive this honor without service as an elected official.[117] The bronze sculpture, created by G. Julian Zolnay, stands on view in the National Statuary Hall.[118]

WILL ROGERS

Will Rogers became a household name in 1930s America. His combination of telegrams, films, radio broadcasts, columns, Broadway performances, and live shows offered a variety of high-profile platforms for his political commentary and biting comedy. He is remembered today as "America's favorite cowboy" and "America's favorite humorist."[119]

Born in 1879 on his father's ranch, Rogers was raised within his Cherokee Nation in Indian Territory, later the state of Oklahoma. Although he belonged to an affluent family, Rogers nevertheless witnessed firsthand the systemic oppression of Native peoples at the hand of the federal government, such as when the family's 60,000-acre ranch shrank to a mere 140 acres as a result of allotment policy under the 1887 Dawes Act.[120] As a young adult Rogers again felt the reach of federal powers into his personal life when he became a naturalized US citizen as a result of the attempted dissolution of his Cherokee Nation—and the Chickasaw, Choctaw, Seminole, and Creek Nations—under the 1898 Curtis Act.[121] These distinct experiences shaped the political perspective the rising star brought to mass audiences throughout his career.

Beginning in his early adulthood, Rogers traveled the United States and, later, the world, as a trick roper. Some of his first international endeavors as a cowboy took him to South Africa, Argentina, New Zealand, and across Europe.[122] Ironically, while across the Atlantic in South Africa in 1902, he joined the touring Texas Jack's Wild West Show.[123] From there he quickly developed the well-known persona of "The Cherokee Kid: The World's Champion Lassoer."[124]

In 1915 Rogers took on a role with more artistic freedom by entering the world of vaudeville performance and joining the Ziegfeld Follies.[125] While performing on Broadway, Rogers published his first newspaper articles in the summer of 1916 and released his first book, *Roger-isms: The Cowboy Philosopher on the Peace Conference*, in 1919. In October 1921 he launched his own film production company. The star left his New York City lifestyle and ten-year run on the stage to begin anew in Southern California in 1930.[126]

Ultimately, Rogers rose to fame in each medium he engaged. Rogers's newspaper column single-handedly generated an audience of forty million— nearly half of the adult population of the nation. His more than 3,600 columns appeared across more than 550 newspapers. On the silver screen, Rogers topped the box offices as the most highly paid actor in the country. His radio broadcast career became the most popular in the nation.[127]

Similarly, Rogers never lost sight of his Cherokee roots and identity. Writes literary scholar Roumiana Velikova, "His direct involvement in U.S. politics, as an ironic commentator, places Rogers within the framework of Native intellectual independence.... Rogers writes from within a tradition of Native intellectuals who engage critically with U.S. political and patriotic discourse."[128] Indeed, he spoke at and weighed in on such weighty events as Cuba's Pan-American Conference in 1928, multiple Democratic and Republican National Conventions, the League of Nations meetings in Geneva, a Franklin D. Roosevelt campaign rally, and President Herbert Hoover's presidential inauguration.[129]

Rogers also leveraged his success to support others during the hardships of the Great Depression. In 1931 he raised $220,000 for his cause through an aviation tour of Mexico, Central America, and the Caribbean. He also completed world tours of Japan, Thailand, China, Greece, England, and more.[130] Although flying became a passion project and philanthropy outlet for Rogers, an accident on August 15, 1935, claimed his life. Rogers and pilot Wiley Post had just begun the first leg of a worldwide tour when the pair found themselves lost in Alaska and suffered a loss of power of the two-seat plane.[131]

In 1939 Oklahoma donated a statue of Will Rogers for inclusion in the National Statuary Collection.[132] Artist Jo Davidson, a personal friend of Rogers, sculpted the piece at the request of Rogers's wife and with financial support from the state.[133] Davidson first created the piece using clay and had it cast in bronze in Brussels, Belgium. A second replica of the statue, personally paid for and donated by Davidson, stands at the Will Rogers Memorial in Claremore, Oklahoma.[134]

During the June 6, 1939, unveiling of the Will Rogers statue, the eight hundred seats in the Capitol Rotunda were filled to capacity, with an additional thousand individuals in overflow attendance.[135] A reporter covering the event wrote of the scene that "never before has there been anything like it in Washington."[136] Amid a concert by the Navy Band and lawmakers hanging over balconies and on steps to capture a view of the proceedings, Capitol architect David Lynn confirmed this assessment.[137]

The statue remains on view in the second-floor corridor of the Capitol Building, located between the Rotunda and the House. Despite "do not touch" signage, many believe that rubbing the statue's left foot brings good luck. For this reason, visitors will notice gold showing through the bronze on the top of this area. Oklahoma representative Tom Cole, a citizen of the Chickasaw Nation, follows this lighthearted tradition as well.[138] Calling Rogers the "quintessential Oklahoman," Representative Cole adds, "He was an American original. [He] is like Mark Twain. You may be from Missouri, but every American owns Mark Twain, and I think the same thing is true of Will Rogers: Every American has a piece of Will Rogers."[139]

KING KAMEHAMEHA I

King Kamehameha I, also popularly known as Kamehameha the Great, is an icon of Hawaiian history. He is noted primarily for his unification of the Hawaiian Kingdom, which was previously factionalized and war-torn before his rule. Today the Kānaka Maoli (Native Hawaiian) community and the state of Hawaii celebrate Kamehameha the Great on the annual Kamehameha Day. On this state-recognized June 11 holiday, the public participates in lei-draping ceremonies to decorate the many statues of the famed leader.

Kamehameha was born at Kokoiki on the island of Hawai'i around 1758.[140] At the time of his birth, the ali'i, or nobility, of O'ahu, Maui, and Hawai'i Island were engaged in ongoing war.[141] The death of King Kalani'ōpu'u in 1782 prompted the division of power over the island of Hawai'i between his nephew, Kamehameha, and his son, Kīwala'ō. When Kīwala'ō died in a battle between his and Kamehameha's conflicting parties, Kamehameha emerged with control over an increased territory—the first of many conquests to come.[142]

Kamehameha quickly rose to fame as a victorious warrior, visionary leader, and prominent ali'i.[143] By 1790 he had extended his influence over the entirety of Hawai'i Island and went on to bring Maui, Lāna'i, and Moloka'i under his rule.[144] Five years later he accumulated all islands except for Kaua'i and Ni'ihau—the furthest territories from Kamehameha's home base in Hawai'i. These islands were peacefully ceded to Kamehameha in 1810.[145]

With this addition, Kamehameha the Great had achieved the unification of the Kingdom of Hawai'i. His rule was characterized by financial success, peace, and international engagement.[146] He reigned until his death on May 8, 1819.[147] As one of his final acts, the great leader named his son, Liholiho, later known as Kamehameha II, as his successor.[148] The Kamehameha dynasty maintained power for nearly a century, through Kamehameha V.

Nearly five thousand miles away, over the Pacific Ocean and the entirety of the mainland United States, Kamehameha the Great maintains a presence in Washington, DC. The statue appears in the US Capitol Visitor Center's Emancipation Hall and was gifted from the State of Hawaii to the National Statuary Hall Collection in 1969. As in Hawaii, the statue is adorned with leis every Kamehameha Day.[149]

FIGURE 2.4. Statue of King
Kamehameha I at the
US Capitol Building
Kamehameha I, National Statu-
ary Hall Collection, Architect of
the Capitol.

Weighing over six tons, the statue and its granite base make it one of
the heaviest pieces in the collection. The bronze and gold sculpture depicts the
royal leader with his right arm outstretched in a friendly, welcoming gesture—a reminder of Kamehameha's beloved rule. His left hand, by contrast,
holds a spear—a symbol of his might and victory in bringing the Hawaiian
kingdom under his rule, ending years of war between divided islands. Viewers

will note the historically accurate helmet, which would typically feature unique feathers, and cloak of woven yellow feathers.[150]

The statue of King Kamehameha in Washington, DC, is only one of five in the United States. The others are all located across Hawaii, in North Kohala and in Hilo on the island of Hawai'i, at the Grand Wailea resort on Maui, and in Honolulu on O'ahu.[151] The statue in Emancipation Hall is a replica of the figure currently located in Honolulu.[152]

Originally, the Kingdom of Hawai'i commissioned American sculptor Thomas R. Gould to create the piece in 1879. Gould modeled the sculpture in Rome and had it cast in bronze in Paris. While en route to Hawaii, the ship carrying the piece suffered a wreck and the statue was lost. Fortunately, a second bronze casting of the same model successfully arrived in Hawaii in 1883 and was placed at the Judiciary Building in Honolulu. In 1912 the shipwrecked statue was recovered and installed in King Kamehameha's hometown on the island of Hawai'i.[153]

More than half a century later, on April 15, 1969, the state of Hawaii had a replica of Gould's piece installed in the Capitol Rotunda in Washington, DC. The statue was on view in the National Statuary Hall from June 1969 to 2008 and was subsequently relocated to its current position in the Capitol Visitor Center's Emancipation Hall.[154] Together the Kamehameha statue and a bronze sculpture of Father Damien, the canonized priest who dedicated his life to serving the leper colony at Molokai, represent Hawaii's two statutory contributions to the United States Capitol.[155] Unique in its significance as more than a stagnant statue, the ceremonial practices around the Kamehameha statue imbue this piece with a living legacy and unique presence.

WASHAKIE

The man who grew to be the most highly respected chief of the Shoshone people was likely born between 1808 and 1810.[156] His mother stemmed from the Lemhi, or Salmon-Eater, Shoshone people of what today is northern Idaho, and his father had roots among the Salish, also known as Flathead, people of present-day western Montana.[157] Historians believe that the young Washakie resided with his family in his father's home territory until the death of his father at the hands of a raiding enemy tribe. Thus, in search of safety, Washakie took refuge among his mother's Lemhi Shoshone community, away from his place of birth.[158]

As a young man Washakie made his home in the Green River, Bear River, and Cache Valley corridor (now southwestern Wyoming and northeastern

Utah) among the Shoshones and soon rose to be their foremost leader. There he developed skills in the fur trade and distinguished himself as a warrior in the 1830s.[159] His business with settlers further enabled Washakie to learn English and French, along with a host of Indigenous languages—an ability that later proved critical in his service to his people.[160]

In the period between 1840 and 1850, Washakie emerged as the principal chief of the Eastern Shoshone.[161] As a recognized warrior and businessman, Washakie put his knowledge of languages to the benefit of his 1,200-member community by entering into shrewd negotiations with settlers and other tribal nations. From Indian agents, he secured food, obtained supplies, and established goodwill by minimizing conflict between the Eastern Shoshone and white emigrants passing through Shoshone lands on their journeys west along the Oregon Trail.[162] Washakie also entered into a profitable, if shaky, friendship with Brigham Young and the Church of Jesus Christ of Latter-day Saints by maintaining peace between his warriors and Mormon homesteaders.[163] In collaboration with clergy, Washakie assisted in creating a boarding school for Shoshone girls.[164] His peaceful cession of the Green River Valley allowed for the compilation of the first transcontinental Union Pacific railroad. Later in life, Washakie went on to lead a group of 150 Shoshone soldiers fighting alongside the US Cavalry against the Sioux and Cheyenne.[165]

Indeed, land encroachment posed an enormous threat to the physical and cultural survival of the Shoshones during the mid-nineteenth century. In response to the disruptions such encroachment caused, Washakie led his people away on a journey to the Three Forks area of southern Montana and to the Wind River Valley in Wyoming in order to maintain access to buffalo hunting grounds.[166] Washakie permanently relocated the Shoshones to this area by signing the Fort Bridger Treaty on July 3, 1868, establishing the three-million-acre Shoshone and Bannock Indian Agency and Wind River reservation.[167] Here the chief modeled a balance of traditional Shoshone and Euro-American ways of life with the ultimate goal of acting in the best interest of his tribe. For instance, at the urging of government agents, Washakie took up farming but was also astute enough to support the Shoshone community by charging white farmers land usage fees for their own farming efforts.[168]

The arrival of Arapaho residents on the reservation in 1878, however, changed the power dynamics at Wind River forever. Although their presence was intended to be temporary, the federal government violated Washakie's Fort Bridger Treaty by allowing the co-occupants to exercise equal say in reservation affairs.[169] Further land cessions and a specific 1896 incident involving a natural hot spring illustrate the impact of this breach on reservation life: As the United States pressured the tribes to cede a ten-square-mile parcel containing a natural hot spring to the federal government, Washakie fought for the Shoshones and Arapahos to be treated as separate parties in the negotiations. US agents rejected this arrangement and arbitrarily collapsed two sovereign tribal governments into one for legal purposes and in order to advance the sale. Years later, in 1937, the Shoshones successfully won a claim against the United States for these actions, which constituted a violation of their Fort Bridger Treaty rights. The spot—known today as Thermopolis—remains open to the public as a condition insisted upon by Washakie at the time of signing.[170]

Washakie remained heavily involved in Shoshone affairs until his death in late February 1900.[171] By that time the chief had led his people for sixty years.[172] He was buried with full military honors—the only Native American at the time to receive such recognition.[173]

Washakie's leadership offers insight into the challenges all Native American leaders faced as a result of encroaching settler colonialism. As Rep. Steny Hoyer remarked during the congressional hearing on the Washakie statue, "Both warrior and peacemaker, [Washakie] recognized that survival of Indian tribes in the western United States depended upon accommodation with migrating settlers and the United States Government."[174] Through difficult decisions, Washakie laid the foundation for the future of his tribal nation and set an example of leadership for not only Native American leaders but for all Americans.

The state of Wyoming honored Washakie's legacy by selecting the Shoshone chief as the subject of their second contribution to the US National Statuary Hall Collection. Wyoming-born sculptor Dave McGary completed the statue, which was installed in a dedication ceremony on September 7, 2000.[175] This was the ninety-seventh statue, out of one hundred, to be donated to the US Capitol.[176] Visitors can view the statue in the US Capitol Visitor Center's Emancipation Hall.[177] Speaking to Washakie's presence here, US senator Mike Enzi of Wyoming reflected that "for me, the Capitol is more than the place where our nation's leaders meet to govern the nation, it is a classroom for the young people of our nation and the repository not only of our history but of the spirit that made this nation great as well."[178]

SAKAKAWEA

Despite being one of the most widely recognized figures in early American lore and Native American history, Sakakawea's story remains shrouded in mystery. Debates rage over subjects ranging from her name to her death, and about the precise nature of her contributions to Meriwether Lewis and William Clark's northwest expedition. In all interpretations of her life, however, the themes of bravery, strength, and resilience characterize this young Shoshone woman.

Sakakawea's joining the Lewis and Clark expedition stands out as her most shining achievement, but few recognize how young she was at the outset of the journey. Historians estimate that she was born in the Lemhi River Valley in present-day Idaho around 1788. She grew up as a member of the Shoshone community, likely the Agaideka or Salmon-Eater band.[179] At twelve years old, the neighboring Hidatsa of the Knife River Village, located in what today is North Dakota, captured Sakakawea and held her captive.[180] She remained in Hidatsa possession for approximately four years, until being purchased by— and, by extension, becoming the wife of—French Canadian fur trapper and trader Toussaint Charbonneau.[181]

Around the same time, the Louisiana Purchase in 1803 nearly doubled the size of the United States and necessitated the charting and exploration of the newly acquired territory, which spanned west of the Mississippi River to the Pacific coast. President Thomas Jefferson tasked Lewis with this assignment, who soon sought out Clark as an accomplice.[182] While traveling in North Dakota, the pair brought Charbonneau into their expedition party as a hired interpreter.[183] Charbonneau, in turn, onboarded Sakakawea to the team.[184] Two short months before their departure, Sakakawea gave birth to her and Charbonneau's son, Jean Pierre, on February 11, 1805.[185] Together, along with more than three dozen men, they formed the Corps of Discovery.[186] The crew departed Fort Mandan on April 7, 1805. Sakakawea was the only woman present during the journey, and Jean Pierre the only infant.[187]

Although seemingly out of place, Sakakawea proved indispensable to the northwest expedition. She served in the critical role of interpreter and translator between the corps and Native American groups they encountered. Her knowledge of edible plants helped sustain the men as well.[188] Sakakawea also drew on her personal family connections to further the expedition, as demonstrated by the horses and guides she procured from her brother, Shoshone chief Cameahwait, as the corps approached difficult terrain in the western Rockies and Bitterroot Mountains in August 1805.[189] And her mere presence—a Native woman carrying a child—assisted in warding off hostile encounters and facilitated peaceful meetings.[190] Clark's own writings describe her as the journey's "pilot" and admit that Sakakawea "diserved [sic] a greater reward for her attention and services on that [dangerous and fatigueing (sic)] rout [sic] than we had in our power to give."[191]

The Corps of Discovery accomplished its mission by reaching the Pacific Ocean on November 8, 1805. The team erected Fort Clatsop near the mouth of the Columbia River in present-day Oregon and took shelter here for the 1805–6 winter. Sakakawea and Jean Pierre joined Clark's faction for the return journey along a southern route, while Lewis led a second party on another path. They departed their camp on March 23, 1806, and successfully reunited in mid-August near Sakakawea's Hidatsa village.[192] On August 17 Sakakawea officially concluded her duties in the Corps of Discovery, leaving Lewis, Clark, President Jefferson, and all of America indebted to her seventeen-month service, which forever shaped the development of the United States.[193]

The timeline of the remainder of Sakakawea's life remains contested. Many believe she succumbed to a fever, likely caused by typhus, and passed on at Fort Manuel in South Dakota on December 20, 1812.[194] This sequence of events would have placed her in only her midtwenties at the time of death. By contrast, oral traditions of the Wind River Shoshone, Cheyenne, and Eastern Shoshone suggest that she returned to a tribal community and lived well into old age, perishing on April 9, 1884, at nearly one hundred years of age.[195] This discrepancy actually became the center of a government-initiated investigation in 1925, when the commissioner of Indian Affairs charged Dakota intellectual Charles Eastman with determining the date of death. Eastman's official report supports the 1884 date.[196]

In any case, the brave and courageous Sakakawea lives on in American memory and retains a modern presence through memorialization. The North Dakota state legislature selected the young Shoshone interpreter, mother, diplomat, and "pilot" as one of the state's contributions to the National Statuary Collection. For this purpose, the General Federation of Women's Clubs of North Dakota gathered the financial support to create a replica of a previously existing sculpture of Sakakawea. The original, created by French American sculptor Leonard Crunelle in 1910, was similarly financed by the federation and continues to sit at the entrance to the North Dakota Heritage Center in the state capital.[197]

For this work, Crunelle employed Sakakawea's granddaughter, Mink Woman of the Fort Berthold Indian Reservation, to stand in as the live model. The sculpture features Sakakawea gazing ahead as if charting forward on her famous journey. The artist also pays homage to one of the most impressive aspects of her accomplishment—namely, her care for infant Jean Pierre during the challenging trek—by depicting him riding on her back. The replica was cast in bronze and weighs 875 pounds, not including the two-ton granite base upon which it stands. The statue installation in the Capitol Visitor Center corresponded to the 2003 bicentennial of the Lewis and Clark northwest expedition.[198]

Importantly, the spelling of her name on the statue base, "Sakakawea," offers tribute to specific Hidatsa language spelling and pronunciation. The "Sakakawea" name translates to "Bird Woman," taken from the Hidatsa words "*tsakaka*" (bird) and "*wiis*" (woman). Like many aspects of her life, however, the exact origin of her name remains unknown, and some push back on this theory. For this reason, spellings obtained from Lewis and Clark's journals (Sah ca gah we ah, Sah-kah-gar-wea, Sar kah gah We a, Sahcah-gar-weah) offer phonetic insight into proper pronunciation, while numerous spelling variations (Sacajawea, Sakajawea, Sacagawea, Sakakawea, Tsakakawea, Sacajowa, Saykijawee, Saca tzah we yaa) abound in more recent works. In light of these variations, the adoption of a spelling without the hard sound of the letter "j"—a sound that does not exist in the Hidatsa language—into the statue ensures that the depiction more closely aligns with Hidatsa language.[199]

Anthropologist Sally McBeth reconciles the discrepancies in Sakakawea's story—her life, her death, her name—by emphasizing her legacy, interpretation, and significance today. "There are many different ways of knowing the various tribal understandings of who this young woman was and why she has become so important to the story of Lewis and Clark," she writes.[200] More importantly than determining an absolute truth, McBeth points toward the possibilities for learning from the unknown: "Her story serves to explore issues of tribal identity, to integrate the white and Indian worlds, to highlight the frequently contradictory positions of women as both independent agents and chattel, and to examine Indian worldviews."[201] The Sakakawea statue at the US Capitol offers a reminder to explore such introspective reflections and provides an opportunity to dwell on the impact of a modest young Native woman on both the past and the future of the United States.

SARAH WINNEMUCCA

Sarah Winnemucca, also known by her given name, Thocmetony or "Shellflower," came from a line of Northern Paiute leaders including her father, Chief Winnemucca, and her grandfather, Chief Truckee.[202] Born in 1844, she lived with her community in what today is western Nevada.[203] Winnemucca dedicated much of her life to the defense of this land and safe harboring its significance to her people, spreading her message through lecture tours, advocacy trips, and the circulation of the written word.

Winnemucca's upbringing familiarized her with both Paiute and Euro-American cultures from an early age. She attended a convent school in San Jose, California, at the urging of her grandfather but was rather quickly removed when white parents complained of the presence of an Indian student. Along with her tribal language, she acquired English and Spanish.[204]

In 1859 the US government relocated Winnemucca's people to the Pyramid Lake reservation. Assimilationist policies pushed the Paiutes toward farming and a sedentary lifestyle at Pyramid Lake, and the desert-like geography of the land and lack of resources and supplies yielded a disastrous situation. Witnessing the starvation and devastation of her community, Winnemucca was able to successfully secure help from the US military installation at Camp McDermit.[205] At only fifteen years old, this achievement propelled Winnemucca into a career as an intermediary between Native peoples, settlers, and the colonial government.

The Northern Paiutes were once again shuffled onto a new reservation in Oregon as land encroachment continued in the 1870s.[206] Although they briefly enjoyed a period of relative peace at the Malheur Reservation under Indian Agent Samuel Parrish, Parrish's replacement, William Rinehart, inflicted immense cruelty upon the community.[207] He developed a personal contempt for Winnemucca, and the feeling was mutual.[208]

Winnemucca's outspoken nature and professional position often placed her in precarious and dangerous situations. In 1878, for instance, Gen. O. Howard employed Winnemucca as a scout, interpreter, and messenger in the Bannock War.[209] Her actions led a group of Paiutes on a 230-mile, three-day journey out of Bannock captivity, along with other missions.[210] She reflected on this particular challenge: "I went for the government when the officers could not get an Indian man or a white man to go for love or money. I, only an Indian woman, went and saved my father and his people."[211] The feat received coverage on the front page of the New York Times. At home, however, the Paiutes felt betrayed by Winnemucca when they were once again subjected to the control of the United States, this time manifesting as a 350-mile forced march, in winter, away from Malheur to the Yakama Reservation in present-day Washington state.[212]

As this example demonstrates, Winnemucca's difficult work at times generated disdain from both sides. Native peoples, including the Paiutes, accused her of acting in self-interest, betraying her tribe for monetary benefit, and becoming corrupted by white influence.[213] Indeed, many of these sentiments remain today, and she continues to be regarded in some Native circles as a controversial figure.[214] Winnemucca also made enemies among settlers, who responded to her sharp-tongued critiques of American policy toward Natives with personal attacks and misogynist accusations of being a "notorious liar and malicious schemer" as well as "a drunk, a gambler, and a whore."[215]

In the face of such trials, Winnemucca refused to waiver from her commitment to serving Native communities across the United States in work that took many forms. She participated in military efforts, as discussed above, but also took on education and public action as avenues for advocacy. Over the course of her adulthood, Winnemucca delivered more than three hundred speeches and lectures along both the East and West Coasts. She also served as an educator at Fort Vancouver and the Peabody Institute in Nevada through the 1870s.[216] In the latter years of her life, Winnemucca established a school for Paiute children. Here she instructed students in the English language, reading and writing, and trade skills. Sadly, federal policy mandating boarding schools for Native American children prompted the closure of her institute.[217]

Of particular interest to this text, Winnemucca also brought her advocacy to the halls of Capitol Hill. Winnemucca's petition to Secretary of the Interior Carl Schurz, calling for the return of the Paiutes, at that time being forcibly held at Yakama, to their Malheur Reservation spurred the government to invite her, along with a small delegation composed of her father, brother, and Washo tribal leader Captain Jim, to Washington in January 1880.[218] While in the capital city, Winnemucca recorded her experiences of being constantly watched over by a government accompaniment charged with preventing her from speaking out to the press.[219] Nevertheless, the *Washington Post* did cover her time in DC and noted her dedication to advancing tribal sovereignty by describing her mission as one to "secure recognition and aid [for the Paiutes] by the Government similar to that enjoyed by other nations."[220] Winnemucca met with both President Rutherford B. Hayes and Secretary Schurz and successfully negotiated for the return of the Paiutes to Malheur.[221] Before this promise could come to fruition, however, the United States backed out of its side of the agreement.[222] Winnemucca ventured to DC in April 1884 once again and restated her claims before the House Subcommittee on Indian Affairs, but the Paiutes never returned to their former home.[223]

Winnemucca's most widely recognized achievement, among all of her accomplishments, remains the publication of her 1883 autobiography. *Life Among the Paiutes: Their Wrongs and Claims* was the first book authored by a Native American woman.[224] The book launch further catapulted Winnemucca's growing fame as an acclaimed speaker and spoke to her already established reputation, which captured the attention of influential intellectuals Elizabeth Palmer Peabody and Mary Peabody Mann, who arranged the publication logistics.[225] In her book, Winnemucca offers a scathing critique of the federal government's treatment of the First Americans, outlining the injustices she witnessed firsthand among her Paiute community and specifically as it pertained to reservation life. She writes of the failed promises and broken treaties: "Since the war of 1860 there have been one hundred and three of my people murdered, and our reservation taken from us; and yet we, who are called blood-seeking savages, are keeping our promises to the government."[226]

Sarah Winnemucca passed on in 1891, in her midforties. Nevada honored her outstanding character 114 years later through her nomination to the National Statuary Hall Collection and her statue's installation in the Capitol Visitor Center's Emancipation Hall.[227] With the passage of the statue's legislative proposal in Assembly Bill 267 in March 2001, the Nevada Women's History Project led the fundraising efforts for the bronze statue created by artist Benjamin Victor.[228] The statue shows Winnemucca as the artist imagines her at age thirty-five. Her long hair reaches her waist, the shellflower in her right hand pays tribute to her name, and the book at her left reminds viewers of her status as the first Native American woman to publish a manuscript. The base of the statue also memorializes her as a "defender of human rights."[229]

In her death and commemoration, as in life, Winnemucca remains controversial to some audiences. The process of including Winnemucca in the Capitol was not spearheaded by her tribe, and Native American literary scholar Cari Carpenter further notes that the claiming of Winnemucca as a distinguished "Nevadan" erases not only Winnemucca's tribal identity as her primary identifier but also eludes the very mistreatment she and her people suffered at the hands of the state itself.[230] Thus, the presence of the Winnemucca statue in the US Capitol revives many of the debates occurring at the time of her own visit to Washington. Then, as now, Winnemucca represents a tireless effort in service to Indian Country and an unrelenting dedication to tribal sovereignty, even in the face of mounting oppression.

PO'PAY

For nearly one hundred years, Spanish colonization ravaged the Pueblo peoples of what would become the American Southwest. In 1680 Ohkay Owingeh (San Juan Pueblo) leader Po'pay took a stand against Spanish tyranny by forming the first-ever coalition of Pueblo forces to successfully drive out the settlers. The resulting Pueblo Revolt is considered by some to be the first American

Revolution—fought nearly a century before the eighteenth-century uprising for American independence.[231] In the words of Native studies scholar Elizabeth Archuleta, "Like the revered actions of George Washington, Thomas Jefferson, and Abraham Lincoln committed on behalf of the American Revolution or the United States, Po'pay fought to free Pueblo communities from Spanish tyranny and to keep Indian nations united."[232]

Beginning with the search for riches in the mid-sixteenth century, Spanish settlers systematically decimated Pueblo lifeways, cultural practices, and populations. Spanish cattle grazing destroyed Pueblo crop production and disrupted Indigenous farming techniques. The Spanish tribute system further extracted precious reserves from the desert-dwelling communities, leaving the Pueblos unable to continue the subsistence lifestyle that had sustained them in their arid homeland since time immemorial.[233] Forced labor exploited Pueblo strength and manpower for the benefit of Spanish expansion into Pueblo territory.[234] Furthermore, the Spanish imposition of Catholicism left those practicing their own religions subject to torture or execution.[235]

Indeed, Pueblo resistance to any of these cruel conditions was met with direct violence from the settlers. When Don Juan de Oñate led a sizable settlement of soldiers and their families, livestock, and missionaries to the upper Rio Grande Valley in 1598, for instance, the local Acoma Pueblo retaliated that same year by killing twelve Spanish. Oñate's crew then killed hundreds of Acomas and enslaved six hundred more. All men over twenty-five years of age were sentenced to having their right foot severed; two Hopis who participated also had their right hands cut off. Men, women, and children over twelve were forced into a twenty-year period of servitude. This particular backlash represents merely one of the numerous atrocities committed against the Pueblo by Spanish settlers.[236] In all, the Pueblo community experienced a loss of 62 percent of their population under the colonizing power.[237]

Po'pay came of age within this oppressive system and experienced Spanish violence firsthand. As a spiritual leader in his community, Po'pay was among the forty-seven Pueblo men convicted by Spanish authorities of practicing witchcraft in 1675. Three were hanged, one committed suicide and the remainder—including Po'pay—were publicly lashed.[238]

Five years later Po'pay accomplished what had never been done before: the unification of more than twenty-four autonomous Pueblos scattered over four hundred miles and across six languages as well as their Apache allies.[239] Using a communications technology of knotted ropes to coordinate the Pueblos' simultaneous uprising on August 10, 1680, Po'pay orchestrated the first and only successful ousting of a foreign oppressor in Native American history.[240] More than four hundred Spanish were killed and another two thousand fled to El Paso. The Pueblos enjoyed twelve years of liberation after the revolt, and when Don Diego de Vargas led another Spanish exposition to Pueblo territory, the two groups moved forward with a more peaceful coexistence.[241]

Po'pay's nomination as New Mexico's second contribution to the National Statuary Hall in Washington, DC, was not without controversy. Some resisted Po'pay as the recipient of this honor by portraying him as the instigator of a vicious and indiscriminate "massacre," and casting the Spanish settlers as victims, "refugees," and benefactors of Western civilization. As Archuleta notes, however, such contemporary efforts to "valorize, normalize, and moralize" historic Spanish oppression of the Pueblos further perpetuates racial hierarchies of white dominance and marginalizes Native perspectives today.[242] Elena Ortiz-Junes, the vice-chair of the Alfonso Ortiz Center for Intercultural Studies, similarly defends Po'pay as a historical figure worthy of celebration by drawing parallels between the Pueblo Revolt and the foundational ideals— life, liberty, and the pursuit of happiness—behind some of the United States' greatest achievements: the Declaration of Independence and the Emancipation Proclamation.[243]

Despite some pushback, the honorific recognition of the Pueblo leader Po'pay went forth. Inspiration began at the 1980 tricentennial celebration of the Pueblo Revolt, during which a number of tribes came together to celebrate Po'pay's accomplishment. This gathering prompted the San Juan Pueblo tribal council to officially nominate Po'pay for inclusion in the National Statuary Hall in November 1996. San Juan leadership then brought their tribal government resolution to New Mexico representative Nick Salazar and senator Manny Aragon, who in turn introduced Senate Bill 404 to the New Mexico State Legislature in 1997. In a few short months, the bill was signed into law on April 10, 1997, by Gov. Gary E. Johnson. The New Mexico State Legislature appropriated $100,000—approximately half of the total estimated cost— to making the Po'pay statue a reality.[244]

The New Mexico Statuary Hall Commission selected Jemez Pueblo artist Cliff Fragua for the commission based on his model submission. After being chosen for the job in December 1999, the artist completed the Po'pay sculpture in May 2005.[245] The installation at the US Capitol Visitors Center's Emancipation Hall took place on September 22 of that same year—a celebration marked by buffalo dances, blessings, and the attendance of tribal leaders from all nineteen Pueblos.[246]

Working without a historical account of his likeness, Fragua figured Po'pay wearing a humble deerskin, necklace, and Pueblo-style moccasins—pieces that all reflect his identity. His *chongo* hairstyle is similarly characteristic of Pueblo culture. Fragua depicted Po'pay holding "items that will determine the future existence of the Pueblo people": in his left hand, the knotted cord used to determine the start of the Pueblo Revolt, and in his right, a bear fetish to symbolize the Pueblo religion. The artist also notably relays the trials that Po'pay and his people suffered for carrying on their traditions and faith by carving scars into his back. Out of the one hundred statues in the collection, Fragua's seven-foot sculpture is the only one that features a colored (pink Tennessee) marble.[247] The black granite pedestal describes Po'pay as a "Holy Man," "Farmer," and "Defender."

In the words of the sculptor, the statue "depicts a simple man, one who is concerned for survival of his family, his culture, and the history and beliefs of the Pueblo People. His actions against the Spaniards were not acts of defiance, but rather, acts of survival.... Po'pay was not a trained fighter, but a man who tended gardens, hunted, and participated in the Kiva ceremonies."[248] In this same spirit, it is appropriate that his inclusion in the US Capitol proved the final contribution to the National Statuary Hall Collection, bringing each state up to two representative statues for a total of one hundred pieces in the holding, and coming full circle with recognition of a national Native American hero. It is similarly fitting because Fragua is the only Native American artist to have a piece included in the National Statuary Hall Collection.[249] Thus, Po'pay's presence in Washington, DC, embodies the essence of the American spirit while simultaneously interjecting a critical Native perspective on the evils of colonial oppression.

STANDING BEAR

Born Manchú-Nanzhín, or Macunajin, historians place Standing Bear's birth between 1829 and 1834.[250] He was brought up among his Ponca community in what is today northeastern Nebraska.[251] By the time Standing Bear was a young adult, he had achieved leadership status as a chief. However, this time also proved tumultuous for his tribe, which lost nearly all of its land to forceful cessions and retained only a small parcel by the Niobrara River. Such changes had transformed the Ponca lifestyle from subsistence buffalo hunting to sedentary farming and trading.[252]

Land disputes intensified in 1868. At the signing of the Treaty of Fort Laramie, the United States mistakenly included nearly all of the remaining Ponca land base in a treaty to create a reservation for neighboring tribal bands. The loss of these 96,000 acres of Ponca territory violated their own 1865 treaty with the United States and instigated violence and tension between the Ponca and the Sioux.[253] In 1877 the federal government again infringed on the tribe's land by mandating Ponca removal to Indian Territory in present-day Oklahoma. The tribe arrived in its new territory the following year but a full third of the community had perished from starvation, disease, and other hardships associated with the forced march.[254]

During this journey, Standing Bear suffered two devastating losses: the deaths of his eldest son, Bear Shield, and of his wife, Zazette Primeau.[255] Standing Bear aspired to fulfill his late son's final wish to be buried at his birthplace among his ancestors and in January 1879 set out for Ponca homelands in Nebraska.[256] In doing so, however, Standing Bear and those accompanying him violated federal mandates that confined Native Americans to reservations.[257] Brig. Gen. George Crook arrested the party while en route and detained them at Fort Omaha.[258]

Despite his history of conflict with Native peoples, historians note that Crook was sympathetic to the plight of Standing Bear's family and their losses.[259] He arranged for a meeting with *Omaha Daily Herald* editor Thomas Henry Tibbles, who published a widely read interview with the tribal leader.[260] The media coverage in turn inspired two lawyers to appeal Standing Bear's detention in Omaha's US District Court and to represent the Poncas pro bono.[261] The resulting case, *Standing Bear v. Crook*, named Brigadier General Crook as the defendant as he had detained the party, no matter his personal sympathies toward the group.[262]

The proceedings of the case distinguished Standing Bear as a civil rights advocate who changed the course of law in the United States. Judge Elmer Dundy oversaw the May 1 and 2, 1879 proceedings.[263] In response to the suit, the US attorney purported that Standing Bear could not sue the government because he was not a US citizen—or even, in the eyes of the law, a person.[264] Standing Bear rebutted this claim as the first Native American to testify in court.[265] Speaking through Omaha interpreter Susette (Bright Eyes) La Flesche, Standing Bear relayed a powerful message of racial equality.[266] "My hand is not the color of yours, but if I pierce it, I shall feel pain. If you pierce your hand, you also feel pain," he explained, "The blood that will flow from mine will be the same color as yours. The same god made us both. I am a man."[267] This appeal to a shared humanity so moved Judge Dundy that he ruled ten days later in favor of Standing Bear and the Poncas.[268] This opinion, although still littered with racism describing Native peoples as a "weak, insignificant, unlettered, and generally despised race," nevertheless determined for the first time in United States court that "an Indian is a 'person.'"[269]

Standing Bear returned to his homelands by the Niobrara to inter his son's remains; the Ponca funerary party was released from captivity.[270] In October of that same year, the chief embarked on a national and international speaking tour with his interpreter, which ran until 1883. Standing Bear grew old in his homelands in Nebraska. When he passed on in 1908, the tribal leader was buried alongside his son and ancestors.[271]

The state of Nebraska selected Chief Standing Bear as one of the state's two citizen statue contributions to the United States Capitol 111 years later. The unveiling ceremony took place on September 18, 2019, making Standing Bear the most recent Indigenous American to be added to the National Statuary Hall Collection. This statue replaced that of former Secretary of State William Jennings Bryan, which had been installed in 1937.[272]

Idaho-based sculptor Benjamin Victor completed the Standing Bear tribute and is also the artist behind the US Capitol's Sarah Winnemucca statue. Victor created the model based on how the tribal leader would have appeared during the *Standing Bear v. Crook* trial. The eagle feather in Standing Bear's hair represents his status as a warrior, while the bear-claw necklace signifies strength and the sacred power of the bear. On top of his breastplate, Standing Bear also dons two Presidential Peace Medals gifted from the United States. While one hand holds a pipe and blanket, the other reaches out "as he asserts that his hand and the judge's hold blood of the same color."[273] The statue looms over nine feet tall and sits atop a base featuring etchings of Standing Bear's wise words.[274]

National Native American Veterans Memorial

Commemorations of military engagements are one of the features for which Washington, DC, is most known. The DC War Memorial, Korean War Veterans Memorial, World War II Memorial, US Navy Memorial Plaza, Vietnam Women's Memorial, and Vietnam Veterans Memorial are some of the most visited and most visible landmarks in the capital city. The latest addition to these iconic tributes is the National Native American Veterans Memorial.

Commissioned by Congress and spearheaded by the NMAI, the National Native American Veterans Memorial honors American Indian, Alaska Native, and Native Hawaiian veterans who served in every branch of the US Armed

Forces. This memorial is the first national tribute to this powerful legacy.[275] "Recognition of Native Americans' service is long overdue. Accounts of their bravery in the armed forces are not widely known, represented in textbooks, or discussed in classrooms," wrote Sen. Ben Nighthorse Campbell (Northern Cheyenne) and Jefferson Keel (lieutenant governor of the Chickasaw Nation), co-chairs of the National Native American Veterans Memorial Advisory Committee. "If we don't keep these stories alive, they will fade away."[276]

The process to establish the memorial began with Congress's passage of the Native American Veterans' Memorial Establishment Act of 1994.[277] This legislation outlined the memorial's "monumental mission" thus: "[The National Native American Veterans Memorial would] give all Americans the opportunity to learn of the proud and courageous tradition of service of Native Americans in the Armed Forces of the United States."[278] In this original language, however, Congress only paved the way for the creation of a memorial within the NMAI interior structure, and space limitations and funding made this arrangement challenging.[279] To resolve this issue and propel the creation of the memorial forward, Rep. Markwayne Mullin (R-OK) (Cherokee) sponsored a successful amendment on June 11, 2013, to enable the NMAI to place the memorial in the museum's outdoor space.[280]

With new possibilities secured by this congressional development, the NMAI went to task. The first step of manifesting the vision for the memorial first unfolded with the establishment of an advisory committee in 2015.[281] The committee represented a broad range of experiences and interests: all twenty-one members were Native American or Alaska Native from twenty-one different tribes. Three individuals represented military family members, and eighteen of the committee were veterans themselves, having served in Iraq, Vietnam, and Korea. Eleven of the veterans served in the Army, three in the Navy, one in the Air Force, and three in the Marine Corps; one of the family members on the advisory committee represented the Coast Guard. The committee was co-chaired by Sen. Ben Nighthorse Campbell (Northern Cheyenne) and Lt. Governor of the Chickasaw Nation Jefferson Keel. Senator Campbell and Lieutenant Governor Keel served in the Air Force in Korea and in the Army in Vietnam, respectively.[282]

The advisory committee played a significant role in engaging Indian Country early in the creation of the memorial. Beginning in 2016 the committee conducted thirty-five community consultations over a nearly two-year period.[283] Between October 2015 and June 2017 the committee hosted sessions across sixteen states and in each of the twelve regions outlined by the

National Congress of American Indians and the Bureau of Indian Affairs.[284] In total, these events engaged approximately 1,200 tribal leaders and Native community members and allowed for feedback that shaped the design requirements put forth in the next stage of the memorial's development.[285]

A shared vision for the National Native American Veterans Memorial emerged from this nationwide consultation campaign. The theme of inclusivity ensured the representation of all of the United States' First Peoples, including American Indians, Alaska Natives, and Native Hawaiians, as well as veterans from all branches of service, all ages, men and women alike. The meetings determined that the families of veterans—their sacrifices, struggles, and support—would also be recognized by this memorial. Those consulted expressed a desire for the memorial to offer a space for healing and reflection as well as spiritual connectedness. Accordingly, the collective selected the serene northern portion of the museum lands, complete with a flowing water feature, as the location for the memorial.[286]

In November 2017 the committee launched an open, international design competition to artists, architects, designers, and many more who hoped to lend their ideas to the appearance of the memorial.[287] More than 120 designs were entered.[288] By early the following year, the competition had narrowed to five finalists—James Dinh, the Dan Jones and Kelly Haney team, Harvey Pratt, Stefanie Rocknak, and Leroy Transfield—who presented their designs before an eight-member jury and a public forum in February.[289] Four months later, in June 2018, the jury unanimously named Harvey Pratt (Cheyenne and Arapaho), and his Warriors' Circle of Honor design, the winner.[290]

Pratt had become aware of the plans for a new memorial after attending two of the Smithsonian's community meetings in Oklahoma. At the time, however, he reflected that he "really wasn't interested" in being involved. That all changed, he recalled, when inspiration for the design came to him in a dream.[291] This spark led Pratt to imagine a memorial that offered an interactive space for healing, ceremony, gathering, and community building.

The final design reflects Pratt's original vision in many of its features. Specifically, the memorial is focused around a towering stainless steel circle—a traditional Indigenous motif—balanced vertically atop a drum carved from stone.[292] The drum sits in a circular pool of water, symbolizing "the constant pulse of Native American spirit and sacrifice across the breadth of U.S. history."[293] To commemorate special occasions, a flame leaps up into the center of the steel ring above the drum head.[294] Here the water is also incorporated as an element of many Indigenous communities' traditional ceremonies, and the four stone benches surrounding the circle encourage gathering with the community.[295] Lances surrounding the circle offer a tribute to military might, and visitors engage with these installations by attaching prayer ties to them.[296] Each is oriented toward the four directions and dons the sacred color affiliated with each: the southeast lance flies a white ribbon to signify new beginnings and the start of each day; the southwestern lance marks the home of the Creator and is identified by a red ribbon; the northwestern lance carries a yellow ribbon for Mother Earth, and the northeastern lance is for the ancestors, represented by a black ribbon.[297] In keeping true to its purpose of inclusivity, insignia for all branches of the armed forces pay tribute to the Army, Air Force, Navy, Coast Guard, and Marine Corps.[298] *Indian Country Today*, a major Native news outlet, reported the memorial "is like a spiritual container that [Pratt] hopes will grow into a location of pilgrimage for those who want to remember the thousands of Native American soldiers who honored the warrior traditions of their tribes and fought to protect the land of our ancestors."[299]

Pratt drew inspiration for his winning design from his own life and knew intimately of the subject at hand. After enlisting with the US Marine Corps, Pratt served in Vietnam from 1962 to 1965, specializing in Air Rescue and Security at Da Nang Air Base.[300] After spending three years in the service, Pratt returned to his home state of Oklahoma intending to reenlist as an officer after continuing his education. Pratt's career path instead shifted to a life of service closer to home: law enforcement. Over the course of more than fifty years, Pratt worked primarily as a forensic artist at the Midwest City Police Department and Oklahoma State Bureau of Investigation. His military background prepared him well for assignments to such high-profile, critical cases as the Green River Killer, Ted Bundy, and the I-5 Killer.[301]

Having earned his political science degree from Oklahoma State University and receiving special training at the FBI National Academy in 1981, Pratt identifies as a self-taught artist. His commissioned and collected works include a seven-foot bald eagle and tribal shield relief at the Oklahoma State Bureau of Investigation; a thirty-seven-foot mural of the Oklahoma State Bureau of Investigation's case history; a painting of the 1868 Washita Massacre in historic Cheyenne, Oklahoma; numerous paintings among the National Park Service's permanent holdings; and a life-sized sculpture in Denver honoring the victims of the 1864 Sand Creek Massacre. Pratt has also held leadership positions related to the arts on a national level, serving as chair of the Indian Arts and Crafts Board of the Department of the Interior, and has received the

FIGURE 2.5. The National Native American Veterans Memorial outside the National Museum of the American Indian
National Native American Veterans Memorial at the National Museum of the American Indian, by Michael Perrin, licensed under CC BY-SA 4.0.

highest recognition of his Cheyenne Nation by becoming a peace chief.[302] With themes of justice, service, and Native American history running throughout Pratt's portfolio, it is clear to see how the artist's military background and Cheyenne culture inform one another in his work.

Pratt's vision, the NMAI grounds, and the input of so many veterans and military families across the nation culminated with the breaking of ground for the memorial's construction in 2019.[303] Its location at the foot of Capitol Hill on the National Mall on the grounds of the Smithsonian's National Museum of the American Indian draws approximately twenty-four million visitors each year and is central to raising awareness of the often overlooked sacrifices made by the United States' original peoples.[304] The memorial was to be publicly dedicated on Veterans Day 2020.[305]

No one could have anticipated that the dedication ceremony would be interrupted by the COVID-19 pandemic. Rather than gathering in person, the November 11 opening event took shape in a virtual format. Distinguished tribal leaders, federal officials, and team members behind the memorial contributed video speeches looking back on the process and expressing their hopes for the new National Native American Veterans Memorial.[306] Tulalip Tribe councilman and Vietnam veteran Mel Sheldon discussed the proud legacy of the warrior tradition, while Fawn Sharp, president of the National Congress of American Indians and president of the Quinault Nation, explained that before Native peoples were US citizens, tribal warriors defended the fundamental notions of freedom, justice, equality, and liberty. NMAI director Kevin Gover (Pawnee) and secretary of the Smithsonian Institution Lonnie Bunch reflected on the role of the NMAI in leading this national tribute to Native veterans. With Sen. Brian Schatz speaking to the need for this memorial, Secretary of the Department of Veterans Affairs Rob Wilkie expressed gratitude to Native veterans on behalf of Veterans Affairs. US representatives Deb Haaland (Laguna Pueblo) and Sharice Davids (Ho-Chunk), the first Native women elected to Congress, highlighted contributions of Native veterans to the shaping of the United States, including family members. As Rep. Tom Cole (Chickasaw) communicated national pride in Native veterans, Rep. Markwayne Mullin offered thanks to veterans' families for their support of these warriors. Co-chairs of the Memorial Honorary Committee, John Herrington (Chickasaw) and Wes Studi (Cherokee), wished all a happy Veterans Day and recognized all who have served in times of war and peace, past and present. Sen. Ben Nighthorse Campbell (Northern Cheyenne) and Lt. Gov. Emeritus Jefferson Kee (Chickasaw), co-chairs of the National Native American Veterans Memorial Advisory Committee, elaborated on the history of Native peoples' service in the armed forces since the American Revolution. To conclude, Harvey Pratt (Cheyenne), designer of the memorial, shared the experience of dreaming his vision for the memorial and its ceremonial uses for healing. The virtual ceremony has been viewed by thousands.[307]

As millions of visitors spend time at the National Native American Veterans Memorial, many will undoubtedly wonder: Why, given such rife mistreatment by this country and abuse by its government, would Native peoples continue to serve in the military at such high rates? The answer, in the words of Army veteran Allen K. Hoe (Native Hawaiian), is land. "This is our land and this is our culture, and we all have a spirit of defending our homeland," he declared, "In the end . . . we do this . . . because we love our homeland."[308] Indeed, the profound love of the land is the constant that unites Sgt. 1st Class John Raymond Rice, who was denied burial because of his race, and servicemembers like Navajo code talker Pvt. Carl Gorman, who was punished for speaking his tribal language as a schoolchild. The commitment to defend land connects Ira Hayes, who is forever memorialized in the US Marine Corps War Memorial, and heroes like M.Sgt. Woodrow Wilson Keeble, the first Sioux servicemember bestowed a Medal of Honor. A mutual understanding of land joins together those who continue this work today, such as Harvey Pratt, designer of the National Native American Veterans Memorial, and active members like Col. Wayne Don, who oversees 1,200 Alaska National Guard soldiers. A shared dedication to this land binds together all the Indigenous leaders whose statues grace the US Capitol and who welcome young Native leaders like 1st Lt. Nainoa K. Hoe, who was killed in action in Iraq, into their ranks and legacy.[309]

NOTES

1. National Museum of the American Indian (NMAI), *National Native American Veterans Memorial: Honoring Native American Military Service* (Washington, DC: National Museum of the American Indian, n.d.), 3.

2. Native Americans have served in the post-9/11 period at a higher percentage than people of other ethnicities: 18.6 percent compared to 14 percent. NMAI, *Honoring*, 3.

3. Lauren Monsen, "Native American Veterans Memorial coming to Washington," *ShareAmerica*, November 6, 2019, https://share.america.gov/native-american-veterans-memorial-coming-to-washington/.

4. NMAI, *Honoring*, 3.

5. NMAI, *National Native American Veterans Memorial: Consultation Report* (Washington, DC: Smithsonian National Museum of the American Indian, 2018), 8.

6. Tom Holm, *Strong Hearts, Wounded Souls: Native American Veterans of the Vietnam War* (Austin: University of Texas Press, 1996), 30–65.

7. Tom Holm, "Strong Hearts, Wounded Souls Revisited: The Research, the Findings, and Some Observations of Recent Native Veteran Readjustment," *Wicazo Sa Review*, 32, no. 1 (Spring 2017): 119.

8. Quoted in Robert Sanderson, "More Indian Voices from Vietnam," American Native Press Archives and Sequoyah Research Center.

9. John A. Little, "Between Cultures: Sioux Warriors and the Vietnam War," *Great Plains Quarterly* 35, no. 4 (Fall 2015): 362.

10. Little, 364–67.

11. Dean J. Kotlowski, "Burying Sergeant Rice: Racial Justice and Native American Rights in the Truman Era," *Journal of American Studies* 38, no. 2 (2004): 208.

12. Kotlowski, 199, 208.

13. Kotlowski, 208; and Michael Robert Patterson, "John Raymond Rice: Sergeant, United States Army," Arlington National Cemetery Website, accessed July 2, 2020, http://www.arlingtoncemetery.net/jrrice.htm.

14. Kotlowski, 208.

15. Kotlowski, 208.

16. Kotlowski, 209.

17. Kotlowski, 208.

18. Kotlowski, 209.

19. Kotlowski, 199.

20. Kotlowski, 209.

21. Bret Hayworth, "Rice Buried in Arlington—A Rosa Parks for American Indians," *Sioux City Journal*, May 13, 2006, https://siouxcityjournal.com/news/rice-buried-in-arling-ton—a-rosa-parks-for-american-indians/article_1918a4f1-9136-5562-8921-898487b94fd3.html.

22. Chuck Hagel, "Remembering Soldiers and Their Families," speech, May 24, 2006, Arlington National Cemetery website, accessed July 2, 2020, http://www.arlingtoncemetery.net/jrrice.htm.

23. Kotlowski, "Burying Sergeant Rice," 211.

24. Kotlowski, 212.

25. Hayworth, "Rice Buried in Arlington."

26. Kotlowski, "Burying Sergeant Rice," 215.

27. Kotlowski, 215; and Patterson, "John Raymond Rice."

28. Kotlowski, "Burying Sergeant Rice," 215.

29. Hayworth, "Rice Buried in Arlington."

30. For more on the history of Indigenous racialization, segregation, and military service, see Malinda Maynor Lowery, *Lumbee Indians in the Jim Crow South: Race, Identity, and the Making of a Nation* (Chapel Hill: University of North Carolina Press, 2010), 229–30.

31. "History of the Marine Corps War Memorial," National Park Service, February 24, 2020, https://www.nps.gov/gwmp/learn/historyculture/usmcwarmemorial.htm; and "U.S. Marine Corps War Memorial Rehabilitation," National Park Service, last modified February 21, 2020, https://www.nps.gov/gwmp/learn/management/marine-corps-war-memorial-rehabilitation.htm#:~:text=The%20US%20Marine%20Corps%20War%20Memorial%20is%20visited%20annually%20by,use%20the%20park%20access%20road.

32. "U.S. Marine Corps War Memorial Rehabilitation."

33. "U.S. Marine Corps War Memorial Rehabilitation."

34. "History of the Marine Corps War Memorial."

35. "History of the Marine Corps War Memorial."

36. "History of the Marine Corps War Memorial."

37. "Joe Rosenthal of Associated Press," The Pulitzer Prizes, 2020, https://www.pulitzer.org/winners/joe-rosenthal.

38. "History of the Marine Corps War Memorial."

39. "History of the Marine Corps War Memorial."

40. "History of the Marine Corps War Memorial."

41. Corky Siemaszko, "Warrior in Iconic Iwo Jima Flag-Raising Photo Was Misidentified, Marines Corps Acknowledges," *NBC News*, October 16, 2019, https://www.nbcnews.com/news/us-news/warrior-iconic-iwo-jima-flag-raising-photo-was-misidentified-marines-n1064766.

42. "History of the Marine Corps War Memorial."

43. "History of the Marine Corps War Memorial."

44. Siemaszko, "Warrior in Iconic Iwo Jima Flag-Raising Photo Was Misidentified."

45. "Ira Hayes: Immortal Flag Raiser at Iwo Jima," *VAntage Point* (blog), US Department of Veterans Affairs, November 21, 2019, https://www.blogs.va.gov/VAntage/68545/ira-hayes-immortal-flag-raiser-iwo-jima/; and Eric Hammel, *Two Flags over Iwo Jima: Solving the Mystery of the U.S. Marine Corps' Proudest Moment* (Oxford: Casemate, 2018), 58.

46. "Ira Hayes."

47. "Ira Hayes"; and Hammel, *Two Flags over Iwo Jima*, 59.

48. "Ira Hayes."

49. "Ira Hayes"; and Hammel, *Two Flags over Iwo Jima*, 59.

50. Hammel, *Two Flags over Iwo Jima*, 59.

51. "Ira Hayes."

52. "Ira Hayes."

53. "Ira Hayes"; and Siemaszko, "Warrior in Iconic Iwo Jima Flag-Raising Photo Was Misidentified."

54. Chelsea Curtis, "Ira Hayes Raised the Flag on Iwo Jima 75 Years Ago. His Heroism Still Inspires the Gila River Indian Community," *Azcentral.com*, February 22, 2020, https://www.azcentral.com/story/news/local/pinal/2020/02/22/ira-hayes-inspires-gila-river-indian-community-75-years-after-iwo-jima/4843217002/.

55. "Ira Hayes"; and Curtis, "Ira Hayes Raised the Flag on Iwo Jima 75 years ago."

56. Curtis, "Ira Hayes Raised the Flag."

57. Curtis.

58. "Collections," National Museum of the American Indian, accessed December 19, 2020, https://americanindian.si.edu/explore/collections#:~:text=The%20National%20Museum%20of%20the%20American%20Indian%20(NMAI)%20has%20one,indigenous%20cultures%20throughout%20the%20Americas; and Ira Jacknis, "A New Thing? The National Museum of the American Indian in Historical and Institutional Context," in *The National Museum of the American Indian: Critical Conversations*, ed. Amanda J. Cobb and Amy Lonetree (Lincoln: University of Nebraska Press, 2008), 3.

59. "History of the Collections," National Museum of the American Indian, accessed December 19, 2020, https://americanindian.si.edu/explore/collections/history; and "National Museum of the American Indian," Smithsonian Institution Archives, accessed December 19, 2020, https://siarchives.si.edu/history/national-museum-american-indian.

60. "National Museum of the American Indian."

61. "History of the Collections"; and Amanda J. Cobb and Amy Lonetree, eds., *The National Museum of the American Indian: Critical Conversations* (Lincoln: University of Nebraska Press, 2008), xxx.

62. Jacknis, "A New Thing?," 3.

63. Judith Ostrowitz, "Concourse and Periphery: Planning the National Museum of the American Indian," in *The National Museum of the American Indian: Critical Conversations*, ed. Amanda J. Cobb and Amy Lonetree (Lincoln: University of Nebraska Press, 2008), 84.

64. Debbie Ann Doyle, "National Museum of the American Indian Opens in Washington, D.C.," *Perspectives on History*, November 1, 2004, https://www.historians.org/publications-and-directories/perspectives-on-history/november-2004/national-museum-of-the-american-indian-opens-in-washington-dc.

65. "National Museum of the American Indian."

66. "Visitor Stats," Smithsonian Institution, accessed December 11, 2020, https://www.si.edu/newsdesk/about/stats.

67. Mario A. Caro, "The National Museum of the American Indian and the Siting of Identity," in *The National Museum of the American Indian: Critical Conversations*, ed. Amanda J. Cobb and Amy Lonetree (Lincoln: University of Nebraska Press, 2008), 433.

68. "National Museum of the American Indian."

69. Ostrowitz, "Concourse and Periphery," 105.

70. "National Museum of the American Indian"; and "Outdoors at the Museum," National Museum of the American Indian, April 8, 2011, https://blog.nmai.si.edu/main /2011/04/outdoors-at-the-museum.html.

71. "Outdoors at the Museum."

72. "Native Landscape at the National Museum of the American Indian," Smithsonian Gardens, accessed December 9, 2020, https://gardens.si.edu/gardens/native-landscape -nmai/.

73. "Outdoors at the Museum."

74. "Outdoors at the Museum."

75. Jacknis, "A New Thing?," 31.

76. Ostrowitz, "Concourse and Periphery," 107.

77. Caro, "The National Museum of the American Indian and the Siting of Identity," 433–34.

78. "National Museum of the American Indian," *United Kingdom Architecture News*, July 22, 2014, https://worldarchitecture.org/architecture-news/czpgh/national-museum -of-the-american-indian.html.

79. Amanda J. Cobb, "The National Museum of the American Indian as Cultural Sover- eignty," *American Quarterly* 57, no. 2 (June 2005): 494.

80. Cobb, 486.

81. Cobb, 502.

82. Cobb, 503.

83. Doyle, "National Museum of the American Indian Opens in Washington, DC."

84. Cobb and Lonetree, *The National Museum of the American Indian*, xxv.

85. Cobb and Lonetree, xxv.

86. Cobb and Lonetree, xxiv.

87. Jasmin K. Williams, "Hiram Revels," *New York Post*, February 12, 2007, https:// nypost.com/2007/02/12/hiram-revels/.

88. "Campbell, Ben Nighthorse," History, Art & Archives: United States House of Representatives, accessed December 17, 2020, https://history.house.gov/People/Listing/C /CAMPBELL,-Ben-Nighthorse-(C000077)/.

89. "American Indians in the US Army," US Army, accessed December 17, 2020, https:// www.army.mil/americanindians/carson.html.

90. "Native Americans in Art," Architect of the Capitol, accessed December 19, 2020, https://www.aoc.gov/explore-capitol-campus/art/native-americans.

91. Ellen Cushman, "'We're Taking the Genius of Sequoyah into This Century': The Cherokee Syllabary, Peoplehood, and Perseverance," *Wicazo Sa Review* 26, no. 1 (Spring 2011): 70–71.

92. Cushman, 72.

93. Cushman, 73; and "Sequoyah," Architect of the Capitol, accessed December 22, 2020, https://www.aoc.gov/art/national-statuary-hall-collection/sequoyah.

94. Cushman, "'We're Taking the Genius of Sequoyah'," 73.

95. Cushman, 74.

96. Cushman, 72, 74.

97. Cushman, 74.

98. Cushman, 68.

99. Cushman, 72, 74.

100. "Sequoyah."

101. Cushman, "'We're Taking the Genius of Sequoyah'," 68.

Monuments, Museums, and Military Service   91

102. Cushman, 68.

103. Cushman, 75.

104. Cushman, 76.

105. "Sequoyah."

106. Cushman, "'We're Taking the Genius of Sequoyah'," 71.

107. Cushman, 71–72.

108. Judy Baxter, "Bet You Didn't Know This about the Sequoyah Statue in Cherokee!," *Cherokee North Carolina* (blog), accessed December 20, 2020, https://visitcherokeenc.com /blog/entry/bet-you-didnt-know-this-about-the-sequoyah-statue-in-cherokee/.

109. Cushman, "'We're Taking the Genius of Sequoyah'," 73.

110. Cushman, 74.

111. "Sequoyah."

112. Cushman, "'We're Taking the Genius of Sequoyah'," 77–78.

113. Cushman, 77.

114. Cushman, 68.

115. "Sequoyah."

116. Elizabeth Archuleta, "History Carved in Stone: Memorializing Po'Pay and Onate, or Recasting Racialized Regimes of Representation?," *New Mexico Historical Review* 82, no. 3 (June 2007): 320.

117. Gene Curtis, "Only in Oklahoma: Rogers Statue Unveiling Filled U.S. Capitol," *Tulsa World*, February 26, 2019, https://tulsaworld.com/archive/only-in-oklahoma-rogers -statue-unveiling-filled-u-s-capitol/article_b3bf36ee-ec19-575b-bae4-9d6f42afdb08.html.

118. "Sequoyah."

119. Amy M. Ware, *The Cherokee Kid: Will Rogers, Tribal Identity, and the Making of an American Icon* (Lawrence: University of Kansas Press, 2015), 52, 235, 248.

120. Alice George, "Will Rogers Was One of a Kind," *Smithsonian Magazine*, August 5, 2020, https://www.smithsonianmag.com/smithsonian-institution/will-rogers-was-one -kind-180975472/.

121. Roumiana Velikova, "Will Rogers's Indian Humor," *Studies in American Indian Literatures* 19, no. 2 (Summer 2007): 83.

122. George, "Will Rogers Was One of a Kind"; and "Will Rogers Timeline," *Tulsa World*, accessed January 3, 2021, http://tulsaworld.com/app/willrogers/timeline/index.html.

123. Ware, *The Cherokee Kid*, 60.

124. Ware, 61.

125. George, "Will Rogers Was One of a Kind."

126. "Will Rogers Timeline."

127. George, "Will Rogers Was One of a Kind."

128. Velikova, "Will Rogers's Indian Humor," 85.

129. "Will Rogers Timeline."

130. "Will Rogers Timeline."

131. George, "Will Rogers Was One of a Kind."

132. "Will Rogers," Architect of the Capitol, accessed December 22, 2020, https://www .aoc.gov/explore-capitol-campus/art/will-rogers.

133. Talia Mindich, "Will Rogers Still Watches the Lawmakers on Capitol Hill He Loved to Spoof," *The Hill*, October 22, 2013, https://thehill.com/capital-living/329753-will-rogers -still-watches-the-lawmakers-he-loved-to-spoof.

134. Curtis, "Only in Oklahoma."

135. Curtis.

136. Curtis.

137. Curtis.

138. Mindich, "Will Rogers Still Watches."

139. Mindich.

140. "Kamehameha I," Architect of the Capitol, accessed December 22, 2020, https://www.aoc.gov/art/national-statuary-hall-collection/kamehameha-i.

141. Noenoe K. Silva, *Aloha Betrayed: Native Hawaiian Resistance to American Colonialism* (Durham, NC: Duke University Press, 2004), 18.

142. "Kamehameha I."

143. Silva, *Aloha Betrayed*, 18.

144. "Kamehameha I."

145. "Kamehameha I: King of Hawaii," Britannica, accessed January 4, 2021, https://www.britannica.com/biography/Kamehameha-I.

146. "Kamehameha I: King of Hawaii."

147. Silva, *Aloha Betrayed*, 28; and "Kamehameha I."

148. Silva, *Aloha Betrayed*, 28.

149. "Kamehameha I."

150. "Kamehameha I."

151. Matthew Dekneef, "5 Fascinating Facts about the King Kamehameha Statue," *Hawaii Magazine*, June 10, 2016, https://www.hawaiimagazine.com/content/5-cool-facts-about-king-kamehameha-statue.

152. "Kamehameha I."

153. "Kamehameha I."

154. "Kamehameha I."

155. "Father Damien," Architect of the Capitol, accessed December 22, 2020, https://www.aoc.gov/explore-capitol-campus/art/father-damien.

156. Henry E. Stamm, *People of the Wind River: The Eastern Shoshones, 1825–1900* (Norman: University of Oklahoma Press, 1999), 26.

157. Stamm, 8, 25; and "Chief Washakie," Architect of the Capitol, accessed December 22, 2020, https://www.aoc.gov/explore-capitol-campus/art/chief-washakie.

158. Stamm, *People of the Wind River*, 25.

159. Stamm, 27.

160. Placement of the Statue of Chief Washakie in National Statuary Hall, HR 333, 106th Cong., 2nd sess., *Congressional Record* 146, pt. 9, 12518–20.

161. Placement of the Statue of Chief Washakie, 12518–20.

162. Stamm, *People of the Wind River*, 29.

163. Stamm, *People of the Wind River*, 33.

164. "Chief Washakie."

165. Placement of the Statue of Chief Washakie, 12518–20.

166. Stamm, *People of the Wind River*, 41; and Stamm, "Chief Washakie of the Shoshone."

167. Stamm, *People of the Wind River*, ix; and Placement of the Statue of Chief Washakie, 12518–20.

168. Stamm, "Chief Washakie of the Shoshone."

169. Stamm, *People of the Wind River*, 272.

170. Stamm, 243.

171. Stamm, 251; and Placement of the Statue of Chief Washakie, 12518–20.

172. Placement of the Statue of Chief Washakie, 12518–20.

173. "Chief Washakie."

174. Placement of the Statue of Chief Washakie, 12518–20.

175. Dave McGary, *Chief Washakie*, accessed January 5, 2021, https://www.davemcgary.com/chief-washakie/.

176. Placement of the Statue of Chief Washakie, 12518–20.

177. "Chief Washakie."

178. Placement of the Statue of Chief Washakie, 12518–20.

179. Sally McBeth, "Memory, History, and Contested Pasts: Re-Imagining Sacagawea/Sacajawea," *American Indian Culture and Research Journal* 27, no. 1 (2003): 4.

180. McBeth, 13; and "Sakakawea," Architect of the Capitol, accessed December 22, 2020, https://www.aoc.gov/explore-capitol-campus/art/sakakawea.

181. McBeth, "Memory, History, and Contested Past," 13; and "Sakakawea."

182. Teresa Potter and Mariana Brandman, "Sacagawea," National Women's History Museum, accessed January 7, 2021, https://www.womenshistory.org/education-resources/biographies/sacagawea.

183. McBeth, "Memory, History, and Contested Past," 4; and "Sakakawea."

184. McBeth, "Memory, History, and Contested Past," 4; and "Sakakawea."

185. McBeth, "Memory, History, and Contested Past," 4.

186. Potter and Brandman, "Sacagawea."

187. McBeth, "Memory, History, and Contested Past," 4.

188. McBeth, 4.

189. McBeth, 5; and Potter and Brandman, "Sacagawea."

190. "Sakakawea."

191. McBeth, "Memory, History, and Contested Past," 5, 6.

192. Potter and Brandman, "Sacagawea."

193. McBeth, "Memory, History, and Contested Past," 4.

194. McBeth, 6; and "Sakakawea."

195. McBeth, "Memory, History, and Contested Past," 6, 7.

196. McBeth, 11.

197. "Sakakawea."

198. "Sakakawea."

199. McBeth, 3.

200. McBeth, 2.

201. McBeth, 2.

202. "Sarah Winnemucca," Architect of the Capitol, accessed December 22, 2020, https://www.aoc.gov/art/national-statuary-hall-collection/sarah-winnemucca.

203. Rosalyn Eves, "Sarah Winnemucca Devoted Her Life to Protecting Native Americans in the Face of an Expanding United States," *Smithsonian Magazine*, July 27, 2016, https://www.smithsonianmag.com/history/sarah-winnemucca-devoted-life-protecting-lives-native-americans-face-expanding-united-states-180959930/.

204. Eves, "Sarah Winnemucca Devoted Her Life."

205. Eves.

206. Victoria Ford, "Sarah Winnemucca," Nevada Women's History Project, accessed January 9, 2021, https://www.nevadawomen.org/research-center/biographies-alphabetical/sarah-winnemucca/.

207. Cari M. Carpenter, "Sarah Winnemucca Goes to Washington: Rhetoric and Resistance in the Capital City," *American Indian Quarterly* 40, no. 2 (Spring 2016): 93.

208. Carpenter, 87.

209. Eves, "Sarah Winnemucca Devoted Her Life."

210. "Sarah Winnemucca."

211. Eves, "Sarah Winnemucca Devoted Her Life."

212. Eves.

213. Eves.

214. Carpenter, "Sarah Winnemucca Goes to Washington," 98.

215. Carpenter, 95; and Eves, "Sarah Winnemucca Devoted Her Life."

216. Carpenter, "Sarah Winnemucca Goes to Washington," 88.

217. Eves, "Sarah Winnemucca Devoted Her Life."

218. Carpenter, "Sarah Winnemucca Goes to Washington," 87.

219. Carpenter, 91.

220. Carpenter, 92.

221. Carpenter, 88.

222. Carpenter, 89.

223. Carpenter, 93.

224. "Sarah Winnemucca."

225. Eves, "Sarah Winnemucca Devoted Her Life."

226. Quoted in Eves.

227. "Sarah Winnemucca."

228. "Sarah Winnemucca"; and Carpenter, "Sarah Winnemucca Goes to Washington," 98, 99.

229. "Sarah Winnemucca."

230. Carpenter, "Sarah Winnemucca Goes to Washington," 100.

231. Archuleta, "History Carved in Stone," 337.

232. Archuleta, 337.

233. Archuleta, 323.

234. Archuleta, 337.

235. Archuleta, 324.

236. Archuleta, 324.

237. Archuleta, 323.

238. Archuleta, 324.

239. Archuleta, 324.

240. "Po'pay," Architect of the Capitol, accessed December 22, 2020, https://www.aoc.gov/explore-capitol-campus/art/popay; Archuleta, "History Carved in Stone," 330.

241. Archuleta, 324.

242. Archuleta, 330–33.

243. Archuleta, 334.

244. Archuleta, 325.

245. Cliff Fragua, "Po'pay Commission," Singing Stone Studio—Cliff Fragua (blog), March 13, 2017, https://www.singingstonestudio.com/blog/2017/3/14/popay-commission.

246. Fragua; and "Pueblo Leader Completes National Statuary Hall," *Indianz.com*, September 23, 2005, https://www.indianz.com/News/2005/09/23/pueblo_leader_c.asp.

247. "Po'pay."

248. Fragua, "Po'pay Commission."

249. "Pueblo Leader Completes National Statuary Hall."

250. "Standing Bear," Architect of the Capitol, accessed December 22, 2020, https://www.aoc.gov/explore-capitol-campus/art/chief-standing-bear; and Gillian Brockell, "The Civil Rights Leader 'Almost Nobody Knows About' Gets a Statue in the U.S. Capitol,"

Washington Post, September 20, 2019, https://www.washingtonpost.com/history/2019/09
/20/civil-rights-leader-almost-nobody-knows-about-gets-statue-us-capitol/.

251. "Standing Bear"; and Brockell, "The Civil Rights Leader."

252. Brockell, "The Civil Rights Leader."

253. "The Story of the Ponca," NET: Nebraska's PBS and NPR Stations, accessed January 10, 2021, https://www.nebraskastudies.org/en/1875-1899/the-trial-of-standing-bear
/the-story-of-the-ponca/.

254. "Standing Bear."

255. "Standing Bear."

256. Brockell, "The Civil Rights Leader"; and "Standing Bear."

257. "Standing Bear."

258. "Standing Bear"; and Brockell, "The Civil Rights Leader."

259. "Standing Bear"; and Brockell, "The Civil Rights Leader."

260. "Standing Bear."

261. "Standing Bear"; and Brockell, "The Civil Rights Leader."

262. Brockell, "The Civil Rights Leader."

263. "Standing Bear."

264. "Standing Bear"; and Brockell, "The Civil Rights Leader."

265. Brockell, "The Civil Rights Leader."

266. "Standing Bear."

267. "Standing Bear."

268. "Standing Bear."

269. Brockell, "The Civil Rights Leader."

270. Brockell."

271. "Standing Bear."

272. Brockell, "The Civil Rights Leader."

273. "Standing Bear."

274. "Standing Bear."

275. "National Native American Veteran's Memorial," National Museum of the American Indian, accessed January 15, 2021, https://americanindian.si.edu/nnavm/.

276. Ben Nighthorse Campbell and Jefferson Keel, "From the Co-Chairs" (Washington, DC: National Museum of the American Indian).

277. US Congress, House, Native American Veterans' Memorial Amendments Act of 2013, 113th Cong.,1st sess., 2013, H. Rep. 113, 1, https://www.congress.gov/113/crpt
/hrpt287/CRPT-113hrpt287.pdf.

278. NMAI, *Honoring*, 5.

279. US Congress, House, Native American Veterans' Memorial Amendments Act of 2013, 2.

280. US Congress, House, Native American Veterans' Memorial Amendments Act of 2013, 2.

281. NMAI, *Honoring*, 8.

282. NMAI, 18.

283. "National Native American Veteran's Memorial"; and NMAI, *Honoring*, 6.

284. NMAI, *Consultation Report*, 1.

285. NMAI, 1, 3.

286. NMAI, 7.

287. "National Native American Veteran's Memorial"; and NMAI, *Consultation Report*, 7.

288. Kevin Gover, "From the Director" (Washington, DC: National Museum of the American Indian).

289. NMAI, *Consultation Report*, 7; and "National Native American Veteran's Memorial."

290. "National Native American Veteran's Memorial."

291. Frank Hopper, "National Native American Veterans Memorial Artist Explains His Design," *Indian Country Today*, July 23, 2019, https://indiancountrytoday.com /culture/national-native-american-veterans-memorial-artist-explains-his-design -gSMOTYz6RkaSZlXAc8ubKQ.

292. Hopper.

293. Monsen, "Native American Veterans Memorial Coming to Washington."

294. Monsen.

295. "National Native American Veteran's Memorial."

296. Monsen, "Native American Veterans Memorial Coming to Washington."

297. National Congress of American Indians, "Opening of the National Native American Veterans Memorial," YouTube Video, 22:11, November 11, 2020, https://www.facebook .com/ncai1944/videos/461525951485974.

298. Hopper, "National Native American Veterans Memorial Artist Explains His Design."

299. Hopper.

300. "Biography: National Native American Veterans Memorial Design Concept Artist," press release, Smithsonian Institution, Washington, DC, June 26, 2018).

301. Hopper.

302. "Biography: National Native American Veterans Memorial Design Concept Artist."

303. NMAI, *Honoring*, 7.

304. "National Native American Veteran's Memorial."

305. NMAI, *Consultation Report*, 7.

306. National Congress of American Indians, "Opening of the National Native American Veterans Memorial."

307. NCAI, "Opening of the National Native American Veterans Memorial."

308. NMAI, *Consultation Report*, 2.

309. Campbell and Keel.

3 The Tradition of Indigenous Activism and Political Action

Washington, DC, as the United States' capital city, is clearly the national center of law and policy making. But beyond iconic sites from the White House to Capitol Hill and past the local culture of business suits and briefcases, the District also serves as a hub of another force for change: activism. Through direct-action politics, the voices of the people make themselves known through protest signs, megaphones, and the marching feet of thousands. In the best of cases, these grassroots movements generate a legal impact, and the visions of the congressional chambers and the DC streets align.

Martin Luther King Jr.'s 1963 March on Washington and, more recently, the 2017 Women's March are among the most iconic moments of activism in this country. Lesser known, perhaps, are the Indigenous contributions to these actions and dozens more. Further still, history books almost always overlook the Native women who have played formative roles in such movements and brought about meaningful change for their communities. One such activist was Marie Louise Bottineau Baldwin.

A member of the Turtle Mountain Band of Chippewa Indians, Marie Bottineau was born on Anishinaabe lands, now present-day North Dakota, in 1863.[1] She cut her teeth in the legal field as a clerk for her father, Jean Baptiste Bottineau, who came from a mixed Indigenous-French background, also known as Métis, and represented the Turtle Mountain Chippewa as the band's attorney.[2] Bottineau began legal work after the dissolution of her marriage in her midtwenties and by 1893 had relocated along with her father to advocate for her tribe on the ground in Washington, DC.[3] By the turn of the century Bottineau had come into her own and established an independent career as the first Native woman, and second Native employee, to hold a position in the Office of Indian Affairs.[4] She went on to hold leadership in the newly established Society of American Indians and, at nearly fifty years old, enrolled in the Washington College of Law.[5] Bottineau completed her studies with honors and graduated a year ahead of schedule, becoming the first Native woman to earn a law degree.[6]

On March 3, 1913, the day before President Woodrow Wilson's inauguration, Bottineau was among some five thousand suffragists who participated in the first-ever political, organized, and large-scale march in Washington.[7] The Woman Suffrage Procession called for women's right to vote and was led by the National American Woman Suffrage Association. Organizers looked to Bottineau to represent Native women in this action and demonstrate Indigenous women's support for the suffragist cause, but she ultimately played a much larger role.[8] Bottineau added nuance to the mainstream feminist discourse by explaining that, traditionally, in their own communities, Native women have exercised "virtual suffrage, and the power of recall, since time immemorial."[9] Furthermore, when Alice Paul, one of the leaders of the National American Woman Suffrage Association, moved to racially segregate the march and relegate women of color to the end of the procession, Bottineau refused to acquiesce and paraded down Pennsylvania Avenue shoulder-to-shoulder with white women.[10] Despite such attempts to marginalize Indigenous and other women of color from within the suffragist effort itself, Bottineau rose to prominence as an intersectional advocate, organizing not only on behalf of women's causes and Native issues but with an eye toward the specific needs of Native women.

The life and career of Marie Louise Bottineau Baldwin showcase the dynamic overlapping of political advocacy and activism as tools deployed in conjunction with one another to better the lives of Indigenous peoples. Indeed, she was not the only educated Native woman furthering this cause— and straddling these strategies—in the early twentieth century. Others like her include Yankton Dakota activist Zitkála-Šá, also known as Gertrude Bonnin, who asserted tribal self-governance alongside Native American rights to US citizenship and suffrage, and Laura Cornelius Kellogg of the Wisconsin Oneida, whose public speaking and publishing provided a vision of Indigenous land rights and economy as innately linked to the government-to-government relationship between tribes and the United States.[11] Also like Bottineau, these activists' activities unfolded against the backdrop of the District of Columbia. Kellogg delivered multiple testimonies before the Senate Committee on Indian Affairs, and Chicago's *The Day Book* reported on her activities, writing that an "Indian Princess Is Active Lobbyist in Capital."[12] Zitkála-Šá moved to the District in 1917 and later relocated to the Lyon Park area of Arlington Country, Virginia, in 1925, where she lived until her death in 1938.[13] While in the area, she served as secretary of the Society of American Indians at their

FIGURE 3.1. Marie Louise Bottineau Baldwin
Bain Collection, Prints & Photographs Division, Library of Congress, LC-B2- 3194-10.

FIGURE 3.2. Zitkála-Šá
National Portrait Gallery Collection, Smithsonian Institution,
S / NPG. 79.26, licensed under
CC0 1.0.

headquarters location, collaborated with a number of women's and suffrage organizations, and had her words quoted before Congress.[14] In December 2020 the Arlington County Board honored her legacy by voting unanimously to renovate and rename former Henry Clay Park to Zitkála-Šá; the park is located at 3011 7th St. North in the Lyon Park neighborhood and opened in late 2021.[15]

As discussed in chapter 1, Indigenous nations regularly sent political delegations to Washington throughout the nineteenth century, and their legacies live on through the tribal nations that maintain a political presence in the District today. Critically, as evidenced by Bottineau and her compatriots, these efforts are complemented by Indigenous activism and organizing that plays out in the public sphere and that gathers Native individuals together from around the country, brought together by a shared vision. This chapter highlights Washington, DC, as the site of various protests, marches, and actions advancing Indigenous issues on the national level, with particular attention to the ways in which this national component unites tribes geographically and ideologically. These sites include the 1972 Trail of Broken Treaties caravan, which ended in a seven-day occupation of the Bureau of Indian Affairs; the 2014 Cowboy and Indian Alliance Camp and environmental campaign against the Keystone XL Pipeline; the 2016 Oceti Sakowin Youth Relay Run to Washington; the 2017 Native Nations Rise March as part of the Dakota Access Pipeline / #NoDAPL and Standing Rock movement; and efforts to change the name of Washington's professional football team. Taken as a whole, this chapter reveals the ways in which Native organizers have descended, and continue to descend, upon the capital city—the settler seat of power—to make demands for their communities, inspire coalition building between tribal nations around shared federal issues, and complement policy work with grassroots efforts.

Occupation of the Bureau of Indian Affairs

In early October 1972 three caravans set out to traverse the length of the United States, their sights set on Washington, DC.[16] They originated in Seattle, San Francisco, and Los Angeles and convened in St. Paul before heading further east. Men and women, children and elders, made up this parade, representing around 250 tribal nations.[17] The caravan grew as it passed through reservations and tribal communities, raising support for their stand against injustices committed against Indigenous peoples. They called the caravan the Trail of Broken Treaties—a reference to the infamous Trail of Tears of the 1830s that forcibly marched tribal communities onto reservations.

This action came to life at a time of heightened Indigenous activism and national coalition building between tribes and Native organizations across the country. The American Indian Movement, a Minneapolis-based activist organization founded in 1968 to address police brutality among the urban Indian community, for instance, was opening chapters in more than a dozen cities, while the Bay Area–headquartered Indians of All Tribes had recently concluded their highly publicized nineteen-month occupation of Alcatraz Island.[18] The notion for the caravan originated with former Rosebud Indian Reservation tribal chair Bob Burnette that summer and gained support from a dozen Native organizations, including the American Indian Movement, as well as prominent activists Russell Means, Vernon Bellecourt, Hank Adams, and Carter Camp, all of whom Assistant Secretary of Interior for Public Land Management Harrison Loesch would later refer to as "bloody revolutionaries."[19]

The Trail of Broken Treaties drew up a schedule for their time in the nation's capital, which advanced meaningful political agenda items and incorporated culturally relevant events. Planned actions included erecting tipis and sweat lodges in West Potomac Park, evening entertainment at the Sylvan Theater near the Washington Monument, ceremonies at Arlington National Cemetery and the World War II Memorial, a procession around the White House, and delivery of the group's twenty-point platform to high-level federal officials.[20] Styled after the Black Panther Party for Self-Defense's Ten-Point Platform and Program, the activists laid out this list of demands once the three caravans coalesced in Minneapolis. Indigenous fishing advocate Hank Adams (Assiniboine Sioux) took the lead on this effort and focused the platform on issues of tribal sovereignty, self-governance, and the federal-tribal trust relationship.[21] The points position paper demanded:

1. Restoration of constitutional treaty-making authority.
2. Establishment of a treaty commission to make new treaties.
3. An address to the American people and joint sessions of Congress.
4. Commission to review treaty commitments and violations.
5. Resubmission of unratified treaties to the Senate.
6. All Indians to be governed by treaty relations.
7. Mandatory relief against treaty rights violations.
8. Judicial recognition of Indian right to interpret treaties.
9. Creation of congressional joint committee on reconstruction of Indian relations.
10. Land reform and restoration of a 110-million-acre Native land base.
11. Revision of 25 U.S.C. 163; Restoration of right to Indians terminated by enrollment and revocation of prohibitions against "dual benefits."
12. Repeal of state laws enacted under Public Law 280 (1953).
13. Resume federal protective jurisdiction for offenses against Indians.
14. Abolition of the Bureau of Indian Affairs by 1976.
15. Creation of an "Office of Federal Indian Relations and Community Reconstruction."
16. Priorities and purpose of the proposed new office.
17. Indian commerce and tax immunities.
18. Protection of Indians' religious freedom and cultural integrity.
19. National referendums, local options, and forms of Indian organization.
20. Health, housing, employment, economic development, and education.[22]

This twenty-point platform identified historical and ongoing injustices suffered by Indigenous peoples as rooted in the US federal government's practice of treaty breaking and paternalistic posture—the very factors necessitating the group's journey to Washington, DC, and its head-on confrontation with the government. Although little of the group's planned activities or organizing points came to fruition—and perhaps precisely because their itinerary failed—the Trail of Broken Treaties and its spontaneous takeover of the Bureau of Indian Affairs would become "the most important act of Indian resistance since the defeat of Custer at Little Big Horn."[23]

The caravan rolled into the District of Columbia on Wednesday, November 1. The hungry and travel-worn collective first congregated in the Mount Pleasant neighborhood, where they had arranged for lodging at St. Stephen and the Incarnation Church.[24] The welcome they received, however, was the first diversion away from the experience the group had anticipated. Rather than an open-arms reception by a coalition of community activists and a ready supply of provisions furnished by the government, approximately seven hundred Native caravanners were left to stay overnight on thin bedrolls in a dingy, rat-infested church basement.[25] This logistical disaster set the stage for many more mishaps on the horizon.

Only a few of the activists slept through the night; once dawn broke early Thursday morning, the caravan's spiritual leaders determined that the group should relocate to the Bureau of Indian Affairs—a location that had heretofore not been on the group's itinerary. The Bureau of Indian Affairs (BIA) established its headquarters in 1965 in the granite government building spanning the city block between 19th and 20th Streets NW along Constitution Avenue, and this historic site now sits catercorner to the BIA's present-day location within the Department of the Interior.[26] By the morning of Thursday, November 2, 1972, hundreds of caravan participants had made their way to the BIA building; by afternoon, the group had grown to over a thousand.[27] The totality of what was about to unfold would go on to encapsulate "the essence of the BIA'S failure to work with and for Indian tribes."[28]

As Native activists ate in the Bureau of Indian Affairs' cafeteria, congregated in the auditorium, and viewed films from the library, Trail representatives negotiated with BIA leadership to provide better conditions for their party.[29] The activists worked with Assistant Secretary of Interior for Public Land Management Harrison Loesch, a highly despised figure who was not sympathetic to the plight of Native Americans, to secure housing at the Andrews Air Force Base, the Salvation Army, and churches and synagogues, among other locales. As American Indian Movement leader Dennis Banks (Ojibwe) announced the acceptance of this housing offer, his press conference was interrupted by fighting and commotion as General Services Administration riot police attempted to forcibly remove the crowd.[30] This eviction came as the result of a miscommunication: an earlier plan for removing the Trail participants had been called off, but the message had not reached this particular unit. For the Native group, the reasoning behind the onslaught hardly mattered, as the heavy-handedness of the police further elucidated the very reason for their presence in DC.[31]

The energy at the BIA quickly shifted from negotiation to occupation. Former Puyallup Tribal Council chair Ramona Bennett recalls, "We were attacked. . . . [They started] beating people with clubs."[32] Catalyzed by violent intervention into their peaceful assembly, the Indigenous activists took control of the building, blockading the doors and fighting back police who attempted to enter through the windows. Outside, law enforcement officers in riot gear surrounded the bureau.[33] Approximately one hundred US Marshals were flown into DC for tactical support.[34] Snipers took aim from atop the Interior Department across the street, while the General Services Administration concocted a plan to surprise attack the protesters by tunneling from the Department of the Interior to the BIA.[35] President Nixon vetoed this tactic, instead advocating to issue a court order for removal of all occupants by the following morning.[36]

Friday morning, less than twenty-four hours into the action, the protesters conceded to government demands, agreed to step down, and prepared to relocate their crowd to the Labor Department.[37] They were left once again, however, with a feeling of betrayal and suspicion as the first wave of protesters arrived at the new location only to find locked doors. Referencing this third disastrous oversight, authors Paul Chaat Smith (Comanche) and Robert Allen Warrior (Osage) reflect that "perhaps only the BIA could have managed successive failures of this magnitude."[38] Upon return to the BIA, the protesters raised a tipi (on loan from the Smithsonian) on the front lawn and strung up a banner declaring the building the "Native American Embassy."[39] The occupation continued.

Inside, approximately five hundred protesters fortified the building.[40] Protesters set up a system of perimeter security, child care services, food and supplies distribution, and community meetings while the University of Maryland provided medical support. The occupants also readied for police or military attack by making Molotov cocktails, fashioning spears by attaching scissors

FIGURE 3.3. Bureau of
Indian Affairs protest
"Indians Outside of Courthouse,"
Bettmann via Getty Images.

to broomsticks, breaking legs off tables and chairs to be used as clubs, and filling buckets with scalding water. Word of their cause circulated among the city and beyond, drawing hundreds of non-Native supporters to the scene.[41] The Irish Republican Army and the Black Panther Party extended messages of support.

Four days into the occupation, tensions mounted. On Sunday, November 5, federal officials delivered their "final offer and ultimatum," which laid out a plan to remove the Native protesters from the BIA and place them into alternative accommodations. The Trail of Broken Treaties group summarily rejected this proposal.[42] Simultaneously, a court-ordered eviction scheduled for Monday night loomed on the horizon. As the six o'clock deadline drew near, the destruction of the building and its contents escalated from "vandalism" to "war."[43] The protesters organized the group into teams of four and braced themselves with face coverings to prevent possible exposure to tear gas. At one point protesters intercepted a police spy, forcing him out of the building in his own handcuffs. The protesters armed themselves with knives and other makeshift weapons while some reportedly carried firearms. Some individuals took up posts on the rooftop and prepared to drop debris on forces attempting to gain entry into the building. Fearing violence and bloodshed on the eve of President Nixon's election, the government extended the deadline to vacate to Wednesday.[44]

This decision created an opportunity for productive negotiations—ones that would bring the occupation to an end. On Monday evening, nine leaders representing the activists—including men, women, elders, and youth—met with White House officials. Together they agreed that the executive branch would respond to each of the Trail of Broken Treaties' Twenty Points, along with providing financial assistance for transportation out of DC and a recommendation to not prosecute protest participants.[45] Forty-eight hours later federal officials met with Trail leaders at the Riggs Bank in Dupont Circle and issued $66,650 in "small bills" for distribution to participants to fund their travels.[46] With the money distributed and the promise of amnesty secured, the Trail of Broken Treaties concluded their six-day occupation on Wednesday, November 8.[47]

Like any activist moment, the occupation was not universally supported by Native people. On one hand, a handful of Native Americans employed by the BIA joined the takeover to the disdain of their higher-ups. On the other hand, groups like the National Tribal Chairman's Association denounced the action as the work of a rowdy, rogue minority of urban Natives.[48] The government assessed the toll of losses and damages at $2.28 million, which, at the time, was a total cost only surpassed by the 1812 burning of Washington by the British and the 1906 San Francisco earthquake. In their defense, a Trail spokesperson attested that the protesters intentionally did not inflict any property destruction but began tearing down the establishment in earnest on the fifth day of occupation, Monday, November 6, under threat of police force or eviction.[49] Still, others worried about the long-term implications of the loss on a legal level. "Our records of water rights, hunting and fishing treaties, fifty years worth, are gone," chided Yakima Indian Nation chair Robert B. Jim. "This hits at the lowest economic level people," he lamented, referencing the files destroyed during the vandalism and the reservation residents who he feared would suffer as a result.[50]

Indeed, repercussions of the occupation reverberated throughout Indian Country long after the final protester had been evacuated from the BIA. For the government's part, federal officials went back on their settlement agreement to provide amnesty for the BIA occupants and moved forward with indictment proceedings.[51] In the words of the *Montgomery Spark*, "This means the White House has broken yet another treaty with the Indians."[52] The spirit of the Trail of Broken Treaties, however, would not be extinguished. Indigenous leaders organized small and large acts of solidarity across the country, such as a three-day occupation of the Seattle office of the Bureau of Indian Affairs and the fifty-man take over of the Everett, Washington, BIA location.[53] Three months later the American Indian Movement would go on to host their most well-known action: the seventy-one-day occupation of Wounded Knee, South Dakota.

The evening of November 8, 1972, after the last Indigenous activist had vacated the federal building, a sign in the BIA auditorium remained: "When history recalls our efforts here, our descendants will stand with pride knowing their people were the ones responsible for the stand against tyranny, injustice, and the gross inefficiency of this branch of a corrupt and decadent government." It was signed, "Native American Embassy."[54] This proclamation in support of tribal sovereignty harkens back to the delegations of Indigenous leaders who similarly negotiated and struggled with the US federal government more than a century earlier. The fortuitous renaming of the Bureau of Indian Affairs as the Native American Embassy for these few days also foreshadowed the creation of the Embassy of Tribal Nations, which operates in Washington, DC, today. While the Trail of Broken Treaties and the group's occupation of the BIA should be remembered within this continuum of Indigenous advocacy, it also stands apart as a rupture: a turn toward direct-action intervention, a moment of intertribal solidarity, an imprint of Red Power upon the District of Columbia.

Cowboy and Indian Alliance

Indigenous singing and drumming rang out near the US Capitol Building on April 22, 2014.[55] On one side of Third Street NW, between Madison and Jefferson Drives, a line of Indigenous community leaders clad in beaded vests and medallions, wearing feathered war bonnets, and carrying eagle staffs sat atop traditionally decorated ponies.[56] Facing this fierce front, a row of farmers and ranchers sporting blue jeans and cowboy hats lined the opposite side of the street.[57] This powerful scene marked the opening ceremony of Reject and Protect, a 2014 action—part protest and part ceremony—organized by the Cowboy and Indian Alliance. Together, this coalition and its direct-action agenda set out to encourage President Obama to protect the land, water, and climate by rejecting the Keystone XL Pipeline permits.[58]

Hanging in the balance for the Cowboy and Indian Alliance was a 1,179-mile transnational pipeline development that cut across farm and treaty lands spanning the entire country, north to south.[59] From the tar sands of Alberta, Canada, to the Gulf Coast refineries of Texas, the Keystone XL Pipeline would carry 830,000 barrels of tar sands oil per day.[60] The pipeline would route under the United States' largest underground water reserve, the Ogallala Aquifer, and threaten the Missouri River.[61] The Keystone XL, as well as the Dakota Access Pipeline discussed later in this chapter, came to be understood as the fulfillment of a Lakota prophecy: a black snake, Zuzeca Sapa, that would destroy sacred sites, poison the water, and devastate the Earth.[62] Furthermore, tar sands excavation proves particularly dangerous due to the high levels of carcinogens and toxins it emits; at the Fort Chipewyan Indian community located near the originating tar sands in Alberta, for instance, residents report a rate of bile duct cancer 30 percent higher than the national average.[63] Although President Obama had already approved construction of the southern portion of the pipeline, opponents took on the pipeline not only because of the risks posed by this massive construction but also because further assembly signaled the United States' unwillingness to move away from fossil fuel reliance, even at the expense of the five million citizens living along the pipeline's path.[64] Indigenous water protectors—so named "because they weren't simply against a pipeline; they also stood for something greater: the continuation of life on a planet ravaged by capitalism"—would do everything in their power to stop its construction. Summarily, warned Oglala Sioux tribal president Bryan Brewer, "Keystone XL is a death warrant for our people."[65]

While many may perceive an allyship between predominantly white farmers, ranchers, and landowners—the "cowboys"—and Native Americans as an unlikely friendship, the roots of their interest alignment stem from a shared relationship with the land. The Reject and Protect website characterizes the interest convergence plainly: "Farmers and ranchers know the risk first-hand. They work the land every day. Tribes know the risk first-hand. They protect the sacred water every day."[66] Since the 1980s, the two seemingly dissimilar groups had also unified over past issues of environmental degradation, including uranium mining and munitions testing; as new issues emerged in the twenty-first century, the Keystone XL Pipeline took center stage as it fundamentally threatened the values and lifeways for both parties.[67] For Indigenous Environmental Network campaign organizer Dallas Goldtooth (Mdewakanton Dakota and Diné), the land was unifying the improbable allies, literally, on "common ground."[68]

Leading up to Reject and Protect, "cowboy and Indian" coalitions had banded together for actions both large (like the forty-thousand-man Forward on Climate Rally outside the White House) and local (such as the March 2014 Oyate Wahacanka Woecun camp constructed on treaty, yet private, lands along the proposed Keystone XL route).[69] Such collaborative efforts, however, were not without their own internal struggles. Less than a month away from their main Washington, DC, event, Goldtooth received a call from the former Indigenous Environmental Network's Tar Sands campaign coordinator that would rope him into the center of the action. He learned that miscommunications between the two groups, specifically around the narrative of the action and the assurance of a larger decolonial organizing scope, had pushed the Native contingency to the brink of withdrawing its support altogether. Differences between grassroots Indigenous organizations and elected tribal leaders around the merits of direct action versus policy measures further posed heightened tensions. At the time, Goldtooth was not yet employed by the Indigenous Environmental Network, but his ability to navigate these conflicts and to ensure that everyone had a seat at the decision-making table not only ensured that the DC event would go on but also catalyzed his ongoing career in Indigenous organizing. All parties, Goldtooth conveyed, played a distinct role in pressuring the federal government to protect Mother Earth. Overcoming their differences and banding together around climate change actually further amplified the group's moral angle and complimented their political agenda. If predominantly conservative landowners, elected tribal government representatives, and left-leaning Indigenous activists could all agree that the pipeline was a bad idea, the group reasoned, how would it look if politicians—the final decision-makers—refused to work across the aisle?[70]

Over the course of five days between April 22 and 27, 2014, the cowboys and Indians took on Washington in order to stop the progression of the Keystone XL Pipeline. For organizers like Dallas Goldtooth, championing Indigenous rights in Washington, DC, was a precedent modeled by earlier generations that carried a personal family history. His mother had been among the young Indigenous activists who occupied the BIA in 1972, and she was proud to hear that her son would similarly take Indigenous issues to the setter state's national seat of power.[71] "A big part of her story is that she remembers when the police came in [to the BIA] and were making arrests," Goldtooth recalls. "There was actually a police officer that had a baton and was ready to strike her, and a member of the Black Panthers jumped in, took the hit . . . and saved her."[72] More than four decades later, Goldtooth returned to Washington to continue this tradition of Indigenous activism in the capital city, fighting, as his mother had before him, for the future seven generations yet to come.

To gain public attention, the Cowboy and Indian Alliance had timed the inauguration of their DC event to fall on Earth Day. But before any of the activities commenced, the alliance first sought permission from the hereditary chief of the Piscataway Indian Nation, Billy Redwing Tayac, to carry out their mission on traditional Piscataway homelands. At 10:30 a.m., Bob Allpress, a fourth-generation rancher and alliance member, brought forth a blanket as an offering, which was kindly received and the group's plan of action endorsed.[73] The Piscataway leader and his family in turn offered gifts in an exchange of welcome.[74] Then the crowd mobilized. A procession of twenty-four tribal leaders and their non-Native allies rode down Independence Avenue on horseback, leading a group of approximately three thousand.[75] As they trotted down the National Mall, they remained mindful of the original owners and occupants of the land now known as Washington, DC.

The alliance intentionally kept culture at the center of its activities and ensured this guiding vision through the erection of a ceremonial camp that served as the organizers' home base for their time in Washington.[76] Located on the National Mall between 7th and 12th Streets, the activists raised nine tipis in a circle around a fire that burned for the full duration of the activists' stay.[77] Due to the ceremonial nature of the encampment, only members of the Cowboy and Indian Alliance were permitted to reside there.[78] Nevertheless, the camp was a hub of activity. Here a rancher served dinners made from bison raised on lands that the Keystone XL Pipeline would destroy.[79] Photography exhibits, documentary screenings, and TEDx-style presentations showcased the destruction wrought by the tar sands. Two hours each day were reserved for music and storytelling.[80] Looking west from the camp, the alliance members looked out at the Washington Monument; to the east, they could gaze upon the Capitol Building. Through each of their actions, however, the Cowboy and Indian Alliance brought a piece of the Oceti Sakowin homelands to the District of Columbia.

For the Reject and Protect organizers, culture, ceremony, and prayer could not—and would not—be divorced from their political advocacy and direct action. As part of the opening ceremony, for instance, representatives from the cowboy and Indian factions performed a water ceremony as swarms of the press looked on. In this action, nineteen-year-old Gianna Strong of the Sisseton Wahpeton Oyate and rancher and Nebraska Easement Action Team board member Tom Genung each carried a bucket full of water taken from Nebraska

FIGURE 3.4. Cowboy and Indian Alliance Camp on the National Mall
"Cowboy Indian Alliance Encampment on the Mall, Friday morning" by Lorie Shaull, licensed under CC BY 2.0.

family wells to the Capitol Reflecting Pool and, upon their arrival, took turns prayerfully pouring it into the pool.[81] Those behind the action's agenda made certain that water ceremonies were a fixture in their schedule by incorporating them as the first event of each day's itinerary.[82] Other one-time events maintained a spiritual dimension as well. In the early afternoon of Friday, April 25, leaders representing the Sojourner, Protestant, and Jewish faith communities joined with Hereditary Drumkeeper of the Women's Scalp Dance Society of the Ponca Nation of Oklahoma Casey Camp for an interfaith prayer service outside of Secretary of State John Kerry's DC residence.[83] Approximately two hundred participants then marched through the Georgetown neighborhood, blocked the busy intersection of M Street NW and Wisconsin Avenue at peak rush hour, and performed a round dance by joining hands in a circle and side-stepping in time with the drumbeat.[84] As demonstrated by these moments, the Reject and Protect action unfolded with Native peoples and ways at the core and welcomed non-Native allies in the #NoKXL movement to share in Indigenous cultural practices and stand alongside tribal communities in a shared struggle.

Classic protest strategies had their place in the schedule too, of course. On the third day in DC, organizers had planned a "bold and creative action" at an unannounced time released only shortly before the event itself.[85] The activists gathered at the Lincoln Memorial and unraveled a large inflatable black tube signifying the Keystone XL Pipeline and spanning the width of the Reflecting Pool. US Park Police quickly intervened to shut down the action before the participants could inflate the prop and reveal the anti-oil message emblazoned across it.[86] The reflecting pool would not remain untouched, however. Wizipan Little Elk of the Rosebud Sioux Tribe and Nebraska farmer Art Tanderup waded thigh-deep into the middle of the water, each holding one side of a sign proclaiming, "Standing in the water could get me arrested, Trans-Canada pollutes drinking water and nothing happens."[87] That evening the group collaborated with the grassroots network Other 98% to project #NoKXL testimony submitted by members of the public directly onto the Environmental Protection Agency building. In addition to taking to the streets—and reflecting pools—representatives of the Cowboy and Indian Alliance met with White House officials to express their concerns and urge the end of the Keystone XL's construction.[88]

The five days of Reject and Protect culminated on April 26 with a traditional, DC-style march and rally. Approximately ten thousand individuals attended, nearly double the anticipated turnout projections, making it the largest event of Reject and Protect.[89] Tribal leaders, Indigenous activists, ranchers, farmers, environmentalists, and allies from all walks of life came together to make their voices heard. Key allies included major environmental organizations like the Sierra Club, 350.org, the National Wildlife Federation, and Greenpeace as well as Indigenous groups from near and far, such as nations living in proximity to the tar sands origin in Alberta, Canada.[90] Their unity marked one of the first large-scale collaborations between grassroots Indigenous activists, international voices, and major organizations.[91] The protest began at eleven o'clock in the morning, with participants gathering at the headquarters encampment on the National Mall; from there the group processed to the Capitol.[92]

As the march's main event, the Cowboy and Indian Alliance ceremoniously presented a tipi to President Obama, which the National Museum of the American Indian accepted on his behalf.[93] The concept for the tipi originated with the Oyate Wahacanka Woecun, a Rosebud Sioux community, and references the historic visit President Obama made to meet with Lakota and Crow youth in 2008. As a tribute, tribal community leaders in turn named the tipi "Awe Kooda Bilaxpak Kuuxshish," which means in the Lakota language "Man Who Helps the People," and "Oyate Wookiye," which in the Crow language translates to "One Who Helps People Throughout the Land."[94] Traditional artist Steve Tamayo (Sicangu Lakota) designed the tipi and painted it with motifs and symbols relevant to the fight against KXL. Two bands circle the base: blue, representing lifegiving water—in particular, the Ogallala Aquifer—and green, the land with which we are all in relationship. The black top of the tipi stands for the night sky, with stars in the shape of the Big Dipper symbolizing the ancestors and their unwavering guidance even amid absolute darkness. A cedar tree—an entity with deep spiritual significance—appears on the spine of the tipi. Its roots represent the Oceti Sakowin; its green color represents longevity for Mother Earth and for the future generations. The turtle shell in the cedar's trunk symbolizes the earth, interconnectedness between all beings, and humanity's collective responsibility. The decoratively painted horses don imagery specific to individual Indigenous nations, while the horses depicted in solid colors represent the farmer and rancher allies. Their positioning as running together indicates the unification of their power and shared struggle.[95] For the alliance, the tipi represented the "hope that [President Obama] will reject the pipeline, and our promise that we will protect our land and water if he chooses to let the pipeline move forward."[96]

Like so many aspects of the Cowboy and Indian Alliance, the tipi exhibits one of the ways in which the organizers maintained a focus on Indigenous nations and on the particular communities located in the pipeline's path while still finding inventive ways to incorporate the manpower of a much larger movement. Before arriving in DC, the tipi received blessings across Indian Country: first on land located along the Ponca Trail of Tears in present-day Neligh, Nebraska, and again in early April 2014 as part of a "crop art" direct action hosted by the Cowboy and Indian Alliance. In November 2013, furthermore, the tipi—at that time not yet painted—was raised by Ponca, Yankton Sioux, and Rosebud communities along with the activist organization Bold Nebraska as part of an anti-pipeline encampment along the Keystone XL's future path.[97] This inclusive effort only grew in Washington, DC. Organizers achieved this same spirit of solidarity and mass participation by facilitating the contributions of hundreds, if not thousands, of members of the public to the making of this offering: each day of Reject and Protect included a window—at least ten hours over the course of the week—during which organizers invited the public to add their thumb- and handprint to the canvas lining of the structure.[98] "Leave your mark on history," the activists urged President Obama, "as we leave our marks on this tipi."[99] A seven-member cohort of chiefs and tribal council members representing the Oglala Lakota Nation, Upper Brule Sioux Nation, Dakota Nation, Yankton Sioux Nation, and Tsleil-Waututh First

Nation presented the completed gift to the National Museum of the American Indian's curators and historian. The museum agreed to meet the tribal leaders and "exchange gifts with them as is customary" as part of their "[commitment] to documenting Native Americans' participation in the Nation's life."[100]

Having delivered the tipi—and with it a strong message to cease construction of the Keystone XL Pipeline—the activists returned to camp for a blessing and then turned in for their final night in Washington.[101] The next day, Sunday, April 27, the coalition gathered for a final prayer and closing ceremony in Lafayette Park. By noon the activists disbanded and departed the nation's capital.[102] The Cowboy and Indian Alliance's spirit of unity, dedication to the caretaking of Mother Earth for the good of all, and strategic political deployment of Washington, DC, as their site of national action against the Keystone XL Pipeline, however, lived on.

Oceti Sakowin Youth & Allies Relay Run to Washington

Although Indigenous environmental activists won a major victory in President Obama's rejection of the Keystone XL in November of 2015, their celebrations were short-lived. A new oil threat loomed on the horizon, threatening sacred lands, tribal treaty rights, and public drinking water. The target of this new wave of organizing was the Dakota Access Pipeline, a $3.8 billion project by the Texas-based company Energy Transfer Partners designed to transport five hundred thousand barrels of crude North Dakota oil 1,172 miles to a distribution location in Illinois.[103] The DAPL, as it came to be known, snaked through four states along tribal lands, under both the Missouri and Mississippi Rivers, and beneath the lake that supplies drinking water to the Cheyenne River Sioux Tribe and Standing Rock Sioux Tribe.[104] Adding insult to injury, the majority-white community in Bismarck, North Dakota, protested the pipeline's original route, which would have taken the construction closer to their town, prompting the Army Corps of Engineers to reroute the pipeline closer to the Standing Rock Reservation. For tribal members, this action demonstrated that the government and non-Native community took seriously the real "environmental and economic concerns" posed by the pipeline—they were simply willing to acquiesce to the demands of Bismarck and to sacrifice the well-being of the tribes in its path. The DAPL thus reflected environmental racism, plain and simple. The Oceti Sakowin, scholar-activist Nick Estes (Lower Brule Sioux Tribe) concludes, were left to wait to see not *if* but *when* the pipeline would break or leak and devastate their lands.[105]

In April 2016 Native youth, elders, and activists from the Standing Rock Reservation and surrounding communities established the Sacred Stone Camp on Hunkpapa elder LaDonna Brave Bull Allard's land. The water protectors peacefully and prayerfully lived at the camp within their traditional culture and worked to stop construction of the DAPL.[106] Allard recalls the scene at the prayer camp:

> They were roasting deer meat on the grill. The women were cutting meat on the side to dry it. Kids were running and screaming. All of these people sitting around the fire were telling stories and what it was like to live on the river. Here was the catch: Nobody was speaking English. They were speaking Dakota. And I looked at them and I thought, "This is how we're supposed to live. This makes sense to me." Every day I came down to the camp and saw such blessings. I saw our culture and our way of life come alive.[107]

As local life at Sacred Stone blossomed, the Native youth drew strength from this cultural engagement that propelled them to take their message to a national audience. The young leaders determined to travel to Washington, DC.

Bobbi Jean Three Legs, a Standing Rock tribal member in her early twenties organized a series of Native youth–led runs to raise awareness about the #NoDAPL movement that culminated with their arrival in Washington.[108] These runs quickly grew in scale and scope and were carried out in the culturally significant messenger style where an individual completes approximately one mile before handing off the task to another runner and then riding alongside them (traditionally on horseback, in this case in a vehicle) for the remainder of the journey.[109] Thirty youths participated in Three Legs's first eleven-mile run between Wakpala and Mobridge, South Dakota. Only a few weeks later, while living at the Sacred Stone Camp, Three Legs organized a massive five-hundred-mile, eight-day relay that would take twelve runners— and dozens more supporters—from Cannon Ball, North Dakota, to Omaha, Nebraska. Upon their arrival the group delivered a petition to the US Army Corps of Engineers to deny the easement that would allow for drilling under Lake Oahe.[110] Their next journey would be to the nation's capital.

On July 15, 2016, Three Legs and nearly thirty Indigenous youths known as the Oceti Sakowin Youth & Allies strapped on their sneakers, departed the Sacred Stone Camp, and set out for Washington, DC. They carried a petition of 140,000 signatures speaking out against the construction of the DAPL.[111]

FIGURE 3.5. Oceti Sakowin youth and allies relay run to Washington
Oceti Sakowin Youth & Allies Relay Run to Washington, Native Hope.

As they ran nearly two thousand miles across the country, their feat gained international attention and inspired widespread national support from Indigenous communities and non-Native allies alike. The caravan mapped a route that would enable them to visit as many reservations as possible in order to rally additional participants and spread the word of their cause: *Mni wiconi*, "Water is life."[112]

The youth runners arrived in the District of Columbia nearly three weeks later, on August 5, but their work was only beginning. Once in the capital city, Three Legs and her comrades grappled with the news that only two days prior the Army Corps of Engineers had approved easements for drilling under the Missouri River. Activists quickly mobilized the Run for Water Rally, which convened on the steps of the Supreme Court and marched down Constitution Avenue, then up to the US Army Corps of Engineers Headquarters.[113] The youths later that day met with the Corps, the Department of Defense, and the Advisory Council on Historic Preservation to discuss their concerns; the following day, the group delivered their petition to the White House.[114] "[Washington, DC] is where all the officials are, the ones that make these decisions, so why not try and go there and change their minds and hearts about how we see this and what our perspective is?" Three Legs recalled of the cross-country run and the Native youths' work in the capital city. "Educate the people who are non-Native, educate them about us, educate them about how [the DAPL] is going to affect us the most."[115] Still, she reminds, "This isn't just a Native issue. This is an issue for everybody because this is everybody's water."[116] The youth who had mobilized a movement returned to the camps, to their homes, to their reservations, but their strategic use of their journey to the nation's capital had transformed the resistance to the DAPL from a local initiative to an international uprising.

Native Nations Rise March

The Sacred Stone Camp from which the Oceti Sakowin Youth & Allies launched their relay run to Washington, DC, was but one of the several prayer camps developed as hubs for water protectors against the DAPL. Others, such as the Red Warrior Camp, Two-Spirit Nation Camp, the International Indigenous Youth Council, and several others, drew in thousands of campers from around the world. The largest of all, the Oceti Sakowin Camp, developed alongside the Cannonball River, just off the northernmost tip of the Standing Rock Indian Reservation, which sits on the central border between North and South Dakota. Affectionately referred to by some as "Indian City," the Oceti Sakowin Camp grew to between ten and fifteen thousand residents, temporarily qualifying it as the tenth-largest city in the state of North Dakota.[117] Here more than three hundred Indigenous nations—constituting more than half of all federally recognized tribes in the United States—raised their flags in a massive show of Indigenous sovereignty and intertribal solidarity. However inspirational and awe-inspiring to those in support of their cause, the prayer camps suffered a series of grave assaults and attacks by militarized police. Law enforcement and private security deployed flash grenades, rubber bullets, pepper spray, water cannons, tear gas, beanbag rounds, and dogs against water protectors young and old, men and women, all of whom remained peaceful and unarmed throughout each onslaught.[118] As the Standing Rock encampments swelled and tensions rose between Indigenous water protectors and law enforcement, activists continued to draw on Washington, DC, as a site to make their voices heard and their struggle seen.

The Native Nations Rise March took place on March 10, 2017, approximately three years after the Cowboy and Indian Alliance carried out their Reject and Protect action and one year after the Oceti Sakowin Youth & Allies ran from the Sacred Stone Camp to Washington, DC. Drawing enthusiasm from these highly organized and professional interventions, Native Nations Rise became "the biggest Native protest ever seen in DC, ever!"[119] Fittingly, the Standing Rock Sioux Tribe took the lead as the primary organizer and were joined by the Native Organizers Alliance.[120] The Indigenous Environmental Network (IEN), a grassroots organization dedicated to environmental and economic justice for Native peoples, also collaborated in the action's leadership.

The IEN had long been active in the movement against both the Keystone XL and Dakota Access pipelines: organizers from the IEN proved central to the Cowboy and Indian Alliance, and the group had operated behind the scenes providing logistical support and professional training to the youth activists orchestrating the relay run to Washington.[121]

As the name implies, Native Nations Rise encouraged tribal nations to broadly make a collective stand against injustice. "We rise for Indigenous rights. We rise for sovereignty. We rise for the seven generations," a video advertising the march declares.[122] While halting the DAPL certainly consti-tuted the central objective, organizers kept in line with the refrain that the water protectors had long championed: that the #NoDAPL movement was about safeguarding Indigenous peoples, Mother Earth, and her waters at large. The same promotional video illuminates this perspective by pointing to various "attacks on Indigenous rights and people": the mines threatening sacred sites at Oak Flat, fracking at Chaco Canyon, sea-level rise along the Gulf Coast, and the devastation of wildlife by climate change throughout the Arc-tic.[123] The action's all-encompassing emphasis on respect for land and water-ways across the nation made the federal capital a natural rallying point. The scope of the issues at hand, to use the language of the promotional video, "is why we are calling on our Native relatives and all allies to march with us in Washington, DC."[124]

Fortuitous timing nevertheless solidified the action's focus on the DAPL. By the time Native Nations Rise unfolded, nearly all of the 1,172 miles of pipe-line had been constructed, save for the tract located less than half a mile from the Standing Rock Reservation.[125] President Obama ordered a stay on building in the final weeks of 2016, shortly before the end of his time in office, which prompted the Army Corps of Engineers to search for alternate routes and offered a glimmer of hope for the water protectors.[126] This optimism quickly faded in the early days of the Trump administration. Three weeks after the inauguration, President Trump in fact expedited the drilling by issuing an executive order for the pipeline's review and approval, and on February 7 the Army Corps of Engineers granted an easement that enabled the project to move forward.[127] Construction resumed that month; by April, the company announced, oil would be flowing.[128] Three days before the Native Nations Rise March, with the completion of the pipeline looming, a federal judge denied the Standing Rock Sioux and Cheyenne River Sioux tribes' legal efforts to cease construction once more.[129] This particular motion, filed jointly by the tribes in the US District Court for the District of Columbia, had sought a preliminary injunction against the pipeline company after its attempt to secure a restraining order against the company also failed.[130] Such devastating news galvanized the grassroots actors who took the cause from the courtroom into the streets. They demanded that the president meet with Indigenous leaders and called on the government to move beyond the hollow paradigm of tribal consultation to ensure active consent to the pipeline construction.[131]

Activists participating in the Native Nations Rise March flooded into Washington from across the country, some in organized fifty-passenger busloads departing such major cities and Indigenous hubs as Los Angeles, St. Paul, Phoenix, Albuquerque, and Chicago, along with Kadoka, Murdo, and Pierre, South Dakota.[132] Attendees spent the three days leading up to the march participating in a variety of activities: Tuesday featured lobby visits, Native talent open mics, and advocacy training hosted at the National Congress of American Indians; Wednesday offered a solidarity event with the Council of Popular and Indigenous Organizations of Honduras around the assassination of Indigenous environmental leader Berta Cáceres, a Native women's panel discussion, and a round dance; Thursday's events included an allyship workshop, a panel on solidarity with Black Lives Matter, and a special evening prayer at the National Cathedral. Each day kicked off its schedule with a water blessing.[133]

On Friday, March 10, the day of the march, the group congregated at ten o'clock in the morning at the Army Corps of Engineers headquarters at 441 G Street NW, an appropriate origin point given the Corps' involvement in the pipeline construction.[134] That dreary Friday morning brought rain and snow, but the less-than-ideal conditions did not deter the protesters.[135] For many, the wintry mix would recall memories of the freezing weather endured over the past months by those living at the water protector prayer camps. For Ron His Horse Is Thunder, former tribal chair of the Standing Rock Sioux Nation, the weather held a spiritual significance: "People come out here and they think the rain is inclement weather but actually it's a blessing, if you will, because we are talking about the protection of water, and so to have . . . the grandfathers rain on us means that they're here with us. And so this isn't inclement weather. It's a blessing."[136] Huddled under a near-equal number of umbrellas and protest signs, the mood among the crowd remained "celebratory yet defiant."[137]

From the Army Corps of Engineers, the protesters processed westward down the 400 and 500 blocks of G Street NW before turning south onto 6th Street NW along the Capital One Arena. One onlooker observed that it took eighteen minutes for the thousands upon thousands of individuals

FIGURE 3.6. Raising of a tipi during the Native Nations March, 2017
"2017-03-10 Native Nations March 4," by Mike Maguire, licensed under CC BY 2.0.

participating in the march to collectively pass a single vantage point.[138] The
March moved westward on E Street NW and turned South on 10th Street
NW before passing the Trump International Hotel on Pennsylvania Avenue.[139]
This landmark proved significant to the water protectors because, in addition
to the White House representing President Trump's political power used to
propel the pipeline forward, the Trump International Hotel signified all that
the Standing Rock movement organized against: corporate greed, the rich and
powerful class, and financial gain at the expense of the environment. A con-
tingent of Native men known as the Black Snake Killers raised a tipi in front
of the hotel in an impromptu action while protesters coalesced, hand drums
rang out, and Native women led the group in a round dance.[140] After this
brief interlude, the march resumed shape and pressed on down Pennsylvania
toward the South Lawn.[141]

A final right turn northward on 15th Avenue NW concluded the exactly
1.5-mile-long parade route.[142] The group poured into Lafayette Square for a
noontime rally across from the White House.[143] Sixteen-year-old Xiuhtezcatl
Martinez (Mexica) and a representative of the International Indigenous Youth
Council, Eryn Wise (Laguna Pueblo, Jicarilla Apache), emceed the event,
appropriately symbolizing the central role of youth in the cause and calling the

audience to attention with a "people power" call-and-response chant.[144] Judith LeBlanc (Caddo), director of the Native Organizers Alliance, opened the rally by acknowledging the Indigenous activism history in the making, declaring simply that "Standing Rock changed everything."[145] As LeBlanc introduced the next speaker, tribal chair of the Standing Rock Sioux Tribe Dave Archambault, a mixture of "boos" and support for the tribal leader emerged from the crowd. This disunified response arose from internal community conflict over the Standing Rock Sioux Tribe's political leadership and its controversial move to ask the water protectors to vacate the prayer camps.[146] Reiterating his commitment to Indigenous youth and love for his people, Archambault insisted as he left the stage, "Indian Country will come together. We'll be strong and our rights will always be respected!"[147] Multiple of the rally's speakers that day would address the audience's heckling directly, including Standing Rock Sioux Tribe youth activist Alice Brown Otter and Yakima Nation tribal chair JoDe Goudy, who also offered a message of unity. "We must remain of one voice, one heart, one spirit to speak for those things that cannot speak for themselves. There is no dispute in and amongst ourselves . . . that is more important than the future of our generations."[148]

Following Goudy's reading of a proclamation against the Doctrine of Discovery, Quinault Indian Nation president and vice president of the National Congress of American Indians Fawn Sharp returned the audience's attention to the importance of the rally's Washington, DC, location: "The President of the United States, every member of Congress, every justice and judicial officer that sits on a bench takes an oath, and that oath is to uphold [tribal] treaties and to deem and to recognize that they are the supreme law of the land."[149] Elder activist Faith Spotted Eagle (Yankton Sioux) next took the stage to speak of the Standing Rock movement's historical alignment with contemporary activists' ancestors who similarly traveled to Washington to advocate for tribal rights, and she thanked the attendees for doing the spiritual work of returning home the spirits of those ancestors who perished in the nation's capital.[150] Echoing the sentiments around DC's symbolism for the Native Nations March, Rep. Tulsi Gabbard of Hawaii's 2nd District criticized, "We stand in . . . the spirit of peace and in prayer looking upon our nation's Capital, looking upon this White House, sending a message to our nation's leaders that our government belongs to the people. Because too often, as you know, in this town the decisions being made here benefit the powers of corporate money, special interests, and greed on the backs of people, on the back of our planet."[151] Candi Brings Plenty (Oglala Lakota), leader of the Two-Spirit Nation Camp at Standing Rock, then discussed her experiences surviving hypothermia and maintaining ceremony amid oppressive conditions, drawing on that strength to propel the cause forward in DC.[152] "Each and every day here in Washington, DC," Minnesota representative Peggy Flanagan (White Earth Band of Ojibwe) cautioned the crowd, "people [try] to make decisions about us without us at the table.... It matters when we show up and we make our voices heard," she continued, "No more decisions about Indigenous people without Indigenous people!"[153]

Additional rally speakers included Melissa Mark-Viverito and fellow members of the New York City Council, who offered a message of solidarity from Black, Latino, and Asian communities; Maria and Lisa DeVille (Mandan, Hidatsa, and Arikara Nation), who testified to the environmental devastation wrought by oil spills at the Fort Berthold Reservation in North Dakota; anti-fracking youth activist Kim Howe (Diné), who discussed the importance of the Chaco Canyon sacred site; and Cherokee actor Wes Studi, who challenged the notion of corporations receiving human rights.[154] Musical performances by Yaqui classical guitarist Gabriel Ayala, Mexica musician Xiuhtezcatl Martinez, Rosebud Sioux hip-hop artist Prolific the Rapper, Tewa Pueblo / Chumash singer Mayda Garcia, the Akwesasne Mohawk Women Singers ensemble, Taboo (Shoshone) of the Black Eyed Peas, and the Native women's group Ulali punctuated the speeches, all performing songs dedicated to the environment, supporting Indigenous empowerment, and condemning fossil fuel industries. "People come by the hundreds, sing and dance in the streets and shopping malls, to the corners and capitals of city halls," Ulali harmonized, "On this Turtle Island, our presence will break the silence, together, brothers and sisters, Idle No More."[155] As a light snow began to fall, Rosebud Sioux tribal councilmember Royal Yellow Hawk closed the rally with a prayer song to the Four Directions in thanks for the water that gives life.[156]

Rally attendees reconvened at the National Mall tipi camp for pizza, music, and socializing.[157] The following morning, a nine o'clock closing ceremony officially concluded the Native Nations Rise March. Organizers packed up the tipis, and the buses that had chauffeured thousands returned attendees to all corners of the nation.[158]

Washington, DC, offered the ideal location for Indigenous activism surrounding Standing Rock, in part because the issues championed by the movement's "global call to action" proved so holistic.[159] The place-specific details and grassroots efforts at the prayer camps in South Dakota are responsible for mobilizing the masses to action in places like Washington, DC, and the ideas that originated in Oyate lands resonate with much larger challenges around climate change and environmental stewardship, necessitating a broader, nationwide conversation. "The Standing Rock movement is bigger than one tribe," the Oceti Sakowin Camp reflects. "It has evolved into a powerful global phenomenon highlighting the necessity to respect Indigenous Nations and their right to protect their homelands, environment and future generations."[160]

Indeed, the international movement to stop the construction of the Keystone XL and Dakota Access Pipelines brought non-Native communities into the fold of Indigenous affairs in a way that has never been done before or since. Together Indigenous activists and their non-Native allies mobilized around a shared understanding that "we cannot drink oil and we cannot eat money."[161] Nick Estes offers that the resistance to these pipelines and protection of the vital resources under threat constituted "a war story," reminding us that "it is not always with weapons that warriors wage their struggle."[162] While the water protectors and their allies organized on the ground throughout the Great Plains and in Washington, DC, at least 1.5 million more voiced their support from all corners of the United States and chimed in from such varied places as New Zealand, Canada, Australia, Morocco, France, Japan, the United Kingdom, Ecuador, Peru, Mexico, and Belize.[163] Amid this global uproar, Washington, DC, emerged as a focal point of the action, second only to the contested Oceti Sakowin homelands themselves.

Hours after taking the presidential oath as the forty-sixth President of the United States, Joe Biden issued an executive order officially ending construction of the Keystone XL Pipeline. The Dakota Access Pipeline is currently transporting oil within one mile of the Standing Rock Sioux Reservation. Canadian oil company Enbridge Energy's 2021 construction of Line 3, which cuts across Ojibwe lands in Canada, Minnesota, and Wisconsin, is the latest fossil fuel threat to Indigenous lands.

Change the Name Campaign

Professional football may seem an unlikely rallying point for Indigenous activism, but in Washington, DC, the local team has become just that. For nearly fifty years, Native individuals and their non-Native allies in the DC area have rallied, protested, and petitioned to change the Washington team's name. The term under fire—"Redskins," or what many refer to as the "R-word"—is a dictionary-defined racial slur in reference to Native American people.[164] The football team first adopted the name in 1933 while headquartered in Boston and subsequently brought its unsavory namesake with it to the nation's capital in 1937.[165] Thirty-five years before the renaming, however, Webster's Collegiate Dictionary officially recognized the derogatory nature of the term, defining it as "often contemptuous."[166] The historical root of this characterization extends to the eighteenth-century use of the word to indicate a bounty placed upon Native people, such as in a September 25, 1863, announcement run by Minnesota's *Winona Daily Republican*, "The State reward for dead Indians has been increased to $200 for every red-skin sent to Purgatory. This sum is more than the dead bodies of all the Indians east of the Red River are worth."[167] For many, like DC-based tribal attorney Tara Houska (Couchiching First Nation), the historical context of the term represents only part of its offensiveness. In today's culture, Houska simply offers, "if you call someone a Redskin, you know that's a racial slur."[168] Furthermore, the mascot image affiliated with the "Redskins" name reflects racialized stereotypes of Indigenous people; it pictures the profile of a Native man, shown with dark brown skin, braided hair, and feather adornments. For the city's diverse Indigenous residents and within the capital's legacy of Indigenous advocacy, the use of this offensive language and imagery—plastered profusely across the city from billboards to pizza boxes, bumper stickers to T-shirts—inflicted a particularly demoralizing effect.

Activism promoting the end of the use of the football team name began in the 1960s and continued for over fifty years. On March 29, 1972, tribal leaders first made inroads with the team by persuading it to remove racist language—"Scalp 'um"—from its fight song. While they did not secure a commitment to change the team name, the delegation also succeeded in convincing the team to do away with the braided black wigs worn by team cheerleaders.[169] Twenty years later, more than two thousand activists representing the American Indian Movement, National Association for the Advancement of Colored People, the Urban Coalition, National Organization for Women, and more gathered at the 1992 Super Bowl XXVI outside of the Minneapolis Metrodome to protest the team name as Washington faced off against the Buffalo Bills.[170] The *New York Times*'s "Super Bowl XXVI Notebook" column reported on the action, titling the article and referring to the movement to change the name as, "The Protest That Won't Go Away."[171] In early 2015 the Oneida Indian Nation and the National Congress of American Indians collaborated to launch a call-in campaign, encouraging fans who "love the team but hate the name" to contact the NFL's vice president of social responsibility and ask for a rebranding.[172]

One of the individuals speaking on the call, Ian Washburn, was a lifelong Washington football fan, third-generation season ticket holder, and non-Native ally who had reached a crisis of conscience a few years prior. Washburn determined in 2013 that he could no longer cheer for a team organized around the "cancer" of racist mascots and subsequently deployed a combination of black electrical tape, custom tailoring, and overseas textile manufacturing to literally rebrand all of his burgundy and gold memorabilia by removing any trace of the "R-word."[173] By 2015 Washburn's personal conviction evolved into a grassroots advocacy group established with two additional cofounders known as Rebrand Washington Football: Fans for a New Name, which he described as "a natural outlet to channel my passion for Washington football fandom. Changing the harmful mascot today would be a more enjoyable fan experience than any Super Bowl championship. Mascots deny life to Native Peoples. That's not fun to root for."[174] Rebrand Washington Football's goal of securing a name change has taken shape through near-weekly petition signature collections, collaborations with Native activists, rallies, press conferences, white papers, educational and public awareness campaigns, work with local political offices and religious institutions, and delivery of the approximately two thousand petition signatures annually to team owner Dan Snyder.[175]

In addition to this advocacy work on the ground, DC-based activists have brought this local issue to an international platform and generated tremendous direct impact by leveraging the virtual sphere as well. On Wednesday, December 17, 2017, the internet erupted with headlines declaring that the Washington team had rebranded as the Washington Redhawks. Materials showcasing the Redhawks name alongside a hawk head mascot image—all stylized in the brand's iconic font and burgundy and gold colors—flooded social media platforms. A press release on the newly unveiled "WashingtonRedhawks.com" website explained, "The WASHINGTON REDHAWKS is a team EVERYONE can cheer for. The Franchise is proud to be a leader in bringing people together in the DMV and in our country during a time of growing divisions," and continued on to cite "team owner Dan Snyder's deep admiration for Native Americans" as the inspiration behind the rebrand.[176] The content, however, was not legitimate. Rather, this form of digital activism, known as a "culture jam," sought to interrupt media as a cultural institution in order to promote a vision for social justice and was the work of the DC-based, Indigenous woman-led advocacy group Rising Hearts Coalition.[177] Designed to mirror major outlets like *ESPN*, *Washington Post*, and *Sports Illustrated*, the content went viral, receiving half a million unique views in the initial hours after the launch, hundreds of reposts from Indigenous influencers, and coverage by legitimate news sites.[178] By changing four small letters, the coalition offered, the purpose of their action was to demonstrate to team fans "how easy, popular and powerful a name change could be."[179] "Especially as a Native of the Washington, D.C., area," Rising Hearts Coalition organizer Valarie Marie Proctor (Cedarville Band of Piscataway) reflected on her participation in the culture jam, "[the Washington football team] is the only representation we have.... This is the only time you really hear anything about Native people. It's sad that the only representation we have is one that's a racial slur."[180]

In true DC fashion, grassroots efforts to change the hearts and minds of team name supporters have been complimented by legal action. On September 10, 1992, a group of Native rights activists led by Suzan Harjo (Cheyenne and Hodulgee Muscogee) petitioned the Trademark Trial and Appeal Board of the Patent and Trademark Office to revoke six trademarks registered to the team on the basis of the trademarks' disparaging nature. The Native plaintiffs of *Harjo v. Pro-Football, Inc.* proved victorious at the Trademark Trial and Appeal Board, but the case was thrown out by the US Court of Appeals for the District of Columbia Circuit, which ruled that the delay in filing suit resulted in a lack of a claim. As the appeals process for *Harjo* continued to unfold, social worker Amanda Blackhorse (Navajo) was named as a plaintiff in a 2006 suit similarly seeking cancellation of the denigrating trademark.[181] While the Supreme Court declined the *Harjo* appeal in 2009, the Trademark Trial and Appeal Board handed down a two-to-one ruling in favor of the Native parties in *Blackhorse v. Pro-Football, Inc.* on June 18, 2014, and secured another victory in the US District Court for the Eastern District of Virginia the following year.[182] As the team appealed this ruling in the US Court of Appeals for the Fourth Circuit, 2017 Supreme Court case *Matal v. Tam* vacated the *Blackhorse* ruling on findings that earlier disparagement legislation was unconstitutional and violated the First Amendment.

After years of activism and legal action, the Washington team owner Dan Snyder officially announced in the summer of 2020 that the team would review and eventually retire the racial slur name. This change came on the heels of the police killing of an unarmed Black man, George Floyd, in Minneapolis and the eruption of protests against racism and police brutality that swept across the nation. Major funders like Nike, FedEx, and Pepsico had threatened to terminate their hundreds of millions of dollars worth of dealings with Washington football if the team refused to reassess their brand in light of the Black Lives Matter movement for racial justice.[183] While many criticize

Snyder for enacting this necessary development only as a means to continue lining his own pockets—evidenced by his infamous 2013 assertion that "we'll never change the name. It's that simple. NEVER—you can use caps"—the solidarity between Black and Indigenous communities that prompted the name change and material effects stemming from the development remains inspirational and continues to strengthen.[184] Leading up to the name change, for instance, the DC chapter of Black Lives Matter instructed individuals visiting the newly unveiled Black Lives Matter Plaza in downtown DC to not wear to the site clothing reflecting the old team name, and years earlier the 2017 Indigenous Peoples March centered Black and Indigenous solidarity by seeking to "unify tribes and indigenous peoples from North, South, and Central America; the Pacific; Asia; Africa; and the Caribbean."[185] For more than a year and a half beginning July 2020, the team operated under the temporary brand Washington Football Team and retired its Indian head logo; the new name— the Washington Commanders—was unveiled in February 2022. Looking back at her years on the frontlines of this fight, Harjo reflects on the significance of the change: "It is king of the mountain because it's associated with the nation's capital, so what happens here affects the rest of the country."[186]

Be it in the streets, on the National Mall, or in front of federal agencies, the city of Washington has borne witness to Indigenous activism for more than one hundred years. From the Change the Name Campaign to the Oceti Sakowin Youth Relay Run, Native advocates have championed Indigenous issues in DC on the local and national levels alike. From the activist careers of Marie Louise Bottineau Baldwin and Zitkála-Šá in the early twentieth century to the 2014 Cowboy and Indian Alliance Camp, the District has functioned as ground zero for positive change for Indian Country. From the 1972 occupation of the BIA to the Native Nations Rise March in 2017, Indigenous organizers have looked to the nation's capital as the center stage upon which to make their voices heard. Thousands more have traversed the city streets for myriad causes, and as the seven generations teaching suggests, many more are yet to come. Uniting them all is the strength of Indigenous nations and a determination to take a stand for their rights.

NOTES

1. Marie Louise Bottineau Baldwin, "An Ojibwe Woman in Washington, DC," in *Recasting the Vote: How Women of Color Transformed the Suffrage Movement*, by Cathleen D. Cahill (Chapel Hill: University of North Carolina Press, 2020), 83.

2. Baldwin, 83, 86.

3. Baldwin, 86.

4. Baldwin, 88.

5. Baldwin, 93–94.

6. Marie Louise Bottineau Baldwin, "The Indians of Today," in *Recasting the Vote: How Women of Color Transformed the Suffrage Movement*, by Cathleen D. Cahill (Chapel Hill: University of North Carolina Press, 2020), 137–38.

7. Jenn Brandt, "1913 Woman Suffrage Procession," 100 Years of the Women's Vote, California State University, Dominguez Hills, Spring 2020, https://scalar.usc.edu/works /100-years-of-the-womens-vote/1913-woman-suffrage-procession-poster.

8. Cathleen D. Cahill, "Marie Louise Bottineau Baldwin: Indigenizing the Federal Indian Service," *American Indian Quarterly* 37, no 3 (Summer 2013): 74.

9. Cahill, 74.

10. Brandt, "1913 Woman Suffrage Procession."

11. Cathleen D. Cahill, "'Our Democracy and the American Indian': Citizenship, Sovereignty, and the Native Vote in the 1920s," *Journal of Women's History* 32, no. 1 (Spring 2020): 41–51.

12. Cristina Stanciu, "An Indian Woman of Many Hats: Laura Cornelius Kellogg's Embattled Search for an Indigenous Voice," *American Indian Quarterly* 37, no. 3 (Summer 2013): 92; and "Indian Princess Is Active Lobbyist in Capital," *The Day Book*, February 15, 1916, https://chroniclingamerica.loc.gov/lccn/sn83045487/1916-02-15/ed-1/seq-15/.

13. Cahill, "'Our Democracy and the American Indian'," 43.

14. Gertrude Simmons Bonnin, "Americanize the First American," in *Recasting the Vote: How Women of Color Transformed the Suffrage Movement*, by Cathleen D. Cahill (Chapel Hill: University of North Carolina Press, 2020), 184; and Cahill, "'Our Democracy and the American Indian'," 43, 46.

15. Jo DeVoe, "Zitkala-Ša Park Slated to Open by July, Delayed by COVID, Weather," *ARLnow.com*, March 24, 2021, https://www.arlnow.com/2021/03/24/zitkala-sa-park -slated-to-open-by-july-delayed-by-covid-weather/; "December County Board Meeting Agenda Highlights," Arlington County Government, December 5, 2020, https://newsroom .arlingtonva.us/release/december-county-board-meeting-agenda-highlights-2; and Jo DeVoe, "Henry Clay Park Set to Be Renamed for Indigenous Activist Who Lived Nearby," *ARLnow.com*, December 8, 2020, https://www.arlnow.com/2020/12/08/henry-clay-park -set-to-be-renamed-for-indigenous-activist-who-lived-nearby/.

16. Paul Chaat Smith and Robert Allen Warrior, *Like a Hurricane: The Indian Movement from Alcatraz to Wounded Knee* (New York: New Press, 1996), 143.

17. Bob Simpson, "Native Americans Take Over Bureau of Indian Affairs: 1972," *Montgomery Spark*, November 29, 1972, 13–14.

18. *American Indian Movement Past, Present & Future* (Minneapolis: A.I.M. Interpretive Center), 9.

19. Simpson, "Native Americans Take Over Bureau of Indian Affairs"; and "Justice Eyes Way to Charge Indians," *Washington Post*, November 10, 1972.

20. Smith and Warrior, *Like a Hurricane*, 152.

21. Simpson, "Native Americans Take Over Bureau of Indian Affairs."

22. For the full proposal, see "Trail of Broken Treaties 20-Point Position Paper," American Indian Movement, October 1972, Minneapolis, Minnesota, https://www.aimovement .org/ggc/trailofbrokentreaties.html. See also Jerry D. Stubben, *Native Americans and Political Participation: A Reference Handbook* (Santa Barbara, CA: ABC-CLIO, 2006), 69–70.

23. Smith and Warrior, *Like a Hurricane*, 156.

24. Smith and Warrior, 149.

25. Smith and Warrior, 150, 152.

26. Smith and Warrior, 153.

27. Smith and Warrior, 154.

28. Smith and Warrior, 158.

29. Smith and Warrior, 153.

30. Smith and Warrior, 154.

31. Smith and Warrior, 155.

32. Dana Hedgpeth, "The Week Hundreds of Native Americans Took Over D.C.'s Bureau of Indian Affairs," *Washington Post*, January 24, 2021, https://www.washingtonpost.com /history/2021/01/24/native-americans-occupied-bureau-indian-afffairs-nixon/.

33. Hedgpeth.

34. "Justice Eyes Way to Charge Indians."

35. Hedgpeth, "The Week Hundreds of Native Americans"; and Smith and Warrior, *Like a Hurricane*, 156.

36. Smith and Warrior, *Like a Hurricane*, 156.

37. Smith and Warrior, 157.

38. Smith and Warrior, 157.

39. Smith and Warrior, 157, 159.

40. "Justice Eyes Way to Charge Indians."

41. Simpson.

42. Smith and Warrior, *Like a Hurricane*, 161.

43. Smith and Warrior, 162.

44. Simpson, "Native Americans Take Over Bureau of Indian Affairs."

45. Smith and Warrior, *Like a Hurricane*, 163.

46. Smith and Warrior, 164.

47. Simpson, "Native Americans Take Over Bureau of Indian Affairs."

48. Smith and Warrior, *Like a Hurricane*, 160.

49. Jon Katz, "Damage to BIA Third Heaviest Ever in U.S.," *Washington Post*, November 11, 1972.

50. "Justice Eyes Way to Charge Indians."

51. Simpson, "Native Americans Take Over Bureau of Indian Affairs."

52. Simpson.

53. "Indians Take Over Wash. Bureau Office," *Washington Post*, November 10, 1972.

54. Smith and Warrior, *Like a Hurricane*, 166.

55. Jenna Pope, "Cowboy Indian Alliance to Obama: Take Your Pipeline and Shove It," *Vice*, April 27, 2014, https://www.vice.com/en_us/article/7xjd9x/cowboy-indian-alliance -to-obama-take-your-pipeline-and-shove-it.

56. "Reject & Protect: Farmers, Ranchers, and Tribes Protest Keystone XL with Week-Long DC Encampment," *350.org*, April 21, 2014, https://350.org/press-release /reject-protect-farmers-ranchers-and-tribes-protest-keystone-xl-with-week-long-dc -encampment/; and "'Cowboys and Indians' Keystone XL Protest," *Politico*, April 26, 2014, https://www.politico.com/gallery/2014/04/cowboys-and-indians-keystone-xl-protest -001615?slide=30.

57. "Reject & Protect"; and "'Cowboys and Indians' Keystone XL Protest."

58. Dallas Goldtooth, interview with author, September 17, 2020.

59. Naureen Khan, "Cowboys and Indians Ride into U.S. Capital to Protest Keystone pipeline," *Al Jazeera America*, April 22, 2014, http://america.aljazeera.com/articles/2014/4 /22/keystone-xl-protestcowboysindiansranchers.html.

60. "FAQs," Reject and Protect, accessed June 19, 2021, http://rejectandprotect.org/faqs/.

61. Devon Douglas-Bowers, "What the Cowboy-Indian Alliance Means for America and the Climate Movement," *Resilience*, October 29, 2014, https://www.resilience.org/stories/2014-10-29/what-the-cowboy-indian-alliance-means-for-america-and-the-climate-movement/.

62. Nick Estes, *Our History Is the Future: Standing Rock Versus the Dakota Access Pipeline, and the Long Tradition of Indigenous Resistance* (London: Verso, 2019), 14.

63. "FAQs."

64. Khan, "Cowboys and Indians Ride"; "FAQs"; and Douglas-Bowers, "What the Cowboy-Indian Alliance Means."

65. "Thousands March with Cowboy and Indian Alliance at 'Reject and Protect' to Protest Keystone XL Pipeline," *350.org*, April 26, 2014, https://350.org/thousands-march-with-cowboy-and-indian-alliance-at-reject-and-protect-to-protest-keystone-xl-pipeline/.

66. "FAQs."

67. "FAQs."

68. "Cowboys and Indians Stand Together against Keystone XL," *National Geographic*, May 14, 2014, https://blog.nationalgeographic.org/2014/05/14/cowboys-and-indians-stand-together-against-keystone-xl/.

69. Estes, *Our History Is the Future,* 26, 30.

70. Goldtooth, interview.

71. Goldtooth, interview.

72. Goldtooth, interview.

73. Kristin Moe, "When Cowboys and Indians Unite—Inside the Unlikely Alliance that Is Remaking the Climate Movement," *Waging Nonviolence*, May 2, 2014, https://wagingnonviolence.org/2014/05/cowboys-indians-unite-inside-unlikely-alliance-foretells-victory-climate-movement/.

74. Pope, "Cowboy Indian Alliance to Obama."

75. "Cowboy and Indian Alliance Stands against Pipeline," *CBS News*, April 23, 2014, https://www.cbsnews.com/pictures/cowboy-and-indian-alliance-stands-against-pipeline/15/; and "Camp Schedule," Reject and Protect, accessed June 19, 2021, https://rejectandprotect.org/camp-schedule/; Goldtooth, interview.

76. "FAQs."

77. "Reject & Protect"; "Camp Schedule"; "Cowboys and Indians Stand Together Against Keystone XL"; and Mark Hefflinger, "Reject + Protect: Press Resources," *Bold Nebraska*, April 18, 2014, https://boldnebraska.org/reject-protect-press-resources/.

78. "FAQs."

79. "Reject & Protect."

80. "Camp Schedule."

81. Heather Smith, "The Cowboys and Indians Pipeline Protest Was a Throwback—in More Ways Than One," *Grist Magazine*, April 30, 2014, https://grist.org/climate-energy/cowboys-and-indians-pipeline-protest-a-throwback-in-more-ways-than-one/; Pope, "Cowboy Indian Alliance to Obama"; and Hefflinger, "Reject + Protect."

82. "Camp Schedule."

83. Pope, "Cowboy Indian Alliance to Obama."

84. Pope, "Cowboy Indian Alliance to Obama"; "Thousands March with Cowboy and Indian Alliance"; and Goldtooth, interview.

85. "Thousands March with Cowboy and Indian Alliance."

86. "'Cowboys and Indians' Keystone XL Protest."

87. "'Cowboys and Indians' Keystone XL Protest."

88. "Thousands March with Cowboy and Indian Alliance."

89. "Reject & Protect"; and Goldtooth, interview.

90. "About," Reject and Protect, accessed June 19, 2021, http://rejectandprotect.org /about-2/; and "Thousands March with Cowboy and Indian Alliance at 'Reject and Protect' to Protest Keystone XL Pipeline."

91. Goldtooth, interview.

92. "FAQs."

93. "Reject & Protect."

94. "Thousands March with Cowboy and Indian Alliance."

95. "Thousands March with Cowboy and Indian Alliance."

96. "FAQs."

97. "Thousands March with Cowboy and Indian Alliance."

98. "Camp Schedule"; and "Reject & Protect."

99. "Thousands March with Cowboy and Indian Alliance."

100. "Collecting Items Related to the Cowboy and Indian Alliance Protests," National Museum of the American Indian, April 22, 2014, https://americanindian.si.edu/sites/1 /files/pdf/press_releases/Statement_on_Collecting_Items_Related_to_the_Cowboy_and _Indian_Alliance_Protests.pdf.

101. "FAQs."

102. "Camp Schedule."

103. Kolby KickingWoman, "Dakota Access Pipeline: Timeline," *Indian Country Today*, July 9, 2020, https://indiancountrytoday.com/news/dakota-access-pipeline-timeline ?redir=1.

104. KickingWoman; and Nick Estes, "Fighting for Our Lives: #NoDAPL in Historical Context," *Wicazo Sa Review* 32, no. 2 (Fall 2017): 115.

105. Estes, "Fighting for Our Lives," 115.

106. KickingWoman, "Dakota Access Pipeline: Timeline."

107. Nick Estes and Jaskiran Dhillon, eds., *Standing with Standing Rock: Voices from the #NODAPL Movement* (Minnesota: University of Minnesota Press, 2019).

108. "Winona LaDuke: Trump's Push to Build Dakota Access & Keystone XL Pipelines Is a Declaration of War," *Democracy Now*, January 25, 2017, https://www.democracynow .org/2017/1/25/winona_laduke_trumps_push_to_build; and "The Voice of a Genera-tion: Bobbi Jean Three Legs (Part 1)," *Native Hope*, accessed July 2, 2019, https://blog .nativehope.org/the-voice-of-a-generation-bobbi-jean-three-legs-part-1.

109. Alli Joseph, "Running for Their Lives: Native American Relay Tradition Revived to Protest Dakota Access Pipeline," *Salon*, September 12, 2016, https://www.salon.com/2016 /09/12/running-for-their-lives-native-american-relay-tradition-revived-to-protest-dakota -access-pipeline/.

110. "The Voice of a Generation (Part 1)."

111. "Treaties Still Matter: The Dakota Access Pipeline," National Museum of the American Indian: Native Knowledge 360, 2018, https://americanindian.si.edu/nk360 /plains-treaties/dapl.

112. Saul Elbein, "The Youth Group that Launched a Movement at Standing Rock," *New York Times*, January 21, 2017, https://www.nytimes.com/2017/01/31/magazine/the-youth -group-that-launched-a-movement-at-standing-rock.html.

113. "The Voice of a Generation: Bobbi Jean Three Legs (Part 2)," *Native Hope*, accessed July 2, 2019, https://blog.nativehope.org/the-voice-of-a-generation-bobbi-jean-three

-legs-part-2?__hstc=88825988.bcf3fd45afa59c51a92ddbad019005e3.1619994485286
.1619994485286.1619994485286.1&__hssc=88825988.1.1619994485291&__hsfp=
2660841320.

114. Yessenia Funes, "PHOTOS: Native Youth Deliver Petition Against Pipeline to
White House," *Colorlines*, August 8, 2016, https://www.colorlines.com/articles/photos
-native-youth-deliver-petition-against-pipeline-white-house.

115. Braudie Blais-Billie, "6 Indigenous Activists on Why They're Fighting the Dakota
Access Pipeline," *Fader*, September 9, 2016, https://www.thefader.com/2016/09/09
/dakota-access-pipeline-protest-interviews.

116. Blais-Billie, "6 Indigenous Activists."

117. Estes, *Our History Is The Future*, 3.

118. Estes, 55.

119. Gabrielle Tayac, interview with author, October 8, 2020.

120. Rob Capriccioso, "Native Nations Rise March: The Good, the Bad, and the
Ugly," *Indian Country Today*, September 13, 2018, https://www.nytimes.com/2017/01/31
/magazine/the-youth-group-that-launched-a-movement-at-standing-rock.html.

121. Elbein, "The Youth Group that Launched a Movement at Standing Rock."

122. Indigenous Rising, "Naive Nations Rise," YouTube video, 0:58, March 7, 2017,
https://www.youtube.com/watch?v=UrrlMGobvsg.

123. Indigenous Rising.

124. Indigenous Rising.

125. "Native Citizens Rally in Nation's Capital to Send Message to Donald Trump,"
Indianz.com, March 10, 2017, https://www.indianz.com/News/2017/03/10/native-citizens
-rally-in-nations-capitol.asp.

126. Lauren Gambino, "Native Americans Take Dakota Access Pipeline Protest to
Washington," *Guardian*, March 10, 2017, https://www.theguardian.com/us-news/2017
/mar/10/native-nations-march-washington-dakota-access-pipeline.

127. "Native Citizens Rally"; and Rebecca Hersher, "Key Moments in the Dakota Access
Pipeline Fight," *NPR*, February 22, 2017, https://www.npr.org/sections/thetwo-way/2017
/02/22/514988040/key-moments-in-the-dakota-access-pipeline-fight.

128. Gambino, "Native Americans Take Dakota Access"; Cajsa Wikstrom, "Native
Nations Rise Brings DAPL Protest to Washington," *Al Jazeera*, March 11, 2017, https://
www.aljazeera.com/news/2017/03/standing-rock-tribe-takes-dapl-protest-washington
-170310032032028.html; and Hersher, "Key Moments in the Dakota Access Pipeline Fight."

129. Wikstrom, "Native Nations Rise Brings DAPL Protest to Washington."

130. Hersher, "Key Moments In the Dakota Access Pipeline Fight."

131. "March," Standing Rock Sioux Tribe, accessed June 6, 2021, https://
standwithstandingrock.net/march/.

132. "Solidarity Events," #NoDAPL Archive—Standing Rock Water Protectors,
accessed June 9, 2021, https://www.nodaplarchive.com/solidarity-events.html.

133. Toyacoyah Brown, "Native Nations Rise—March On Washing-
ton D.C. March 10th," *Powwows.com*, March 7, 2017, https://www.powwows.com/native
-nations-rise-march-washington-d-c-march-10th/.

134. Andy Rowell, "Native Nations Rise March in DC Takes on 'Tyranny' of Trump
Administration," *Oil Change International*, March 9, 2017, http://priceofoil.org/2017/03/09
/native-nations-rise-march-in-dc-takes-on-tyranny-of-trump-administration/.

135. Adam R. Sings In The Timber, "Native Nations March to Trump's White
House Draws Huge Crowds," *Indian Country Today*, September 13, 2018, https://

indiancountrytoday.com/archive/native-nations-march-to-trump-s-white-house-draws
-huge-crowds-video-sQLTEJ7sqkKUeIei84Ux-Q.

136. Gambino, "Native Americans Take Dakota Access Pipeline."

137. "Native Citizens Rally."

138. "Native Citizens Rally."

139. Brown, "Native Nations Rise."

140. "Native Citizens Rally."

141. Brown, "Native Nations Rise."

142. Brown.

143. Rowell, "Native Nations Rise March in DC."

144. "Native Nations Rise March and Rally," *C-SPAN video*, 2:18;15, March 10, 2017. https://www.c-span.org/video/?425181-1/members-standing-rock-sioux-tribe-hold
-protest-white-house.

145. "Native Nations Rise March and Rally."

146. Estes, *Our History Is the Future*, 64; and "Native Citizens Rally."

147. "Native Nations Rise March and Rally."

148. "Native Nations Rise March and Rally."

149. "Native Nations Rise March and Rally."

150. "Native Nations Rise March and Rally."

151. "Native Nations Rise March and Rally."

152. "Native Nations Rise March and Rally."

153. "Native Nations Rise March and Rally."

154. "Native Nations Rise March and Rally."

155. "Native Nations Rise March and Rally."

156. "Native Nations Rise March and Rally."

157. Sings In The Timber, "Native Nations March."

158. Brown, "Native Nations Rise."

159. "Standing With Standing Rock," Standing Rock Sioux Tribe, accessed June 6, 2021, https://standwithstandingrock.net.

160. "March," Standing Rock Sioux Tribe, accessed June 6, 2021, https://
standwithstandingrock.net/march/.

161. Hefflinger, "Reject + Protect: Press Resources."

162. Estes, *Our History Is the Future*, 25.

163. Estes, 15; Merrit Kennedy, "More Than 1 Million 'Check In' On Facebook to Support the Standing Rock Sioux," *NPR*, November 1, 2016, https://www.npr.org/sections
/thetwo-way/2016/11/01/500268879/more-than-a-million-check-in-on-facebook-to
-support-the-standing-rock-sioux; and Ryan Schleeter, "#NoDAPL Day of Action Draws Tens of Thousands, Lights Up Social Media," *Greenpeace*, November 16, 2016, https://www
.greenpeace.org/usa/nodapl-day-action-draws-tens-thousands-lights-social-media/.

164. "*More Than a Word*—Transcript," Media Education Foundation, 2017, https://www
.mediaed.org/transcripts/More-Than-A-Word-Transcript.pdf.

165. Dan Bernstein, "Redskins Name Change Timeline: How Daniel Snyder's 'NEVER' Gave Way to Washington Football Team," *SportingNews.com*, November 26, 2020, https://
www.sportingnews.com/us/nfl/news/redskins-name-timeline-washington-football-team
/1uk394uouwi631k7poirtq1v1s.

166. Ian Shapira, "A Brief History of the Word 'Redskin' and How It Became a Source of Controversy," *Washington Post*, July 3, 2020, https://www.washingtonpost.com/history
/2020/07/03/redskins-name-change/.

167. Shapira.

168. "*More Than a Word*—Transcript."

169. Shapira, "A Brief History of the Word 'Redskin'."

170. Ken Denlinger, "Protest of 'Redskins' Draws 2,000 at Stadium," *Washington Post*, January 27, 1992, https://www.washingtonpost.com/archive/sports/1992/01/27/protest -of-redskins-draws-2000-at-stadium/39e3ab8d-791f-4531-98ee-e11d7acceb66/.

171. "Super Bowl XXVI Notebook: The Protest that Won't Go Away," *New York Times*, January 21, 1992, https://www.nytimes.com/1992/01/21/sports/super-bowl-xxvi -notebook-the-protest-that-won-t-go-away.html.

172. "Native American Group Launches Anti-'Redskins' Telephone Campaign," *Sports Illustrated*, January 15, 2015, https://www.si.com/nfl/2015/01/15/washington-redskins -name-change-oneida-telephone-campaign.

173. John Woodrow Cox, "A Fierce, Lifelong Redskins Fan Takes a Stand against His Beloved Team's Name," *Washington Post*, November 21, 2014, https://www .washingtonpost.com/local/a-rabid-lifelong-redskins-fan-takes-a-stand-against-his -beloved-teams-name/2014/11/21/34848708-6fb7-11e4-8808-afaa1e3a33ef_story.html.

174. "About," Rebrand Washington Football, accessed July 25, 2021, https://www .rebrandwf.org/about.html.

175. "About," Rebrand Washington Football.

176. "Press Release," Rising Hearts Coalition, December 13, 2017, http:// washingtonredhawks.com/press_release.pdf.

177. "Go Washington Redhawks! Washington Redskins Hit with an Elaborate Culture Jam," *Last Real Indians*, December 14, 2017, https://lastrealindians.com/news/2017/12 /14/dec-14-2017-go-washington-redhawks-washington-redskins-hit-with-an-elaborate -culture-jam; and Kevin Abourezk, "Native Activists Go Viral with 'Redhawks' Campaign Aimed at NFL Team's Racist Mascot," *Indianz.com*, December 13, 2017, https://www .indianz.com/News/2017/12/13/fake-news-about-name-change-for-washingt.asp.

178. Katie Toth, "Rising Hearts Protesters on Why They 'Changed' the Washing- ton NFL Team Name to the 'Redhawks,'" *Teen Vogue*, December 19, 2017, https:// www.teenvogue.com/story/why-rising-hearts-protesters-washington-nfl-team-name -redhawks.

179. "Go Redhawks Pep Rally (+ Twitter Storm) #ChangetheName," 2017, Facebook event, December 17, 2017, https://www.facebook.com/events/371403393297689/.

180. Toth, "Rising Hearts Protesters."

181. Victoria F. Phillips and Ryan M. Van Olst, "The Longstanding Pro Bono Battle Challenging the Washington Football Team Trademarks," *Landslide* 8, no. 3 (January/ February 2016).

182. Shapira, "A Brief History of the Word 'Redskin'."

183. "BLM: NFL's Washington Redskins Announce 'Thorough Review' of Name," *Al Jazeera*, July 3, 2020, https://www.aljazeera.com/news/2020/7/3/blm-nfls-washington -redskins-announce-thorough-review-of-name.

184. Abby Cruz, "What Native American Activists Think about the Washington Foot- ball Team Name Change," *ABC News*, August 8, 2020, https://abcnews.go.com/Sports /native-american-activists-washington-football-team-change/story?id=72188694; and Bernstein, "Redskins Name Change Timeline."

185. Black Lives Matter DC (@DMVBlackLives), "Do not go to #BlackLivesMatter- Plaza take selfies with your Washington football team gear on. Its unacceptable. That is all." Twitter, July 4, 2020, 12:50 a.m. https://twitter.com/DMVBlackLives/status

/1279276374910480385; and Cecily Hilleary, "Indigenous Peoples Stage Solidarity March on Washington," *Voice of America*, January 18, 2019, https://www.voanews.com/usa /indigenous-peoples-stage-solidarity-march-washington.

186. Ken Belson, "Redskins' Name Change Remains Activist's Unfinished Business," *New York Times*, October 9, 2013, https://www.nytimes.com/2013/10/10/sports/football /redskins-name-change-remains-her-unfinished-business.html?ref=us&_r=0.

Native Arts and Artists in the Nation's Capital

The Native American arts exhibited throughout Washington, DC, complement the political advocacy for which the city is known. Surely, however, the arts are not politically neutral—they perform awareness-raising functions, provide educational insights, and relay Indigenous issues to onlookers. Often the creation stories behind the pieces themselves speak volumes about the at-times contested relationship between artist, community, and city.

The styles, mediums, and periods of arts covered in this chapter vary widely. In that way, the pieces reflect the diversity of Indigenous influences on the capital city. Whereas Joerael Numina's *Imprinting Dimensional States of Being* takes up local Piscataway history and culture as its subject, for instance, the dozens of murals at the Department of the Interior each showcase material specific to the Kiowa, Fort Sill Apache, Potawatomie, Navajo, and Zia Pueblo. The *Liberty*, *Freedom*, and *Sovereignty* totem poles, on the other hand, retain a distinctly Lummi design but incorporate Piscataway features to honor their display in Piscataway homelands. Further still, *The Spirit of Haida Gwaii: The Black Canoe* draws in a transnational element of Native art and offers a material representation of Indigenous resistance to state-imposed national borders.

To be sure, Washington, DC, is home to hundreds of additional artworks that take up Native American subject material. These can be found in the archives and collections of the National Gallery of Art, the Smithsonian American Art Museum, the National Portrait Gallery, and more. The purpose of this chapter, however, is to highlight sites of permanent installation available for public view. In this way, the art pieces featured within this chapter constitute sites of Indigenous importance imprinted upon the District's geography.

Imprinting Dimensional States of Being

In 2018 artist Joerael Numina collaborated with the local Piscataway community to design a spray-painted mural for the Corcoran School of the Arts and

Design at George Washington University. The mural spans the length of the basement corridor of the Flagg Building, located at 500 17th Street NW, Washington, DC. *Imprinting Dimensional States of Being* is the most recently established site of Indigenous importance in the capital to be included in this text.

To create the mural, the artist collaborated with members of the Piscataway community local to the Chesapeake Bay region, and upon whose homelands the capital city rests. First, local Piscataway community members took Numina to sacred traditional lands, now Piscataway Park, Maryland, where twenty-seven Piscataway hereditary chiefs are buried under a cedar tree. Next the artist consulted with Piscataway historian Dr. Gabrielle Tayac, who provided Numina with an oral history of the Piscataway people that has since been worked into the mural as a "dense and complex code" of symbolism. "It wasn't the Piscataway that were here, the Piscataway still live here," Numina reflected on his community-engaged artistic process. "That's part of what I've learned through them. A lot of people think, in the history books they're taught—the people who were once here—but they still exist."[1]

This piece at the Flagg Building is part of Numina's larger Mobilize Walls series. Numina intends for the series of murals, launched in 2018 shortly after the election of President Donald Trump, to "out-scale" Trump's proposed border wall.[2] The Corcoran School of the Arts and Design describes Mobilize Walls as "the polar opposite of Trump's proposed wall; it's decentralized, transformative, inclusive, healing—bridging versus building borders between communities."[3] Numina has thus far completed 58,204.5 square feet—an estimated 1,200 square miles—of art.[4] He ultimately plans to install more than 420 million square feet of painting—the size of Trump's proposed wall.[5] In addition to Washington, DC, these murals reside across the United States in Albuquerque, New York City, Denver, Phoenix, Santa Monica, Santa Fe, Los Angeles, Macon (Georgia), and more.[6]

Imprinting Dimensional States of Being weaves together symbols and representations of Piscataway culture and history as well as survival into the contemporary moment. Although landmarks throughout the District of Columbia—rivers, roads, and more—draw from Indigenous language, this mural remains one of the only artistic representations of the Piscataway people in the capital.[7] Indeed, an early image within the mural evokes the topography of Piscataway traditional territory—namely, the Chesapeake Bay area—to center land as a subject of the utmost importance to this piece.[8]

To create the mural, Numina employed graffiti, which he identifies as "the first global networked form of non-discriminating visual expression," as his

FIGURE 4.1. Detail of *Imprinting Dimensional States of Being*
Imprinting Dimensional States of Being, by Joerael Numina, Washington, DC.

medium of choice.[9] The universality behind this medium speaks to the various backgrounds of those represented within and honored by the mural. This particular style reflects the "bombardment" that colonization has wrought upon Indigenous peoples and homelands.[10] Numina adds an additional nod to regional specificity through the use of mid-Atlantic graffiti styles emblematic of go-go music, the official music of DC. This lettering appears highly legible and cartoon-like. Taken as a whole, the many layers of images, colors, and themes come together to create a "busy" aesthetic that the artist intended to evoke the chaos of the US capital.[11]

Numina's signature "handskrit" writing appears throughout the mural, uniting this piece with others in the Mobilize Walls series. Handskrit is a play on Sanskrit, a phonetic language wherein the rhythm and flow of words lend meaning, and "handstyle," the individual tag of a graffiti artist. By merging the two concepts into his own handskrit, Numina creates a "visual phonetics based on rhythm, structure, and flow," which "honors the trajectory of communications and meaning behind expressions."[12]

The mural depicts a number of black-and-white portraits of prominent, contemporary Piscataway figures. These include Mervin Savoy, tribal chair of the Piscataway Conoy Confederacy and Subtribes; Natalie Proctor, tribal chair of the Cedarville Band of Piscataway Indians; and Billy Tayac, chief of the Piscataway Indian Nation. These leaders held these positions at the pivotal time when Maryland governor Martin O'Malley signed executive orders establishing the state recognition of two entities, the Piscataway Indian Nation and the Piscataway Conoy Tribe, on January 9, 2012. The Piscataway Conoy Confederacy and Subtribes and the Cedarville Band of Piscataway Indians are two factions subsumed under the Piscataway Conoy Tribe.[13]

Turkey Tayac (1895–1978), the twenty-seventh hereditary chief of the Piscataway, also appears in various iterations throughout the mural. On one wall a black-and-white rendition of Turkey Tayac shows the tribal leader in casual Western dress. This depiction is stylized as a flat outline and is marked by the dripping black lines that appear throughout the mural. Iconic images from the Indians of All Tribes' 1969–71 occupation of Alcatraz Island surround his figure. This pan-Indian movement originated in San Francisco and reclaimed the nearby Alcatraz Island, the site of an abandoned prison, in an act to uphold provisions held by the Treaty of Fort Laramie. This treaty holds that unused federal lands should be returned to the ownership of Native peoples, and the occupation received national attention. Thus, to each side of Tayac, Numina included graffiti from Alcatraz Island reading, "United Indian Property" and "Indian Land."[14]

In a similar style, the artist also showcases Tayac in his role as a service member. He served in the 42nd Infantry, also known as the Rainbow Division, of the US Army National Guard during World War II. Directly below this figure and in the same style yet again, Numina painted a figurative outline of a Native man based on the renderings of the Piscataway people by early colonist John White.[15] By placing these images so closely together, Numina challenges popular notions of Native peoples as exclusively historical figures.

The artist references Turkey Tayac in various symbolic interpretations, in addition to portraits. At one location in the painting, for instance, Numina includes Tayac in the visualization of the word "Piscataway," which means "confluence of waters." Here the artist portrays Tayac's crossed arms and hands holding a bundle of tobacco—a traditional Indigenous medicine—as two waterfalls converge upon his hands. At another point, interwoven into representations of the Piscataway language, the artist painted a large gray eel in profile. Tayac relied on eels as a source of traditional medicine and is known to have wrapped his joints in eel skin to relieve arthritis pain.[16] As a symbolic gesture toward the hereditary chief, Numina also added a full-color literal depiction of a wild turkey.

In the most visible portrait portrayal, half of Turkey Tayac's face is depicted in full color while the other half is painted in black and white. He wears a headdress styled of upright feathers, as is typical of Indigenous cultures in the eastern United States. On either side of this particular portrait of Tayac, Numina incorporates depictions of Living Solid Face.

Living Solid Face is a spiritual figure found among the Indigenous cultures of the Northeast and is believed to be the deity responsible for allowing only enough animals into the world to meet the needs of human hunger. The half-moon shape framing Living Solid Face represents universal consciousness, and the eyes are portrayed as thunderbirds crying lightning.[17] In the depiction on the left, the lightning bolts appear as symmetrical, flat, stylized shapes on Living Solid Face's cheeks. The image on the right, by contrast, showcases the flash of a lightning strike through the use of bright yellow and more lifelike shaping.

The thunderbirds that appear in Living Solid Face's likeness also appear again in the mural, although many may overlook their presence. In another section of the painting Numina incorporates a large woodpecker whose body melts into a cloud formation. This representation honors the Piscataway spiritual teaching that holds that thunderbirds take on the form of woodpeckers.[18]

In addition to these birds, an eagle and a condor fly together in another portion of the mural to symbolize the unity between the Indigenous peoples of North and South America, which many Native people collectively refer to as Turtle Island.[19] This reference offers a critical resistance to the settler-colonial division of nation-states and pushes back against the violence imposed upon Indigenous peoples by settler state borders.

A large portrait of Joe Tayac forms one of the focal points within the mural. Joe Tayac, son of Turkey Tayac, was a US veteran like his father.[20] Four additional figures appear directly to his left and contextualize the prominence of this figure. In the upper left, two Longest Walkers (discussed below) depicted in outline speak to the spirit of activism within Piscataway territory. To Joe's direct left, a minimalistic cartoon depiction of George Washington with an "X" in place of his eye references the death, destruction, and conflict spurred by colonization and the founding of the United States. To Joe's bottom left, his daughter, Dr. Gabrielle Tayac, appears as a gesture toward the future generations of Piscataway people who keep the memories of their ancestors alive today.

Drawing on his consultative experience with the Piscataway community, Numina depicts the tree under which the past twenty-seven Piscataway hereditary chiefs are buried. Sebastian, or Sebi, Medina-Tayac, the great-grandson of Turkey Tayac, appears in the mural singing and playing the hand drum in front of the Capitol Building. Numina also incorporates a portrait of Dr. Gabrielle Tayac, granddaughter of Turkey Tayac, shown holding a feathered fan.

The Piscataway language, Conoy, appears in the mural in the form of the Ten Commandments. Numina's rendition mirrors the handwriting of Jesuit Father Andrew White, who translated the Commandments into Conoy in the early seventeenth century.[21] The artist speaks to the hypocritical nature of Christian colonization by highlighting four commandments: number five, "Thou shalt not kill"; number seven, "Thou shalt not steal"; number eight, "Thou shalt not bear false witness against thy neighbor"; and number ten, "Thou shalt not covet thy neighbor's goods."[22]

In addition to highlighting Piscataway-specific history and references, Numina dedicates a portion of the mural to a subject that may be more widely recognized by viewers: the American Indian Movement (AIM). Here the artist portrays the cofounder of AIM, Dennis Banks. An upside-down flag appears next to the portrait in a reference to AIM's 1972 Occupation of the Bureau of Indian Affairs (see chapter 3). A cloudy "1978" forms above Banks to commemorate the 1978 Longest Walk action that converged on Washington, DC. The iconic AIM symbol—a red hand giving the peace sign, with a face inscribed on the side of the hand—and a drum reading "AIM" also add to this dedication portion of the mural. Although many may be familiar with the American Indian Movement, some may not realize the close connections between AIM and the Piscataway community.

The Piscataway also embraced Navajo activist Roberta Blackgoat during her travels to Washington, DC. Blackgoat led a resistance movement opposing mining interests and federal efforts to remove nearly fifteen thousand Navajo and Hopi locals from Black Mesa in Arizona.[23] A portrait of Blackgoat, along with her famous slogan, "If you want me to move first you must sue the Creator," offers insight into the sacred relationship between Native peoples and land. Her inclusion within the mural honors her influential relationship with the Piscataway.[24]

Amid all of the complexity and layering within the mural, one section of the painting stands apart. Stylistically and spatially distinct, this portion of the mural is painted on a small wall separated from the larger piece by hallways, relies heavily on text, and features only black, white, and red hues. Numina dedicated this approximately twenty-square-foot area to a replication of a historical poster raising awareness for the 1978 Longest Walk. The original flyer encourages people to support Native populations and to "stop the genocide" by attending a rally in Washington, DC, on July 15, 1978. The Longest Walkers converged upon DC after completing a three-thousand-mile march that originated in California. The purpose of this spiritual protest was to resist anti-Indian legislation and to uphold treaty rights. Weldon Austin and Lone Wolf Willie, two participants in the second iteration of the Longest Walk (2008), also appear in the mural to the upper right of Joe Tayac.[25] Incorporating this historical reference and emphasizing its placement within the mural, Numina calls attention to the ways in which Washington, DC, the homelands of the Piscataway people, has also served as the site of national, pan-Indian activism.

Throughout Numina's massive work, stylistic elements and motifs unite the broad subject matter covered by the artist. Nude-toned rainbows, for instance, swirl around figures and allude to the diversity of appearances and racial backgrounds among Indigenous peoples. Algonquian floral designs also punctuate the canvas and provide regional-specific cultural designs.[26]

Imprinting Dimensional States of Being opened to the public on October 19, 2019. The event included an invocation by a Piscataway community leader, Native American drumming by a DC group, a historical presentation by Dr. Gabrielle Tayac, discussion with the artist, and community viewing.[27] Numina hopes that his mural provides a visual land acknowledgment of Piscataway homelands.[28] In this way, *Imprinting Dimensional States of Being* renders visible the original peoples of Washington, who are far too often neglected in the public sphere despite their ongoing service to their traditional territory. "I hope as you have explored this work," the artist writes, "you have opened yourself up to the ground you walk upon and not only recognize Washington DC as ancestral lands to First Nations like the Piscataway, but all of Turtle Island's First Nations."[29]

The Spirit of Haida Gwaii: The Black Canoe

Of all of prolific Haida artist Bill Reid's sculptures, *The Spirit of Haida Gwaii: The Black Canoe* stands out as his pièce de résistance.[30] The gargantuan work—Reid's final creation—showcases Haida culture and tradition, and the story behind its development speaks to Haida politics as well. *The Black Canoe* sits outside the embassy of Canada in Washington, DC, at 501 Pennsylvania Avenue NW.

Born January 12, 1920, in Victoria, British Columbia, Bill Reid belonged to the Raven clan. His Haida name, Yaahl Sgwansung, translates to "The Only Raven." The internationally acclaimed artist—a celebrated goldsmith, jewelry maker, sculptor, writer, and carver—embraced his identity as a "maker of things" for the entirety of his life.[31]

Reid's formal artistic journey began at the age of twenty-eight, at Ryerson Institute of Technology in Toronto, and later at the London School of Design.[32] There he took up goldsmithing and jewelry making—a craft practiced by various members of his family. Approximately six years into this field of work, Reid was forever changed by viewing one of his great-great-uncles' bracelets carved in the Haida style.[33] Henceforth, he shifted his own designs to incorporate stronger Haida influences, themes, and imagery, and he ventured into new mediums as well.

Over the years, Reid gained popular acclaim as an artist and advocate for the Haida people. Between 1976 and 1978, he carved a totem pole for his mother's village of Skidegate, British Columbia; it was the first totem pole to be raised there in more than a century.[34] Two years later he completed *The Raven and the First Men*, a massive carving of the Haida human creation story in yellow cedar, for the Museum of Anthropology at the University of British Columbia.[35] Reid unveiled his eighteen-foot-tall sculpture of a killer whale titled *Chief of the Undersea World* at the Vancouver Aquarium in 1984 and his twenty-eight-foot-long bronze frieze of Haida spiritual figures, *Mythic Messengers*, at Teleglobe Canada in 1985.[36] He completed another great work, *Lootaas*, or "wave eater" a fifty-foot canoe carved from a single cedar log, in 1986.[37]

The idea for *The Spirit of Haida Gwaii: The Black Canoe* first emerged in 1985, while Reid was engaged in the *Lootaas* project. At the prompting of Reid's colleague, Arthur Erickson, to create a welcome structure for the Canadian Embassy building in Washington, Reid hatched the idea for a sculpture centered around another canoe.[38] The process began with a clay model in the spring of 1986 and advanced to a plaster figure by 1987.[39]

Unlike his other pieces, *The Black Canoe* emerged during a heightened period in Reid's activism on behalf of his Haida community and took on a decidedly political tone.[40] Only weeks before he broke ground on the project, for instance, Reid weighed in on local efforts to protect natural resources, demanding that "the Haida must have their ancient lands back unviolated to reestablish the links with their distinguished past and build a new future. If those remnants of those former riches are not returned, it will make the act of theft a conscious one, perpetuated by the people of today."[41]

FIGURE 4.2. *The Spirit of Haida Gwaii: The Black Canoe*, by Bill Reid
Keith Beaty [Toronto Star] via Getty Images.

In March of 1987 Reid further leveraged his position in support of Haida activism by halting production in protest of clear-cut logging on traditional Haida territory.[42] "I couldn't live with it anymore, using the Haida symbols to advertise a government ... that we felt was not cooperating with us."[43] Speaking specifically to the placement of the piece in the District of Columbia, Reid chastised, "I'm not prepared to enhance your international reputation when you treat my people [Haida] badly."[44] He furthermore stated that he refused to have *The Spirit of Haida Gwaii* reduced to "Canadian window dressing in Washington."[45] Ultimately, the Haida Nation, Canadian federal government, and British Columbia provincial government agreed to implement environmental protections for Haida homelands through the establishment of the Gwaii Haanas National Park Reserve and Haida Heritage Site on the southern half of Haida Gwaii.[46] Reid resumed work on the sculpture in January 1988 after a ten-month protest.[47]

Reid unveiled the final product—cast in bronze and coated in black patina—in 1992.[48] The piece stands a whopping 12 feet and 9 inches tall and is nearly 20 feet long and 11.5 feet wide.[49] In all, the estimated production costs of $275,000 increased more than sixfold by its conclusion, skyrocketing to a total between $1.7 and $1.8 million. Indeed, Reid himself contributed $100,000 of his own funds toward the project.[50]

In addition to its imposing size and costs, *The Spirit of Haida Gwaii: The Black Canoe* proves just as vast in the symbolism and subject matter it takes up. The sculpture is composed of thirteen Haida spiritual figures, "symbols of another time when the Haidas, all ten thousands of them, knew they were the greatest of all nations," together in a canoe traveling "a long way from Haida Gwaii."[51] At the front of the vessel, Reid depicts the Bear family, made up of Grizzly Bear seated at the bow, the Bear Mother in human form holding an oar and facing Grizzly Bear, and their two cubs between them. Beaver—which Reid describes as "doughtily paddling away, hardworking if not very imaginative, the compulsory Canadian content, big teeth and scaly tail, perfectly designed for cutting down trees and damming rivers"—rows behind Bear Mother.[52] Reaching over Beaver's tail, the magical and mysterious Dogfish Woman retains her predominantly human features but also exhibits gill slits on her face, a sharp nose, and a crown that mirrors the snout of a dogfish.[53] Raven sits at the stern, a representation of a traditional trickster figure and of one of the predominant Haida lineages. From beneath the shelter of Raven's wing, the elusive and minuscule Mouse Woman—a traditional guide between the human and nonhuman worlds—peers out. Moving up the starboard side of the canoe, the Ancient Reluctant Conscript pulls his oar.[54] Reid describes the importance of this resilient figure:

> A culture will be remembered for its warriors, philosophers, artists, heroes and heroines of all callings but in order to survive it needs survivors. And here is our professional survivor, the Ancient Reluctant Conscript, present if seldom noticed in all the turbulent histories of men on earth. When our latter day kings and captains have joined their forebears he will still be carrying on, stoically obeying orders and performing tasks allotted him. But only up to a point; it is also he who finally says, "Enough," and after the rulers have disappeared into the morass of their own excesses, it is he who builds on the rubble and once more gets the whole damn thing going.[55]

Wolf stretches his body across the boat, with his front legs rowing in front of the Ancient Reluctant Conscript, hindquarters propped up on Beaver's back, and teeth sunk into Eagle's wing. The "proud, imperial, somewhat pompous" Eagle in turn pecks at Bear's paw.[56] Frog crouches at Bear's feet, tongue outstretched, not paddling but along for the ride. At the center of the canoe, Reid's central, human figure, the Haida *kilstlaai*, or chief, towers over the other passengers. He holds a carved staff, dons a Haida-style basketry hat, and, in the words of Reid, "seems to have some vision of what's to come" on the canoe journey.[57] As a whole, then, *The Spirit of Haida Gwaii* incorporates many creatures that each call up Haida traditions and worldviews and that collectively speak to the various positions individuals inhabit on the journey of life. The sculpture's position outside the Canadian Embassy furthermore serves to welcome visitors and to evoke a sense of travel and movement at this international outpost.

In recognition of his outstanding contributions, including his final masterpiece, *The Spirit of Haida Gwaii*, Bill Reid received the National Aboriginal Achievement Award for Lifetime Achievement in 1994 and was inducted into both the Royal Canadian Academy and the Order of British Columbia.[58] He held honorary degrees from some of Canada's most prestigious universities, including Simon Fraser University, the University of Victoria, York University, the University of Western Ontario, Trent University, the University of British Columbia, and the University of Toronto.[59] After more than twenty years of living with Parkinson's disease, Reid passed on in 1998; his ashes were carried back to Haida Gwaii in *Lootaas*.[60] In 2004 the government of Canada incorporated prints of Reid's artworks—*The Spirit of Haida Gwaii*, *The Raven and the First Men*, *Mythic Messengers*, and *Xhuwaji/Haida Grizzly Bear*—into the twenty-dollar bill.[61]

The Spirit of Haida Gwaii proved to be Bill Reid's last sculpture.[62] An exact replica of *The Spirit of Haida Gwaii*—cast in jade rather than black patina and appropriately subtitled *The Jade Canoe*—was installed in the Vancouver International Airport in 1994.[63] With Bill Reid's works displayed so prominently throughout Canada, *The Spirit of Haida Gwaii: The Black Canoe* offers a unique display of this Indigenous maker's mastery in Washington, DC. "The sheer size, complexity, and polished finish of the black canoe," write art historians Karen Duffek and Charlotte Townsend-Gault, "give it a charisma that is only enhanced by its 'power' location [in Washington, DC]."[64]

Liberty, *Freedom*, and *Sovereignty* Totem Poles

Washington, DC's Congressional Cemetery is the final resting place of more than two dozen tribal leaders hailing from tribes across the nation (see chapter 1). In 2004 this site also became host to the *Liberty*, *Freedom*, and *Sovereignty* totem poles—Lummi carvings dedicated to the 184 individuals who lost their lives on Flight 93 during the September 11, 2001, terrorist attack on the Pentagon.[65] "The poles are meant to connect the past and present. While it may commemorate a tragedy or honor the dead," the placard installed next

FIGURE 4.3. Lummi Totem Poles in the Congressional Cemetery
"Lummi 9-11 Healing Poles—Congressional Cemetery—Washington DC—2012," by Tim Evanson, licensed under CC BY-SA 2.0.

to the poles reads, "its power reaches beyond the loss to actually touch each viewer with the power to heal grief."[66] Accordingly, this installation offers comfort to the families whose loved ones perished and honors members of the US Armed Forces.[67] The totem poles are located at the corner of 18th Street SE and H Street SE/Prout Street SE, as part of the Ward 6 September 11 Memorial within the Congressional Cemetery.

Master carver Jewell James and the team making up the House of Tears Carvers have produced totem poles out of Bellingham, Washington, just west of the Lummi reservation, for more than thirty years.[68] *Liberty*, *Freedom*, and *Sovereignty* were carved out of cedar trees with a history longer than the United States itself.[69] James used a 250-foot-tall and 20-foot-wide red cedar tree, aged between five hundred and eight hundred years, for two thirteen-foot base poles and a second, smaller tree for the thirty-four-foot crossbeam, *Sovereignty*.[70] The carving process took approximately 2,500 hours, the equivalent of 312 8-hour workdays, and was completed in five months.[71] In total, eighty individuals lent their contributions toward the poles' creation.[72]

James's *Liberty*, *Freedom*, and *Sovereignty* totem poles exude symbolism. *Liberty* sits on the left, *Freedom* on the right, and the *Sovereignty* crossbar connects the two. This structure forms the shape of a house, "reminding all Americans we live under one roof."[73] This organization of poles also suggests that, conceptually and literally, freedom and liberty uphold and support sovereignty.[74] *Liberty* takes shape as a male bear, which represents Father Sky, with Grandfather Sun depicted on his belly. On *Freedom*, James established balance by carving a female bear to signify Mother Earth, and a representation of Grandmother Moon on the back of a turtle appears on her abdomen. *Sovereignty* rests upon the tops of these poles. James carved each end of *Sovereignty* into an eagle shape, which symbolizes vision, courage, and protection. The female eagle on the left end of *Sovereignty* depicts peace, and the male eagle on the right end stands for war.[75] James carved both eagles with seven feathers on their wings, in reference to those who were killed on board Flight 77.[76] A small human figure situated inside the female eagle's mouth represents "the men and women in uniform that gave their lives for our freedom and our liberty—whether it was a policeman, fireman or soldier."[77] The designs are all depicted in red, yellow, black, and white paint—a nod to the racial diversity of the United States.[78]

While creating the piece, the carvers felt compelled to include a turtle into the carving but were unsure as to where this inspiration came from. When they arrived in DC and vested the poles into the care of the Piscataway community, they realized that the turtle is a Piscataway clan symbol. Appropriately, this animal also spoke to the poles' new home alongside the Anacostia River.[79]

Although the piece is distinctly Lummi in style, nearly fifty tribal nations across the United States had a hand in the poles' evolution.[80] James brought the piece to tribes in California, Oklahoma, Arizona, Oregon, New Mexico, Tennessee, North Carolina, and Pennsylvania to receive blessings.[81] To honor the poles, the Salt River Pima-Maricopa Indian Community conducted ceremonies that had not been held in half a century; in Tahlequah, Oklahoma, Cherokee community members and veterans prayed over the piece.[82] *Liberty*, *Freedom*, and *Sovereignty* arrived at its final destination, the District of Columbia, only after this 4,485-mile journey.[83]

The Pentagon welcomed the four-vehicle caravan transporting the poles on September 19, 2004.[84] In a ninety-minute ceremony, James and other Lummi representatives presented *Liberty*, *Freedom*, and *Sovereignty* to Secretary of the Interior Gale Norton and Deputy Secretary of Defense Paul Wolfowitz. Lisa Dolan, the wife of the late Navy captain Robert Dolan, received the totem poles as a representative for the families who had lost loved ones in the September 11, 2001, attack on the Pentagon.[85] The poles were originally planned to sit at the Pentagon near the Flight 77 crash site but due to security reasons were relocated to the Congressional Cemetery with plans for eventually incorporating them into the 9/11 Pentagon Memorial Grove on Kingman Island in the Anacostia River.[86] Raymond DuBois, director of Pentagon Administration and Management, described the piece as "a national treasure."[87]

Liberty, Freedom, and *Sovereignty* are the third and final pieces in a series by the House of Tears Carvers in commemoration of the September 11, 2001, attacks. The thirteen-foot *Healing* pole, the first in the series, honors those who lost their lives in the World Trade Center.[88] It was presented at the attack site to the victims' families and permanently erected in 2002 in the Sterling Forest, one hour north of Manhattan in New York.[89] The second in the series, the 2003 *Honoring* pole, pays tribute to the fourth hijacked plane, United Flight 93, and its crash site in Shanksville, Pennsylvania.[90] Together these Lummi totem poles "are a symbol of something that we all have within us. We have the power to heal, the power to love each other, the power to unite."[91] This proves an inspiring message in the US capital city, where the poles now rest in the hands of the Piscataway community and the carved turtle rests at home on the banks of the Anacostia.

Department of the Interior Murals

The US Department of the Interior (DOI) has a long and challenging history with Native communities. Housing the Bureau of Indian Affairs, the majority of federal actions affecting Indian Country originate here. In 1972 Native American activists occupied the bureau in peaceful protest as part of the Trail of Broken Treaties campaign (see chapter 3). Today the DOI welcomes hundreds of tribal leaders visiting DC each year and lends its space to critical meetings and tribal consultations. Built between 1935 and 1937, the prominent building is located less than half a mile from the White House South Lawn. It encompasses two entire city blocks between C and E, and 18th and 19th Streets NW.

Those visiting the DOI will notice the numerous murals throughout the building. Within its walls lies one of the largest collections of New Deal art, curated largely by Secretary of the Interior Harold L. Ickes (1933–46). Amid the Great Depression, President Hoover slashed the budget for the DOI's construction, but Ickes fought to have it reinstated, setting aside a reserve of costs exclusively to art. Today the DOI contains more Public Works Administration art than any other federal office.[92]

Along with this commitment to art came a newfound interest in representing the works of Native American artists. The brainchild of DC-based muralist Margaret Austin, the proposal to feature Native American art met with Ickes's approval in the early planning stages of the DOI's decoration, and Ickes quickly made this task a priority.[93] A planning committee dedicated to installing art in the DOI obtained pieces through a threefold process: first, the committee commissioned established artists; second, they solicited works through a public competition; and, third, the team incorporated Native American artists selected by a board of experts and with input from the Bureau of Indian Affairs.[94]

The board reserved 2,200 square feet exclusively for these Native American painters.[95] Together, selected muralists James Auchiah (Kiowa), Stephen Mopope (Kiowa), Allan Houser (Fort Sill Apache), Woodrow Wilson Crumbo (Potawatomi), Gerald Nailor (Navajo), and Velino Herrera (Zia Pueblo) depict scenes of life specific to their five tribal nations. Each artist received $2,000 for their works, a sum equivalent to what non-Native artists received. Despite the enthusiasm for Native American arts at the time, anti-Indian paternalism still ran deep, as evidenced by the fact that the payment was delivered in installments, due to the belief that the Indigenous artists would not be able to manage the large sum.[96]

As a result of Austin's vision and Ickes's leadership, the DOI features more than two dozen murals by six Native American artists. The tribal-specific pieces by Auchiah, Mopope, Houser, Crumbo, Nailor, and Herrera reflect some of the best New Deal Indian arts produced nationally and offer visual representations of the cultures, traditions, and people of the United States' first Americans. The oil paint murals were completed in the secco style and created using a process that established a sketch with punctuated outlines and then transferred the outline onto the plaster walls using the full-sized stencil.[97]

JAMES AUCHIAH

Kiowa artist James Auchiah, also known as Tse-Koy-Ate (1906–74), was born in Meers, Oklahoma.[98] He is the grandson of the noted nineteenth-century Kiowa chief Satanta, or White Bear.[99] Auchiah attended the government-run Raining Mountain Indian School before studying art under the instruction

FIGURE 4.4. *Harvest Dance*, by James Auchiah; Department of the Interior
Photographs in the Carol M. Highsmith Archive, Prints & Photographs Division, Library of
Congress, LC-DIG-highsm-24754.

of School of Art director Oscar B. Jacobson at the University of Oklahoma,
Norman in 1927.[100] The same year he began completing commissions for his
artwork.[101]

By the late 1920s Auchiah and a cohort of five of Jacobson's other students—Spencer Asah, Jack Hokeah, Stephen Mopope, Louise Smoky, Monroe Tsatoke—had developed international acclaim as the "Kiowa Six."[102] The
group originated as an art club at Saint Patrick's Mission School, where they
caught the attention of Jacobson.[103] Under his tutelage the Kiowa Six's work
displayed in such prominent shows as the American Federation of Arts con-
vention in 1927 and traveled nationally to Portland, Seattle, San Francisco,
Boston, Houston, Denver, Kansas City, Milwaukee, Memphis, Minneapolis,
and New York as well as abroad to Prague, Czechoslovakia, and Paris, France.[104]

At the peak of his career, Auchiah won a bid from the Treasury Section of
Fine Arts to complete a mural in Washington, DC.[105] Auchiah completed *Harvest Dance*, an eight-foot by fifty-foot lunette for the DOI in May 1939. *Harvest
Dance* features twenty nearly life-sized members of the Kiowa community—
children and adults, men and women—engaged in daily activities. On the far-
left side of the scene, a group of men in feathered bustles, porcupine roaches,
and bells dance to the music of two drummers who kneel on a hide. In the
center, men, women, and children gather around baskets full of fruit and a
stack of corn. This center portion is demarcated by a tree on either side and
set apart by the inclusion of tipis in the background. Bookending this image,
the right third of the mural depicts a woman roasting meat or tanning hide
over a fire, accompanied by a man ladling a warm liquid into his bowl. Art
and architecture historian David W. Look notes that the location of the mural
above doorways and its stylistic design of figures against a flat backdrop gives
the mural the effect of a frieze.[106] *Harvest Dance* remains on view in the basement cafeteria of the DOI.

In 1940 Auchiah returned to his native Oklahoma and turned his attention to arts instruction, taking a post at the Riverside Indian School in Anadarko. He then served in the Coast Guard during World War II.[107] Afterward Auchiah joined the US Army Artillery and Missile Center Post Engineer Department, Installations Section at Fort Sill as a civil painter until his retirement in 1967, whereupon he began work as a consultant and curator for the Fort Sill Museum.[108]

STEPHEN MOPOPE

Born in Anadarko, Oklahoma, in 1898, Stephen Mopope is also known by his Kiowa name, Wood-Coy or Qued Koi, which translates to "Painted Robe."[109] Beginning at age ten, Mopope attended a Catholic boarding school, St. Patrick's Indian Mission, on the Kiowa reservation.[110] He grew up around support for the arts and identified his great-uncle, another well-known Kiowa artist, Silver Horn, as his first fine arts instructor.[111] Mopope took an active role in Kiowa cultural and ceremonial life through art, such as when he joined his great-uncles in refurbishing and painting a Kiowa battle tipi in Redstone, Oklahoma, in 1916.[112] He later recalled this moment in his youth as a foundational moment that set the stage for the rest of his life.[113]

Like James Auchiah, Mopope operated as a member of the Kiowa Six. He received art training through programs organized by the Kiowa Agency and later joined the cohort at the University of Oklahoma, Norman, where he studied under Oscar B. Jacobson in the late 1920s.[114] Mopope was the eldest member of the cohort. Jacobson's writings reference Mopope's early artistic expressions as paintings and drawings "in the sand and on hides," describing his background as "the purest of Indian tradition."[115] He has since been identified as the most prolific artist of the group.[116]

Mopope's murals can be found in various locations in Oklahoma. In 1927 he completed his first commissioned mural for his alma mater, St. Patrick's Mission School.[117] Three years later, in 1930, Mopope partnered with another member of the Kiowa Six, Monroe Tsatoke, to install two murals in the University of Oklahoma auditorium. Shortly thereafter he secured another commission for a piece at the Southwestern State College library. In 1937, with support from the Public Works Administration, Mopope initiated a mural at the US Post Office in his hometown of Anadarko, Oklahoma, along with the backing of Kiowa Six members Auchiah and Asah.[118]

This impressive portfolio positioned Mopope for selection as one of the Native American partners brought in to paint for the DOI. In 1939 he secured

FIGURE 4.5. *Ceremonial Dance (Indian Theme)*, by Stephen Mopope; Department of the Interior
Photographs in the Carol M. Highsmith Archive, Prints & Photographs Division, Library of Congress, LC-DIG-highsm- 24753.

the recommendation of the Treasury Department Section of Fine Arts for this New Deal project.[119] His piece, *Ceremonial Dance (Indian Theme)*, is signed and dated November 18, 1939.

Ceremonial Dance sits on the eastern wall of the DOI's basement cafeteria, just opposite Auchiah's *Harvest Dance*. A number of parallels exist between the two pieces, with Mopope's work also taking on the style of a frieze.[120] The six-foot by fifty-foot oil-on-rough plaster painting portrays fifteen Kiowa figures engaged in ceremony. In the middle, a man seated on a blanket and with his back to the viewer raises his arms above his head, holding a pipe. The image of a buffalo head covers his back, gazing at the onlooker. On either side of the seated figure are fires, followed by a row of six dancers. These men and women, dressed in traditional regalia and donning feathers, face inward toward the central figure. Bringing up the end of the rows of dancers are two seated drummers; their open mouths indicate singing. Outside of this scene the artist added three smaller images on separate panels located below the lunette. These panels are set back in space from the main painting, providing a sense of framing. The central secondary image is a replica of the buffalo head from the seated man's back; the positioning of this image lines up underneath that main figure on a column supporting the wall of the main image. Below each row of dancers are the two additional images, which depict shields with crossed spears behind them. These two shield pieces are set back even further than the buffalo head, on the wall behind that of the frieze.

ALLAN HOUSER

Allan Capron Haozous ("Houser"), of the Fort Sill Apache Tribe in Oklahoma, was born on June 30, 1914, to two Chiricahua Apache parents in Apache, Oklahoma.[121] Having pursued other interests earlier in life, Houser turned his attention to art at age twenty by following up on an advertisement for the

Santa Fe Indian School's Painting School. In 1934 he was accepted to attend this institution, also known as the Studio School.[122] "The more I learned [about my tribal customs]," the artist reflected, "the more I wanted to put it down on canvas."[123] It was during his four-year tenure at the school when the artist adopted the last name "Houser" at the urging of the administration.[124]

Houser opened his first solo exhibit—a feature on watercolor painting hosted by the Museum of New Mexico—one year before his graduation, in 1937. He then went out to showcase his works in Chicago, New York, and San Francisco.[125] The Treasury Section of Fine Arts coordinated Houser's study of murals under acclaimed Swedish artist Olle Nordmark in advance of his commissions with the DOI.[126] Houser installed a total of five murals throughout the DOI in the two-year period between 1938 and 1940.

Buffalo Hunt (1938) and *Breaking Camp at Wartime* (1938) are both painted on the northern wall of the DOI's first-floor Indian Arts and Crafts Shop.[127] *Buffalo Hunt* features two Apache men on horseback in pursuit of a pair of buffalo, bows and arrows at the ready. All figures appear nearly suspended in space, with minimal foliage in the foreground. In *Breaking Camp at Wartime*, a Native couple also rides horseback. The man carries a rifle and leads the family, his wife following behind on a second horse and carrying a baby in a cradleboard. A packed donkey brings up the tail of the miniature caravan.

Next Houser painted his *Apache Scenes* trio as part of the 1939 DOI commissions along with the other five Native American artists.[128] This set of paintings is located on the northern and western walls of the eighth-floor penthouse.[129] *Singing Love Songs*, on the north wall, is an ode to Apache courting and love. Houser described the inspiration for the piece:

> In the early days of the tribe when a boy was interested in a certain girl he would watch for the girl leaving camp, and at the first chance he would saddle up his pony and follow. The songs were very similar to those of the whites telling how beautiful she is, or something nice. The design shows two couples, one boy sings love songs to a maiden who you notice is quite bashful, while her riding partner and little sister are teasing.[130]

The mural is spatially divided in the middle by a doorway, with two women and a girl on the left side, and two men on the right. The figures all face the center doorway, which emphasizes the space between the lovers.

On the adjacent west wall *Apache Round Dance* displays five Apache women in a line, shoulder to shoulder, one of whom carries a child on her back. Balance

FIGURE 4.6. *Singing Love Songs*, by Allan Houser; Department of the Interior Photographs in the Carol M. Highsmith Archive, Prints & Photographs Division, Library of Congress, LC-DIG-highsm-18476.

and symmetry define this mural: the women are all wrapped in shawls, wear cool-toned prairie dresses, and don yellow high-top moccasins. While their black hair and bangs blow freely in various directions and the women gaze about, their feet remain unified in measured sidestep. Three baskets of Indian bread and boiled beef sit before the dancers, which Houser noted serve as a base for the lunch that traditionally followed the depicted late-night dancing. Three-pronged plants frame the bottom corners of the image. In the words of the artist, the mural is an homage to the role of women in the Round Dance.[131]

The final component of the Apache Scenes Trio, *Sacred Fire Dance*, shows three rows of four men, each engaged in a sacred dance used for ceremonial purposes. Only the column of men on the far-right side face left into the group while the others look back at them. Three of the figures play Apache water drums, and many appear to be singing. The group is dressed in modern clothing, primarily trousers and button-up shirts, and all wear long hair. Houser conveys the high energy of the dance through the figures' smiles, bent knees, and engaged arms.[132]

After experiencing great success in painting, Houser began studying sculpture under Olle Nordmark back in his home state of Oklahoma. This interest in a new medium continued to grow after relocating to California, where he became involved in the Pasadena Art Center, and then blossomed into full force in 1948, when the Haskell Institute of Lawrence, Kansas, commissioned one of his modernist sculptures. Houser enjoyed a successful career as a Guggenheim Fellow, artist-in-residence at the Intermountain Indian School in Utah, and faculty at the Institute of American Indian Arts, where he established a sculpture department. At sixty-one, he rededicated his career to sculpting full time.[133]

Houser was the first Native American to receive the National Medal of Arts, an award bestowed upon him in 1992.[134] He is also the recipient of the French government's Ordre des Palmes académiques (1954) and the Waite Phillips Trophy for Outstanding Contributions to American Indian Art (1969). In 1975 Secretary of the Interior Stewart L. Udall commissioned Houser to paint his official portrait.[135]

WOODROW WILSON CRUMBO

Woodrow Wilson Crumbo, more commonly known as "Woody," was born near Lexington, Oklahoma, in 1912.[136] Potawatomi by birth, Crumbo grew up around a variety of tribal cultures after his parents passed on by the time he was seven years old. This exposure led to the development of his talent not only as a painter but also as a dancer and wood flute player.[137]

Crumbo graduated from the government-run Chilocco Indian boarding school in 1930. From there he enrolled in the American Indian Institute of Wichita, Kansas—the first Native American college preparatory school in the nation, founded by Yale graduate and federal Indian policy advocate Henry Roe Cloud (Ho-Chunk)—in 1934.[138] Here the emerging artist thrived. He earned a scholarship to support his study and graduated valedictorian. After completing this program Crumbo continued his educational journey by attending Wichita University from 1933 to 1936, where he, like Allan Houser, studied painting under Olle Nordmark.[139]

The University of Oklahoma at Norman played a transformative role in Woody Crumbo's life. From 1936 through 1938, Crumbo received instruction here from the noted Oscar B. Jacobson, mentor of the Kiowa Six.[140] Also while at the University of Oklahoma, Crumbo received his first taste of teaching by leading the institution's first silversmithing class.[141] This experience foreshadowed future career endeavors. In 1938 Crumbo installed a commissioned

FIGURE 4.7. *Buffalo Hunt*, by Woodrow Crumbo; Department of the Interior Photographs in the Carol M. Highsmith Archive, Prints & Photographs Division, Library of Congress, LC-DIG-highsm- 18480.

mural for the university and a year later, under Nordmark's guidance and in collaboration with James Auchiah, Stephen Mopope, Allan Houser, and other Native artists, completed a mural at the Fort Sill Indian School.[142]

Interior Secretary Ickes personally advocated for Crumbo's involvement in the DOI's 1939 Native artist commissions.[143] Crumbo's paintings, completed in 1940, include six murals: *Buffalo Hunt, Deer, Courting, Flute Player, Peyote Bird,* and *Wild Horses.* All can be viewed in the DOI's eighth-floor South Penthouse, formerly the employee lounge.

Buffalo Hunt is a five-foot by eleven-foot installation located on the eastern wall of the room. The scene depicts two men engaged in hunting a herd of five stampeding buffalo. One of the hunters brings up the back of the pack on his horse, his bow and arrow drawn and eyes focused on making the shot. The other hunter appears to have leapt off his horse and onto the back of one of the animals, where he drives a knife into its back and draws blood. This mural delivers a strong sense of plains Indian life through the flat landscape punctuated by small rocks, patches of wild grasses, and a dried buffalo skull under one of the shrubs.

Deer and *Courting* are located at the corner of the eastern and southern walls. A serene image of a doe and her fawn, *Deer* is a celebration of the natural world. Framed by a bright yellow sun, the doe looks down at her fawn, who meets eyes with its mother. The two creatures stand at the edge of a pond, where water lilies and other flowers blossom. The scene is framed by a symmetrical background of two brightly colored birds in the upper corners, who appear to be flying down to join the deer, as well as by geometric designs outlining the sky.

Only a few inches away from *Deer* on an adjacent wall, *Courting* shows a face-to-face couple looking longingly into each other's eyes. The two are dressed in traditional attire that includes buckskin, moccasins, and face paint, and they are shielded in part by a geometrically decorated hide. As the man wraps the hide behind his back, he appears to beckon the woman inside the wrap with him. Their modest smiles lend this mural a very happy tone.

Crumbo painted *Flute Player* and *Peyote Bird*, opposite these two pieces, on the corner of the southern and western walls of the penthouse. *Flute Player* is a portrait of a musician playing a traditional Native American wood flute. Crumbo himself also played this instrument. Wrapped in what appears to be a buffalo hide robe, only the musicians' hands, holding the flute, and head are visible to the onlooker. A brilliant yellow sun outlined in orange frames the figure's head, much like a nimbus or halo does around depictions of holy figures. Tall grasses grow high above the stature of the man.

Of all the murals in Crumbo's DOI installation, *Peyote Bird* stands apart as the only piece that does not depict a life scene. Rather, this painting is purely design-based and symbolic. *Peyote Bird* is a symmetrical and geographic representation of this Native American spiritual creature. In Crumbo's rendition, the bird takes on brown, orange, green, and blue hues. Two peyote fans are located on either side of the bird, under its wings. The bird also appears above a spotted peyote button at the bottom center of the mural. The peyote bird, also known sometimes as the water bird or thunderbird, is the symbol of the Native American Church and also holds deep significance to followers of traditional Indigenous spiritual ways.

The final piece in Crumbo's series, *Wild Horses*, is located on the western wall of the eighth-floor DOI penthouse. This piece shares many similarities with *Buffalo Hunt*, such as Crumbo's iconic sparse plains landscape as the setting to an action sequence. In *Buffalo Hunt* a single figure chases a group of beautiful tan and brown horses, attempting to capture them with a blanket. Crumbo conveys the high speed of this venture by showing the blanket held high above the man's head, as well as the man's clothing and the horses' tails, all horizontal. The scene incorporates the tall grasses also found in *Flute Player* and *Courting*.

After completing this work for the DOI, Crumbo went on to enjoy a successful career in the Indian arts. He joined Bacone College as the director of art from 1938 to 1941, and again from 1943 through 1945.[144] One of his successes during this tenure included the design and construction of a thirteen-foot stained-glass window in the college's Rose Chapel, a creation that stands out for its peyote bird motifs within a church and that is distinguished as one of the very few Native American religious stained-glass windows in the world.[145]

From 1945 to 1948 Crumbo worked with art collector and philanthropist Thomas Gilcrease to curate an American Indian art collection and served as artist-in-residence at the Gilcrease Museum in Tulsa.[146] After leaving the museum, the artist relocated from Oklahoma to Taos, New Mexico, for more than a decade before settling in Texas.[147] Crumbo joined the El Paso Museum of Art first as a curator and later as the director, working there between 1960 and 1974.[148] In 1974 he once again returned to Oklahoma as a partner in his tribe's establishment of the Citizen Potawatomi Nation Cultural Heritage Center in Shawnee, Oklahoma.[149] Crumbo was inducted into the Oklahoma Hall of Fame in 1978.[150]

GERALD NAILOR

Navajo artist Gerald Nailor was born in 1917 in Pinedale, New Mexico, and raised on the Navajo Nation reservation.[151] He attended the Albuquerque Indian School from 1930 to 1934, the Phoenix Indian School, and then the Santa Fe Indian School from 1936 to 1937.[152] Here Nailor adopted the Santa Fe Studio Style of painting, characterized by a minimal background, blocked color without shading, highly stylized scenes, and pronounced subject outlines.[153] He became involved in the DOI project through the recommendation of his Santa Fe Indian School teacher Dorothy Dunn and the sponsorship of the Sector of Fine Arts.[154]

Once selected for the gig, Nailor proposed to paint a mural of Navajo weavers engaging tourists in a sale of traditional weavings. The review board, however, denied this submission.[155] Art historian Jennifer McLerran posits that these oversight boards forbid artistic representations of interaction between Native peoples and non-Natives.[156] In the case of Nailor, this instance illustrates how art produced by Native artists for New Deal projects was confined by parameters that "glossed over historically complex interactions and relations of power between native and nonnative peoples, erasing traces of the colonial encounter."[157]

Nailor completed murals for the DOI in both the Indian Arts and Crafts Shop and in the South Penthouse. On the first floor *Deer Stalking* shares space in the Indian Arts and Crafts Shop along with Houser's works and is located on the shop's southern wall. The artist painted *Deer Stalking* in 1938, the first of his DOI murals.[158] The piece depicts three Navajo men sneaking up on an unsuspecting deer. While two of the men take cover behind a bush, the other reins in the horses. The crouching men appear to have just discovered their target, as indicated by one pointing at the animal and the other signaling to hush the group with an outstretched arm. The hunters are prepared with bows and arrows, although they are not yet drawn. An onlooking bird flies overhead, observing the scene.

Two years later Nailor finished his three-part Navajo Scenes upstairs in the eighth-floor penthouse. The 1940 Navajo Scenes series is made up of three pieces: *Preparing Yarn for Weaving, The Hunting Ground*, and *Initiation Ceremony*. In *Preparing Yarn for Weaving*, the artist showcases the traditional methods of carding, spinning, and winding wool.[159] The three women—all dressed in long skirts, turquoise jewelry, Navajo-style moccasins, traditional buns, and white face paint—work together in this endeavor. A loom and partially finished geometric weaving provide a unique element to the mural by breaking from the flat presentation of figures and lack of shading. This piece honors weaving as a strong element of Navajo culture.

The Hunting Ground is the largest of the trio. In this piece Nailor makes use of a wall with a doorway and incorporates the negative space into the design of the painting. The left side of the scene depicts two Navajo men observing a wildlife oasis. The men are characterized by their traditional Navajo hair bun and typical Navajo-style moccasins. While one points toward the animals from horseback, the other crouches low to the ground, holding a bow in one hand and raising an eagle feather fan in the other. Above the human subjects, on the upper left corner, Nailor painted a Navajo sun and cloud symbol.[160] A pair of animals—either skunks or squirrels—appear to the right of the men. One raises his nose and appears to sniff the light switch on the wall, a choice by the artist that McLerran reads as a humorous jab at federal Indian policy and government oversight of Native communities.[161] Further engaging the wall canvas, the artist painted a pair of antelope standing in the narrow space above the doorway in order to connect the two portions of the mural. Between them, a ceremonial plant and bird serve as the mural's central, pivot point.[162] Each antelope peers down to either side of the doorway and locks eyes with the animals below. On the far right a pair of deer, a bison, and a calf lounge and graze. The piece is further united by symmetrical grasses stemming out of the inner corners of the walls and by the red and blue stripes lining the bottom of the frame.

FIGURE 4.8. *Initiation Ceremony*, by Gerald Nailor; Department of the Interior Photographs in the Carol M. Highsmith Archive, Prints & Photographs Division, Library of Congress, LC-DIG-highsm- 18479.

Finally, *Initiation Ceremony* takes up the spiritual elements of Navajo life as its subject matter. Here Nailor depicts two ceremonial leaders engaging a woman with two children. The two spiritual figures wear feather head-dresses and white buckskin masks, extend their arms outward toward the children, and hold yucca branches. While the smaller of the two children clings to the woman's leg, the older child observes the spiritual figures with finger in mouth, still unsure of what to make of their presence. This scene reflects the Navajos' traditional nine-day Yei Bi Chei ceremony and winter dances.[163]

In 1943 Nailor completed an eight-panel mural of Navajo society for the Navajo Nation Council chambers in Window Rock, Arizona.[164] This piece is one of his most masterful, and it advanced the political cause for the Indian New Deal federal policy under Commissioner of Indian Affairs John Collier.[165] One year later, Nailor installed a mural at the Mesa Verde National Park post office in Colorado.[166] Nailor passed on at the tragically young age of thirty-five, succumbing to injuries sustained in a fight with his sister's abusive husband.

VELINO HERRERA

Also known by his Pueblo name, Ma Pe Wi, artist Velino Shije Herrera was born at Zia Pueblo in 1902.[167] Herrera started painting as a self-taught artist at the Santa Fe Indian School between 1917 and 1922.[168] Although also a rancher, Herrera made his career in art by opening his own studio in 1932, painting at the School of American Research in Santa Fe, and serving as faculty at the Albuquerque Indian School in 1936.[169]

Herrera came to the DOI initiative at the recommendation of the Section of Fine Arts. He was originally slated to paint in the cafeteria, but Secretary Ickes later assigned Auchiah to this space.[170] Herrera ultimately installed eight murals in the eighth-floor DOI penthouse as part of his Pueblo Life series.

On the eastern wall of the penthouse, *Buffalo Chase* and *Buffalo Dance* speak to the importance of buffalo to the cultural practices and lifeways of the Pueblo people. *Buffalo Dance* commemorates the ceremonial celebration of the same name that signals the completion of a buffalo hunt.[171] In this piece a row of four drummers provides the music for six buffalo, deer, and antelope dancers. The dancers appear in the traditional Pueblo regalia for the dance styles, including donning buffalo headdresses, body paint, and horned headpieces. Although the figures appear against a blank background, Herrera conveys a high-energy scene through the use of space and perspective. Today Buffalo Dances are held each winter. *Buffalo Chase* appears to the right of *Buffalo Dance*, separated by a doorway. In this piece the artist showcases three hunters tracking a buffalo herd. Two buffalo face the onlooker head-on, along with one hunter who has just released an arrow from atop his horse. Farther right a second hunter armed with a spear pursues another faction of the herd, all shown in profile. This scene appears separate from a final huntsman depicted on the far side of a second doorway. He appears to look over at the others while his horse rears.

On the opposite wall Herrera painted *Pueblo Woman and Child*, *Women Making Pottery*, *Pueblo Girls Carrying Water*, and *Pueblo Corn Dance*. *Pueblo Girls Carrying Water* depicts three women proceeding forward in line, all transporting pottery on their heads. Only the woman in the middle uses her hand to

FIGURE 4.9. *Buffalo Chase*, by Velino Herrera; Department of the Interior
Photographs in the Carol M. Highsmith Archive, Prints & Photographs Division, Library of
Congress, LC-DIG-highsm- 18473.

steady the object; the other two masterfully balance the pot atop their heads.
As in *Women Making Pottery*, Herrera details the pottery with the highly recognizable Zia bird on the frontmost figure. A minimal landscape design of two
small flowers frames the diagonal procession.

    Women Making Pottery depicts three Pueblo women at work in making
pottery. The women all feature traditional Pueblo hairstyles and dresses with
moccasins and shawls. This painting shows the pottery at various stages of
completion: some are being shaped and smoothed by the women, others await
decoration, and five pieces in the foreground of the mural demonstrate the

beauty and intricacy of finished Pueblo pottery. One pot, for instance, features the Zia bird commonly found in pottery produced by this pueblo, and they all include the standard color combination of black, white, and clay.

In *Pueblo Woman and Child* Herrera painted a traditionally dressed Pueblo mother walking with her baby wrapped to her back. As the woman looks ahead in portrait, the child tilts their head at an angle toward the viewer. This is by far the simplest piece on the western wall, featuring no scenic embellishment, landscape features, or framing. The figures occupy a space only as large as one side of a column, making this piece also the smallest of his murals.

Herrera makes use of these same columns as the canvas for *Pueblo Corn Dance*. Although this installation was originally designed as one continuous, long mural along the back wall, the piece was not completed as planned. Rather, four figures from the original composition were excerpted from the scene and pained as individuals on the various sides of two columns. On the side adjacent to *Pueblo Woman and Child*, Herrera painted one male dancer in action, viewed from head-on. He also incorporated a solitary, traditionally dressed drummer on another column a few feet away and two other dancers at additional locations. When the DOI renovated this area, the figures were all painted over.[172]

Finally, Herrera installed two highly stylized, design-centric murals. The *Eagle Dance Design* appears on the northern wall. In this piece, the artist portrays an eagle dancer with his head down and face obscured, arms forming a circle around his body, raised up on his toes with knees bent into a squat. The piece is perfectly symmetrical and emphasizes the dancer's intricate regalia, which includes feathered wings attached to the dancer's arms. The figure appears alongside a geometric background design with symbols. The *Shield Design* also appears on the north wall, nearby. Here Herrera pays homage to corn.[173] The piece depicts many symbols—corn, squash blossoms, stars, eagle feathers, crescent moons, footprints, handprints, a snake figure—and is organized around the shield as the central figure of the work.

Outside of his work for the DOI, Herrera enjoyed a successful career in art. One of his main achievements included the painting replication of kiva drawings discovered at the Kuaua archaeological site in New Mexico.[174] There is some controversy surrounding Herrera's use of sacred symbols throughout his career, such as when he granted the New Mexican government permission to use the Zia sun in the state logo that can now be found commonly around the state.[175] Nevertheless, Herrera remains widely celebrated for his commissions for the Koshare Kiva museum at La Junta, Colorado; Boy Scouts of America;

and the Albuquerque Indian School. In 1954, Herrera received the Ordres des Palmes académiques from the government of France.[176]

Arts in the Interior, Expanded

At the DOI, the works of Auchiah, Mopope, Houser, Crumbo, Nailor, and Herrera stand out as highlights the building's multitude of artistic offerings. In fact, on May 5, 1940, three years after the DOI's opening, the *Washington Post* featured the new building in a photographic essay and showcased both the artists and their works.[177] In one snapshot Mopope and two other Native men are dressed in their traditional regalia and appear to be describing a hand drum to Secretary of the Interior Ickes.[178] Another image captures three Native women enjoying coffee in the employee's lounge, with Velino Herrera's *Buffalo Dance* ornately decorating the background.[179] A full image of *Buffalo Dance*, along with Herrera's *Buffalo Chase* and Woodrow Wilson Crumbo's *Wild Horses*, also appears as part of the photographic banner under the headline, "Indian Murals in Interior Building Are among Finest in Washington."[180]

However, the DOI has consistently demonstrated its commitment to Native arts and artists through a variety of venues beyond these murals. One such example of this work is the Indian Arts and Crafts Shop, located on the first floor of the DOI. This shop promotes Indigenous artists from across the country and remains one of the only outlets for the purchase of authentic Native American pottery, jewelry, fine arts, music, and more in the District. Interestingly, the Indian Arts and Crafts Shop appears in the original DOI architectural designs at the request of Secretary Ickes himself.[181] It has been operational since the DOI's opening and remains open to the public.

Another instance of commitment in the Native American arts is evident in the functions of the DOI's seventh-floor Art Gallery. World War II necessitated the closure of this space in order to make room for document storage related to war efforts, and it remained shuttered for more than two decades. On May 11, 1964, the Art Gallery finally reopened and showcased its first exhibit, *Schools of Contemporary American Indian Art*. This installation highlighted pieces from the Denman Collection of Contemporary Indian Paintings at the Museum of Modern Art. With this show occupying the Center Gallery, the West Gallery simultaneously exhibited works from Native American students at the Institute of American Indian Arts.[182]

Finally, dozens of the DOI's artworks created by non-Native artists feature themes and tributes to Indigenous life. Among the most notable are two pieces that explore "themes of the Bureau of Indian Affairs," *Indian and Soldier* (1939) and *Indian and Teacher* (1939) by Maynard Dixon (1875–1946). These images depict the conflicting ideological clashes between Native peoples and white settlers as part of western expansion.[183] Taking up a different medium, Mary Ogden Abbott's (1894–1981) *Western Gates*, also known as *Indian Gates*, pays respect to Plains Indians cultures.[184] In these two wood-carved teak doors, the artist showcases one Native man in a buffalo headdress and holding a gourd rattle, and another in an eagle feather headdress with an eagle staff, a shield decorated with a picture of a deer, and a bear claw necklace.

As the headquarters of the Bureau of Indian Affairs, these features, pieces, and histories imbue this federal work building with poignant reminders of the government's obligations to Indigenous peoples. Today the DOI murals by Velino Herrera, Allan Houser, Gerald Nailor, James Auchiah, Woody Crumbo, and Stephen Mopope offer evidence of the long history between tribal nations and the United States and speak to the ways in which Washington has been at the center of many of those relationships. Reid's nearby sculpture, *The Spirit of Haida Gwaii: The Black Canoe*, installed at another government building, offers an international angle from which to further understand the role of settler nation-states in relation to contemporary Indigenous struggles. The story behind the creation of the *Liberty*, *Freedom*, and *Sovereignty* totem poles—much more extensive than the carving elements alone—eloquently combine Lummi specificity with national Indigenous influence and local Piscataway culture. Finally, across the city, the more recently installed *Imprinting Dimensional States of Being* pays homage to the Piscataway, upon whose lands these pieces all remain today. Together these artistic creations and their makers confront what Kevin Bruyneel has termed "settler memory"—the "rendering [of] Indigenous peoples and settler colonialism [as] invisible or barely visible as active contemporary forces"— by relaying Indigenous stories, telling Indigenous truths, and testifying to an ongoing Indigenous presence in the city.[185] Perhaps nowhere is this work more essential than on the national stage in Washington, DC.

NOTES

1. Margot Dynes, "New Mural Honors Local Native American Group in the Flagg Building," *GW Hatchet*, November 15, 2018, https://www.gwhatchet.com/2018/11/15/new-mural-honors-local-native-american-group-in-the-flagg-building/.

2. "Our Wall," Mobilize Walls, accessed August 19, 2020, https://www.mobilizewalls.com/.

3. Aseeli Coleman, "The Ground Floor of the Corcoran Gets a Historically Significant Addition," *GW Hatchet*, September 23, 2019, https://corcoran.gwu.edu/ground-floor -corcoran-gets-historically-significant-addition.

4. "Our Wall."

5. Dynes, "New Mural Honors."

6. "Our Wall."

7. Dynes, "New Mural Honors."

8. Joerael Numina, *Imprinting Dimensional States of Being*, 2019, https:// spark.adobe.com/page/X3wfjMF36zlm8/?fbclid=IwAR15UQcUsvgnItA6YJlum -wEtQmTkJo3FocFqWsq-ksyuqlGEWeuSUiLcpY.

9. Numina.

10. Coleman, "The Ground Floor of the Corcoran."

11. Numina, *Imprinting Dimensional States of Being*.

12. Joerael Numina, personal communication with author, July 2, 2020.

13. "Culture," Piscataway Conoy Tribe, accessed August 21, 2020, http://www .piscatawayconoytribe.com/history.html; and Associated Press, "Md. Formally Recognizes 2 American Indian Groups," *Deseret News*, January 9, 2012, https://www.deseret.com/2012 /1/9/20243213/md-formally-recognizes-2-american-indian-groups.

14. Numina, *Imprinting Dimensional States of Being*.

15. Numina.

16. Numina.

17. Numina.

18. Numina.

19. Numina.

20. Numina.

21. "The American Mission: Maryland Jesuits from Andrew White to John Carroll," Georgetown University Library, accessed August 13, 2020, https://www.library .georgetown.edu/exhibition/american-mission-maryland-jesuits-andrew-white-john -carroll.

22. Numina, *Imprinting Dimensional States of Being*.

23. Numina.

24. Numina.

25. Numina.

26. Numina.

27. "Dedication Ceremony for Imprinting States of Being: A Mural by Joerael Numina," George Washington University Calendar, accessed August 9, 2020, https://calendar.gwu .edu/dedication-ceremony-imprinting-states-being-mural-joerael-numina.

28. Coleman, "The Ground Floor of the Corcoran."

29. Numina, *Imprinting Dimensional States of Being*.

30. Karen Duffek and Charlotte Townsend-Gault, *Bill Reid and Beyond: Expanding on Modern Native Art* (Vancouver, B.C.: Douglas & McIntyre, 2005), 100.

31. "Who Was Bill Reid?," Bill Reid Gallery of Northwest Coast Art, accessed August 10, 2020, https://www.billreidgallery.ca/pages/about-bill-reid#:~:text=Bill%20Reid%20(1920 %2D1998),at%20the%20age%20of%2023.

32. "About Bill Reid," Bill Reid Foundation, accessed August 10, 2020, http://www .billreidfoundation.ca/bill_reid.htm.

33. "Who Was Bill Reid?"

34. "Who Was Bill Reid?"

35. "Who Was Bill Reid?"; and Anne Cross, *Raven and the First Men: From Conception to Completion* (Vancouver: University of British Columbia Museum of Anthropology, 1990), 12.

36. "Chief of the Undersea World," Simon Fraser University: The Bill Reid Center, accessed August 10, 2020, https://www.sfu.ca/brc/online_exhibits/bill-reid-carves-a -whale.html#:~:text=Bill%20Reid%20holds%20the%20boxwood,Chief%20of%20the %20Undersea%20World; and "Mythic Messengers," Bill Reid Foundation, accessed August 10, 2020, http://www.billreidfoundation.ca/banknote/mythic.htm.

37. Carlito Pablo, "Black Eagle Canoe of Legendary Artist Bill Reid Marks End of Its Journey at SFU," *Georgia Straight*, October 22, 2015, https://www.straight.com/arts /562696/black-eagle-canoe-legendary-artist-bill-reid-marks-end-its-journey-sfu.

38. Duffek and Townsend-Gault, *Bill Reid and Beyond*, 98.

39. Joel Martineau, "Autoethnography and Material Culture: The Case of Bill Reid," *Biography* 24, no. 1 (Winter 2001): 249, 251.

40. Duffek and Townsend-Gault, *Bill Reid and Beyond*, 100.

41. Martineau, "Autoethnography and Material Culture," 250.

42. Duffek and Townsend-Gault, *Bill Reid and Beyond*, 99.

43. Martineau, "Autoethnography and Material Culture," 251.

44. Martineau, 251.

45. Duffek and Townsend-Gault, *Bill Reid and Beyond*, 99.

46. Duffek and Townsend-Gault, 35, 99.

47. Martineau, "Autoethnography and Material Culture," 252.

48. Duffek and Townsend-Gault, *Bill Reid and Beyond*, 99; and Martineau, "Autoethnography and Material Culture," 249.

49. Duffek and Townsend-Gault, *Bill Reid and Beyond*, 98.

50. Duffek and Townsend-Gault, 99.

51. Bill Reid, "The Spirit of Haida Gwaii," in *Solitary Raven: The Essential Writings of Bill Reid*, ed. Robert Bringhurst (Seattle: University of Washington Press, 2000), 228.

52. Martineau, "Autoethnography and Material Culture," 252.

53. "The Dogfish Woman (Qqaaxhadajaat)," Simon Fraser University: The Bill Reid Center, accessed August 10, 2020, https://www.sfu.ca/brc/imeshMobileApp/imesh-art -walk-/dog-fish-woman.html.

54. "Grand Hall Tour," Canadian Museum of History, accessed August 12, 2020, https://www.historymuseum.ca/cmc/exhibitions/aborig/grand/gh04eng.html.

55. Martineau, "Autoethnography and Material Culture," 254.

56. Martineau, 253.

57. Martineau, 253.

58. "Bill Reid," Inuit Gallery of Vancouver, accessed August 13, 2020, https://inuit.com /collections/vendors?q=Bill+Reid&page=2.

59. "Biographical Notes," Canadian Museum of History, accessed August 12, 2020, https://www.historymuseum.ca/cmc/exhibitions/aborig/reid/reid06e.html#:~:text =During%20his%20career%2C%20he%20received,and%20the%20University%20of %20Toronto.

60. "Bill Reid."

61. "Bill Reid's Art Graces the $20 Banknote," Bill Reid Foundation, accessed August 10, 2020, http://billreidfoundation.ca/banknote/index.htm.

62. Duffek and Townsend-Gault, *Bill Reid and Beyond*, 98.

63. Martineau, "Autoethnography and Material Culture," 249.

64. Duffek and Townsend-Gault, *Bill Reid and Beyond*, 100.

65. "Secretary Norton Accepts Liberty and Freedom Totem Poles from Lummi Nation," US Department of the Interior: Department of the Secretary, September 20, 2004, https://www.doi.gov/sites/doi.gov/files/archive/news/archive/04_News_Releases /040920a.htm.

66. Posted sign, September 11 Healing Poles, Washington, DC.

67. Will Chavez, "Memorial Totem Poles Visit Tahlequah," *Cherokee Phoenix*, September 30, 2004, https://www.cherokeephoenix.org/Article/index/668.

68. Chavez.

69. "Secretary Norton Accepts Liberty and Freedom."

70. Chavez, "Memorial Totem Poles Visit Tahlequah."

71. Chavez; and Jennifer Lash, "Healing Poles Arrive in D.C.," *Roll Call*, September 21, 2004, https://www.rollcall.com/2004/09/21/healing-poles-arrive-in-d-c/.

72. Lash, "Healing Poles Arrive in D.C."

73. Posted sign, September 11 Healing Poles, Washington, DC.

74. Lash, "Healing Poles Arrive in D.C."

75. Posted sign, September 11 Healing Poles, Washington, DC.

76. Lash, "Healing Poles Arrive in D.C."

77. Rudi Williams, "Pentagon Presented 9/11 'Healing Poles,'" US Department of Defense, September 20, 2004, https://archive.defense.gov/news/newsarticle.aspx?id= 25256.

78. Posted sign, September 11 Healing Poles, Washington, DC.

79. Posted sign, September 11 Healing Poles, Washington, DC.

80. Williams, "Pentagon Presented 9/11 'Healing Poles.'"

81. Lash, "Healing Poles Arrive in D.C."

82. Chavez, "Memorial Totem Poles Visit Tahlequah."

83. Lash, "Healing Poles Arrive in D.C."

84. Chavez, "Memorial Totem Poles Visit Tahlequah."

85. "Lummi Healing Poles Presented to the Pentagon."

86. Lash, "Healing Poles Arrive in D.C."

87. Williams, "Pentagon Presented 9/11 'Healing Poles.'"

88. Lash, "Healing Poles Arrive in D.C."

89. Williams, "Pentagon Presented 9/11 'Healing Poles.'"

90. Chavez, "Memorial totem poles visit Tahlequah"; and Gregory P. Fields, Introduction to *A Totem Pole History: The Work of Lummi Carver Joe Hillaire*, Pauline Hillaire (Lincoln: University of Nebraska Press, 2013), xxxiii.

91. Williams, "Pentagon Presented 9/11 'Healing Poles.'"

92. David W. Look and Carole L. Perrault, *The Interior Building: Its Architecture and Its Art* (Washington, DC, U.S. Department of the Interior, National Park Service, Preservation Assistance Division, 1986), 16.

93. Look and Perrault, 16.

94. Look and Perrault, 111.

95. Look and Perrault, 111.

96. Jennifer McLerran, *A New Deal for Native Art: Indian Arts and Federal Policy, 1933–1943* (Tucson: University of Arizona Press, 2009), 176.

97. Look and Perrault, *The Interior Building*, 112.

98. Look and Perrault, 114.

99. J'Nell Pate, "Kiowa Art from Rainy Mountain: The Story of James Auchiah," *American Indian Quarterly* 1, no. 3 (1974): 193.

100. Pate, 196–97.

101. Look and Perrault, *The Interior Building*, 114.

102. Pate, "Kiowa Art from Rainy Mountain," 197.

103. McLerran, *A New Deal for Native Art*, 162.

104. Pate, "Kiowa Art from Rainy Mountain," 197.

105. Pate, "Kiowa Art from Rainy Mountain," 198; and Look and Perrault, *The Interior Building*, 115.

106. Look and Perrault, *The Interior Building*, 115.

107. Pate, "Kiowa Art from Rainy Mountain," 198.

108. Pate, 199.

109. Look and Perrault, *The Interior Building*, 116; and Mary Jo Watson, "Mopope, Steven (1898–1974)," Oklahoma Historical Society, accessed August 28, 2020, https://www.okhistory.org/publications/enc/entry.php?entry=MO017.

110. Gunlög Maria Fur, *Painting Culture, Painting Nature: Stephen Mopope, Oscar Jacobson, and the Development of Indian Art in Oklahoma* (Norman: University of Oklahoma Press, 2019), 108.

111. Steven L. Grafe, *American Indian Painting: Twentieth-Century Masters* (Goldendale, WA: Maryhill Museum of Art, 2015), 1.

112. Vanessa Paukeigope Jennings, "Kiowa Battle Tipi," *Whispering Wind* 34, no. 6 (2004): 16.

113. Fur, *Painting Culture, Painting Nature*, 4.

114. Grafe, *American Indian Painting*, 1.

115. Gunlög Fur, "'The Earrings': Friendship across Ethnic and Gendered Boundaries in the American West," *Women's History Review* 28, no. 1 (2019): 33; and Les Kruger, "The Kiowa Five," HistoryNet.com, accessed August 31, 2020, https://www.historynet.com/the-kiowa-five.htm.

116. Kruger, "The Kiowa Five."

117. Look and Perrault, *The Interior Building*, 116.

118. Pate, 197.

119. McLerran, *A New Deal for Native Art*, 176.

120. Look and Perrault, *The Interior Building*, 116.

121. "Udall Department of the Interior Building: Houser Murals—Washington, DC," The Living New Deal, accessed August 31, 2020, https://livingnewdeal.org/projects/department-of-the-interior-building-houser-murals-washington-dc/; "Biography," Allan Houser Gallery, accessed August 31, 2020, https://allanhouser.com/the-man; and Look and Perrault, *The Interior Building*, 162.

122. "Biography," Allan Houser Gallery.

123. "Biography."

124. "Biography."

125. "Biography."

126. "Udall Department of the Interior Building."

127. McLerran, *A New Deal for Native Art*, 177.

128. McLerran, 162.

129. McLerran, 177.

130. McLerran, 177.

131. McLerran, 178.

132. McLerran, 179.

133. "Biography," Allan Houser Gallery.

134. "Biography."

135. Look and Perrault, *The Interior Building*, 162.

136. Look and Perrault, 155.

137. "Woody Crumbo: The Third Chapter," The Harwood Museum of Art, accessed August 31, 2020, http://www.harwoodmuseum.org/exhibitions/view/106.

138. "Crumbo, Woodrow Wilson—1978," The Oklahoma Hall of Fame and Gaylord-Pickens Museum, accessed August 31, 2020, https://oklahomahof.com/member-archives /c/crumbo-woodrow-wilson-1978.

139. "Crumbo, Woodrow Wilson (1912–1989)," Oklahoma Historical Society, accessed August 28, 2020, https://www.okhistory.org/publications/enc/entry.php?entry=CR021.

140. "Crumbo, Woodrow Wilson (1912–1989)."

141. "Crumbo, Woodrow Wilson—1978."

142. McLerran, *A New Deal for Native Art*, 265.

143. McLerran, 176.

144. "Crumbo, Woodrow Wilson—1978"; and "Crumbo, Woodrow Wilson (1912–1989)."

145. Cathy Spaulding, "Artist Donates Painting to Bacone College," *Muscogee Phoenix*, December 4, 2018, https://www.muskogeephoenix.com/news/artist-donates-painting-to -bacone-college/article_f97c5566-5008-54bb-a472-175e4a1312d6.html; The window was destroyed by a fire in December 1990.

146. "Crumbo, Woodrow Wilson—1978"; and "Crumbo, Woodrow Wilson (1912–1989)."

147. "Crumbo, Woodrow Wilson—1978."

148. "Crumbo, Woodrow Wilson—1978"; and "Crumbo, Woodrow Wilson (1912–1989)."

149. "Crumbo, Woodrow Wilson—1978."

150. "Crumbo, Woodrow Wilson (1912–1989)."

151. Jennifer McLerran, "The History and Progress of the Navajo People: Dual Signification in Gerald Nailor's Navajo Nation Council Chambers Murals," *American Indian Art Magazine* 4, no. 37 (2012): 43; and Look and Perrault, *The Interior Building*, 158.

152. McLerran, "The History and Progress of the Navajo People," 43; and Look and Perrault, *The Interior Building*, 158.

153. McLerran, "The History and Progress of the Navajo People," 43.

154. McLerran, *A New Deal for Native Art*, 176.

155. McLerran, 18.

156. McLerran, 176.

157. McLerran, 19.

158. Look and Perrault, *The Interior Building*, 126.

159. McLerran, "The History and Progress of the Navajo People," 46.

160. Look and Perrault, *The Interior Building*, 159.

161. McLerran, "The History and Progress of the Navajo People," 48.

162. Look and Perrault, *The Interior Building*, 159.

163. Look and Perrault, 159.

164. McLerran, "The History and Progress of the Navajo People," 41; and Look and Perrault, *The Interior Building*, 158.

165. McLerran, "The History and Progress of the Navajo People," 41.

166. McLerran, 42.

167. Look and Perrault, *The Interior Building*, 165.

168. Look and Perrault, 165; and Ann Clark, *Young Hunter of Picuris* (Washington, DC: United States Department of the Interior, 1943), 56.

169. Look and Perrault, *The Interior Building*, 165–66.

170. McLerran, *A New Deal for Native Art*, 176.

171. Look and Perrault, *The Interior Building*, 166.

172. Look and Perrault, 166.

173. Look and Perrault, 171.

174. Look and Perrault, 166.

175. "Velino Shije Herrera," Smithsonian American Art Museum, accessed August 30, 2020, https://americanart.si.edu/artist/velino-shije-herrera-2187.

176. Look and Perrault, *The Interior Building*, 166.

177. McLerran, *A New Deal for Native Art*, 168.

178. "Photo Standalone 22—No Title," *Washington Post*, May 5, 1940, https://search.proquest.com/hnpwashingtonpost/docview/151303093/D4004836F41A4045PQ/31?accountid=11243.

179. "Photo Standalone 23—No Title," *Washington Post*, May 5, 1940, https://search.proquest.com/hnpwashingtonpost/docview/151289114/D4004836F41A4045PQ/23?a.

180. "Photo Standalone 23."

181. Look and Perrault, *The Interior Building*, 15–16.

182. Look and Perrault, 101.

183. Look and Perrault, 145.

184. Look and Perrault, 140.

185. Kevin Bruyneel, *Settler Memory: The Disavowal of Indigeneity and the Politics of Race in the United States* (Chapel Hill: University of North Carolina Press, 2021), 3.

Conclusion

The Capital of Indian Country

Snake River, Idaho. Bears Ears, Utah. Chaco Canyon, New Mexico. Black Hills, South Dakota. Missouri River, South Dakota. Standing Rock Indian Reservation. White Earth Indian Reservation. Line 5, Michigan. These eight locations encapsulate some of the most sacred sites across the land now known as the United States of America. They also represent some of the most fraught natural resource extraction and hotly contested development projects in the country. The work happening in these places threatens traditional food sources for Native peoples and creates inhabitable living conditions for nonhuman relations such as salmon. Mining, drilling, logging, and damning destroy ancient sacred sites and desecrate tribal burial grounds. Continued operations of these industries disregard treaty rights, and executives are dismissing Native leaders from legally mandated consultation and collaboration in the planning and execution processes. For these very reasons, the sites included on this docket are ground zero for Indigenous communities who are fighting for their very futures.

While it may be difficult to see how Washington, DC, fits on this list, it is indeed the ninth and final locale. Together these sacred sites made up the itinerary for the Lummi carvers and community members who toured a totem pole across the nation to raise awareness and generate opposition to environmental degradation.[1] Artists and activists together stopped at each location, rallying support for their cause. Finally, the group concluded their venture by traveling to the District of Columbia. Their journey is known as the Red Road to DC. The Red Road to DC brings together the four themes discussed in this book: Native American political issues advanced in the capital city, representations of First Americans presented in monuments and museums, the cultural footprint made by Indigenous arts, and intertribal activism leaving a powerful legacy. In this way, the Red Road to DC exemplifies the claim that Washington, DC, is not only Indian land but, indeed, that it is the political capital of Indian Country.[2]

For more than twenty years leading up to the Red Road to DC, artists from the Lummi Nation have carved totem poles and toured them across the United States in order to raise awareness of pressing social issues.[3] The House of Tears Carvers, based out of Lummi Nation and led by head carver Jewell James and carving assistant Douglas James, spearheads this initiative. They are the same group who carved and caravanned the totem pole that sits in the District's Congressional Cemetery in honor of the victims of the September 11, 2001, terrorist attacks, as is elaborated in chapter 4. Community connectedness for the Lummi is at the center of the House of Tears' carving processes as they bring in many individuals—from toddlers to elders—to carve, paint, or otherwise contribute.[4] The purpose of this intensive labor has been the same: to raise awareness and inspire opposition to fossil fuel projects that threaten the waters, lands, and sacred sites upon which Indigenous—and non-Indigenous communities—live and depend. "We are all coming together, like figures on a totem pole," offered James of the Red Road to DC, "to produce an end vision: the protection of Native American sacred sites."[5] James and his collaborators carved the pole from a four-hundred-year-old cedar tree grown on Lummi lands. The pole, in its finished state, stands at twenty-four feet and eight inches and weighs approximately five thousand pounds.[6] The artists carved each figure from the top of the totem on down over the course of three months, taking their inspiration from spiritual guidance and dreams rather than predetermined blueprints.[7]

The topmost image on the pole features an Indigenous man in profile, wearing eagle feathers and kneeling before a fire in prayer. The fire pays tribute to Pueblo spirituality by depicting the flames emerging from a "giant pearle" rather than from wood logs. This scene appears in front of a pure white background carved into a circle, symbolizing a full moon. The moon depicted here is significant for its powers in shaping the course of the winds, waters, and women. It also speaks to traditional Star Child stories that appear across Indigenous cultures.[8]

A row of white eagle tailfeathers blends the bottom of the full moon with the next image: the diving eagle. The overlap with the moon suggests the heights to which the eagle flies and its spiritual power. This figure is centered on the pole, comprising approximately a quarter of the totem space. The eagle is depicted diving down toward the earth, and his head projects out from the pole. Here the eagle stands in as the Father Sky power, and his position flying downward represents his union with Mother Earth. His black-, red-, turquoise-, and bronze-painted wings depict traditional Northwest coast-style "salmon head" designs, encouraging viewers to reflect on the stories of the Salmon Children.[9]

Relatedly, two parallel depictions of silver and bronze chinook salmon sit below the eagle head, their heads meeting in the middle of the pole, similarly appearing to swim downward. One of these salmon represents the food supply of the local killer whale pod, while the other symbolizes the salmon that swim up the Columbia and Snake Rivers.[10] Along the right side of the pole under the chinook is an eight-foot bear, painted brown and shown in a crouching position. The bear figure also relates to the salmon, with Pacific Northwest cosmology identifying Bear as the brother-in-law to Salmon Woman. A black wolf is carved on the left side of the pole, opposite the bear. Both Wolf and Bear are intended by the artist to convey sacred male powers—that of the scout and of strength, respectively—and to serve as a reference to Indigenous stories and beliefs whereby humans coexist peacefully with their nonhuman relatives and live in community with them. For the carvers, these figures are also included due to their at-risk status stemming from the human destruction of their habitats.[11]

In the center, between the wolf and bear, appears Canadian copper: a symbol of the Northwest coast potlatching, or gift-giving, culture.[12] "The image is intended to remind us that only by giving all you own away to others can you show the true power of your spiritual endowment," James offers.[13] The copper also serves as a statement of international connection with Indigenous relatives living across the northern US border as well as in Alaska.[14]

Another kneeling figure appears as the bottommost image. This individual—"praying mother kneeling with rattle"—sits in front of a blue background with one hand holding a rattle. She can also be read as a medicine woman or grandmother. The woman's other hand appears outstretched, showing a red palm: the symbol of the Missing and Murdered Indigenous Women and Girls. To her right are seven peyote buttons, representative of the peyote religion, and gouge marks representing falling rain. Below her hands and under the peyote buttons appears a small figure, "Mexican child in a cage." This figure is laying on its back with feet and arms in the air; a black square cage surrounds the figure, and bars of varying lengths appear to press down upon it from above. This image specifically honors and raises awareness of the Indigenous migrant children who have been separated from their parents at the southern US border; more than fifty thousand unaccompanied minors remain in US custody, living in incarceration facilities today. On the opposite side of the (grand)mother figure is a second, smaller kneeling woman representing her

FIGURE C.1. Detail of Red Road to DC totem pole
Author photo, 2021, Washington, DC.

daughter or granddaughter. She is placed behind the older woman to demonstrate that she is learning from the elder, bringing traditional teachings to the next generations. Seven "tears of trauma"—one for each Indigenous generation that has been traumatized under colonialism—appear between the two, figuratively showing how trauma can divide generations. One of the blue teardrops doubles as the (grand)daughter's rattle in order to symbolize her intergenerational trauma and her use of traditional spirituality for healing. All three figures rest upon a dark blue band at the bottom of the pole, stylized as flowing waters of the River of Life.[15]

In the three months before the Red Road journey began, the House of Tears Carvers met with more than one hundred communities across the nation "to gather the hopes, prayers and support from communities to protect sacred places and the natural world, for generations to come."[16] Then, on March 25, the cross-country journey officially began. The group first visited a number of neighboring tribal nations in the western Washington area before arriving in traditional Nez Percé lands along the Snake River in Idaho on July 15, marking the first sacred site stop on the list.[17] Next the totem visited Bears Ears, located on lands traditionally used by the Hopi, Navajo, Ute, and Zuni peoples, before heading to Chaco Canyon. On July 21 the Lakota community welcomed the caravan to their sacred Black Hills; the following day, organizers gathered on the banks of the Missouri River.[18] A five-member escort riding horseback next led the totem into the Standing Rock community on July 24.[19] One day later the totem visited water protectors rallying against Line 3 pipeline in White Earth, Minnesota, and then met at Bay Mills Indian Community to fight Line 5 on July 27.[20]

Finally, on July 29, 2021, the caravan arrived in Washington, DC.[21] The crowd gathered on the grounds of the National Museum of the American Indian for a ceremony to open the exhibit featuring the Red Road to DC journey. Later that afternoon, Chief Jesse James Swann of the Piscataway Conoy Tribe of Maryland and Julie Yates representing the Piscataway Indian Nation opened the event with a land recognition, followed by honor songs and speeches by various event organizers, artists, activists, tribal leaders, and politicians, including Judith LeBlanc (Caddo), director of the Native Organizers Alliance; Brenda Mallory, chair of the Council on Environmental Quality; the House of Tears Carvers, including Doug James, who spoke on behalf of master carver Jewell James; PaaWee Rivera (Pueblo of Pojoaque), White House senior adviser for intergovernmental affairs and director of tribal affairs; Fawn Sharp (Quinault), president of the National Congress of American Indians; Lawrence Solomon, Lummi Nation chair; and many more.[22] In following this program of events, the gathering concluded the Red Road to DC's journey with a presentation of the totem pole to Secretary of the Interior Deb Haaland and the delivery of a 75,000-signature petition to the Biden administration calling for the protection of sacred Indigenous sites. By completing its caravan across the United States with a final stop in the nation's capital, the totem pole "[carried] the spirit of the lands it visits and the power and prayers of communities along the way" and gifted these "prayers, power and demands" to political leadership in Washington.[23]

The totem sat on view on Maryland Avenue outside the National Museum of the American Indian between the afternoon of July 29 and the morning of July 31.[24] Accompanying its presence, the museum also installed a temporary exhibit, *Kwel' Hoy: We Draw the Line*, from July 2 through September 9, 2021.[25] This traveling exhibit highlighted the work of the carvers and their collaborations with communities nationwide. Included in this exhibition were testimonies to the significance of the Red Road journey. Reuben George of the Tsleil-Waututh First Nation, for instance, reflected, "I want our kids to realize how rich our ancestors were. . . . That's why we joined the Totem Pole

Journey.... I've seen people come up to the totem pole of all walks of life and touch that and put prayers into that and feel the holiness of the story of that tree.... Somebody put energy and spirit into something like this and made it beautiful and alive—showed me that we lived abundant, and we're going back to that. We're going to thrive and we're going to win and we're going to stop [industrial development] and we're going to continue to live abundant in the good ways of our ancestors."[26] On July 31 the totem was relocated to sit outside of the US Department of the Interior, overseen by Secretary Haaland.[27] At the time of writing, the final home for the totem pole has yet to be determined.

"As the pole travels, it draws lines of connection," declares the Red Road to DC organizers, "honoring, uniting and empowering communities working to protect sacred places."[28] And just as this totem pole made its way across Indian Country before finalizing its journey in DC, so too do cohorts of emerging tribal leaders venture to Washington, connecting the political capital of Indian Country with Indigenous nations across Turtle Island. I first came to the capital city myself as part of such tradition, interning for my tribe, the Chickasaw Nation, in the Department of the Interior. I returned each subsequent summer before permanently relocating and have called this city my home ever since. As a Chickasaw person in this city, I occupy a position of being Indigenous to the lands now incorporated into the United States but not to the land base now known as the District of Columbia, upon which I live and work. I made it a priority to learn about this place. Each site and story incorporated into this book came to my attention by connecting with the city's Indigenous community and by traversing both the built and natural environments of this territory. I have come to understand this process—Indigenous individuals and our allies directing me to "must-see" sites—as community-centered curation.

In my role directing the George Washington University's AT&T Center for Indigenous Politics and Policy as well as the center's Native American Political Leadership Program and the Inspire Pre-College Program, I administered educational opportunities that brought American Indian, Alaska Native, and Native Hawaiian students to Washington, DC, for a semester of political leadership learning. Later I continued teaching and mentoring Indigenous students in my position as a faculty member at American University. Unfortunately, however, it was not uncommon for my Native students to report feeling invisible, out of place, and unrepresented during their time here. This feedback—the painful erasure of Indigenous peoples in the nation's capital, of all places—struck me as a travesty. To redress this sense of not belonging,

I set out to share with my students the knowledge I had gained through my own time as an Indigenous person in the District of Columbia.

In 2019 I entered over one dozen sites of Indigenous significance into a digital map and rendered this map into a free, publicly facing mobile application format. My intention was to provide this map and app—the Guide to Indigenous DC—as a visual representation of Native imprints upon the capital city, with pinpoints spanning the full terrain within District limits. Not only did these sites stretch the full span of the city space, but they confronted the one-dimensional myth of Indigenous peoples as mere historical subjects; these sites, by contrast, centered tribal sovereignty, highlighted memorializations dedicated to Native heroes, spotlighted the amplified First Nations arts, and recalled the tradition of Indigenous activist organizing in the capital. This interdisciplinary approach to the digital mapping project made clear that Native peoples belong in fields of inquiry beyond history, anthropology, and archaeology and instead offer invaluable contributions in areas ranging from political science to fine arts.

In practice, mapping sites of Indigenous significance to Washington, DC, opens pathways for understanding the past as a way to empower Native communities today. Many sites included in my map and in this text are not celebrated with any form of public commemoration—there are no plaques dedicated to the occupation of the Bureau of Indian Affairs, statues depicting the tribal leaders buried at the Congressional Cemetery, or signage contextualizing Dumbarton Bridge, to name but a few sites. The Guide to Indigenous DC deploys a digital space to do precisely that work and, indeed, facilitates this process unfolding beyond the digital sphere. When I have taken my students out of the classroom to use the mobile application, we take to the National Mall and analyze pictures of Indigenous activism on the land where the events occurred. Orienting ourselves to the perspective of the photographer, we look toward the Washington Monument and hold up our phones to look at images depicting the tipis that once sat in its foreground during the Native Nations Rise March. Turning the opposite direction, toward the US Capitol, we scroll through the app's photo gallery of the Cowboy and Indian Alliance and share the perspective of our tribal leaders who rode horseback on this very spot. Within the larger national context of settler colonialism and Indigenous stereotypes, this act of remembering and our physical return to a place becomes particularly salient. By commemorating these sites, this mapping project empowers us as Indigenous peoples because, in the words of Lumbee scholar and my partner on the Guide to Indigenous Baltimore Ashley Minner, "Stories connect us to our places. Our stories and our places connect us to ourselves and each other."[29] We have been in these places, and we belong in these places as Native people. By learning and repeating the stories affiliated with each site, we confront the settler-colonial project of Indigenous erasure. We find power in the knowledge of our stories and pride in our continued presence in this place. In sum, these sites revealed to my Native students—and to all readers who have since accessed the app or picked up this book—that Washington, DC, is Indian land.

Mapping as the methodology for this project has also offered a new possibility for Indigenous storytelling and the centering of Indigenous ways of knowing in the settler state capital. By demarcating pinpoints on a map, I fundamentally orient the narrative of Native contributions to Washington around this place and this space. This site-specific framework resists linear unfoldings of time and, as previously mentioned, resists neat disciplinary boundaries in a strategic decision to unite and place into conversation Indigenous visions for our communities across time. In practice, the act of visualizing Indigenous imprints upon this space enables the up-and-coming tribal politicians, advocates, thought leaders, and activists to see themselves as part of this ever-evolving story. In what ways will they leave their own marks upon this land? How will their actions here in Washington, DC, reverberate across the nation to affect positive change on the ground in their home communities? Instead of suffering from isolation in this space, these stories enable the Native youth who travel here to align their own experiences with those who came before them and to draw power and strength from that knowledge. For some time after creating this map, I used to say that our next generations of Indigenous leaders who come to Washington are following in their ancestors' footsteps. Now I've come to understand that as they carry on this tradition and embark upon the paths blazed before them, they also leave their own footprints for future generations yet to come.

In this way new pinpoints representing Indigenous imprints upon the District of Columbia emerge every day. The work of mapping is never done; it is continuously evolving. Certainly, there exist many more sites across Washington that hold significance to Indigenous peoples but do not appear in my analysis. This manuscript contains additional histories and places that do not make their way into the Guide to Indigenous DC mobile application, and, even still, the list included herein is not exhaustive. In many ways, this is precisely the purpose of this work: the fact that the entirety of this land base is Indigenous inherently precludes the possibility of relaying every significant site. Every piece of this land is imbued with Indigenous stories and is shaped by Native footprints.

NOTES

1. "Background: Sacred Sites on the Red Road to DC," Red Road to DC, accessed November 3, 2021, https://redroadtodc.org/wp-content/uploads/2021/07/RR2DC-sacred -sites_final.pdf.

2. Gallup, New Mexico, is at times colloquially referred to as the capital of Indian Country for its large Indigenous population and connection to Navajo, Zuni, Pueblo, and Hopi communities.

3. "#RedRoadtoDC Totem Journey at National Museum of the American Indian," Facebook video, 34:51, July 29, 2021, https://www.facebook.com/totempolejourney/videos /349454480117715/.

4. Lynda V. Mapes, "Lummi Nation Carvers and Allies to Embark on National Tour to DC, Give Totem Pole to President Biden," *Seattle Times*, April 12, 2021, https://www .seattletimes.com/seattle-news/environment/lummi-nation-carvers-and-allies-to-embark -on-national-tour-to-d-c-give-totem-pole-to-president-biden/.

5. Jewell Praying Wolf James, "Sacred Sites Totem Pole 2021," Red Road to DC, March 20, 2021, https://s3.documentcloud.org/documents/20613355/sacred-sites-totem -pole-2021.pdf.

6. James.

7. James; and Dana Hedgpeth, "Lummi Nation Totem Pole Arrives in DC after Journey to Sacred Lands across U.S.," *Seattle Times*, July 29, 2021, https://www.seattletimes.com /nation-world/nation/lummi-nation-totem-pole-arrives-in-d-c-after-journey-to-sacred -lands-across-u-s/?fbclid=ˆIwAR3ivIyYtQV9VpZEruHQRvhfqmKjMGV3zxX805HgiEGpd _SDqyjNJy5P3uM.

8. James, "Sacred Sites Totem Pole 2021."

9. James.

10. Freddie Lane, "Red Road to DC TPJ—Description of Symbols," Youtube video, 14:04, April 7, 2021, https://www.youtube.com/watch?v=0LsOweAedgo.

11. James, "Sacred Sites Totem Pole 2021."

12. James.

13. James.

14. James.

15. James.

16. "Background: Sacred Sites on the Red Road to DC"; and Mapes, "Lummi Nation Carvers and Allies to Embark on National Tour to DC."

17. Mapes, "Lummi Nation Carvers and Allies to Embark on National Tour to DC."

18. Jason Mark, "Some Highlights from the Red Road to DC," *Sierra*, July 29, 2021, https://www.sierraclub.org/sierra/some-highlights-red-road-dc?fbclid= IwAR2yKITK6Yxvy26kVDftiacZ6CDyb94ZJXBQJM34W7ivC9VG2nGG2yO_TP8# .YQQc2kZlPrY.facebook.

19. Jason Jones, "Yesterday the Red Road to DC Caravan Arrived at Standing Rock Escorted by Horses," Facebook, July 25, 2021, https://www.facebook.com /totempolejourney/.

20. Our Shared Responsibility: A Totem Pole Journey, "Quick Update from the #RedRoadtoDC as We Make Our Way to Bay Mills Indian Community for a Blessing Ceremony Tomorrow . . . ," July 26, 2021, https://www.facebook.com/totempolejourney/; and Our Shared Responsibility: A Totem Pole Journey, "#RedRoadtoDC Stop Line 3 Blessing Ceremony," July 28, 2021, https://fb.watch/9AXYItcLoA/.

21. Mapes, "Lummi Nation Carvers and Allies."

22. "#RedRoadtoDC Totem Journey at National Museum of the American Indian."

23. "About & Press," Red Road to DC, accessed November 3, 2021, https://redroadtodc .org/about-press/.

24. Exhibit, *Kwel' Hoy: We Draw the Line*, National Museum of the American Indian, Washington, DC.

25. *Kwel' Hoy: We Draw the Line*, Smithsonian Institution, accessed November 3, 2021, https://www.si.edu/exhibitions/kwel-hoy-we-draw-line%3Aevent-exhib-6549.

26. Exhibit, *Kwel' Hoy: We Draw the Line*.

27. Totem Pole Journey RedRoadtoDC, 2021, "#RedRoadtoDC Pole at Dept. of Interior . . . ," Instagram, July 31, 2021, https://www.instagram.com/p/CSAW56ql-1b/.

28. "About & Press."

29. Ashley Minner, "The Lumbee Community: Revisiting the Reservation of Baltimore's Fells Point," in *Baltimore Revisited: Stories of Inequality and Resistance in a US City*, ed. P. Nicole King, Kate Drabinski, and Joshua Clark Davis (New Brunswick, NJ: Rutgers University Press, 2019), 193. The Guide to Indigenous Baltimore is the second mobile app and digital mapping project under my Guide to Indigenous Lands Project; the Guide to Indigenous DC was the first.

BIBLIOGRAPHY

Archuleta, Elizabeth. "History Carved in Stone: Memorializing Po'Pay and Onate, or Recasting Racialized Regimes of Representation?" *New Mexico Historical Review* 82, no. 3 (June 2007): 317–42.

Baird, W. David. *Peter Pitchlynn: Chief of the Choctaws*. Norman: University of Oklahoma Press, 1986.

Baker, Marcus. "The Boundary Monuments of the District of Columbia." *Records of the Columbia Historical Society* 1 (May 1897): 215–24.

Baldwin, Marie Louise Bottineau. "The Indians of Today." In *Recasting the Vote: How Women of Color Transformed the Suffrage Movement*, by Cathleen D. Cahill, 131–41. Chapel Hill: University of North Carolina Press, 2020.

———. "An Ojibwe Woman in Washington, DC." In *Recasting the Vote: How Women of Color Transformed the Suffrage Movement*, by Cathleen D. Cahill, 83–96. Chapel Hill: University of North Carolina Press, 2020.

Batton, Gary. "Congressional Cemetery Final Resting Place for Two Honored Choctaw Chiefs." *Biskinik*, July 2011.

Benedict, John Downing. *Muskogee and Northeastern Oklahoma: Including the Counties of Muskogee, McIntosh, Wagoner, Cherokee, Sequoyah, Adair, Delaware, Mayes, Rogers, Washington, Nowata, Craig, and Ottawa*. Chicago: S. J. Clarke, 1922.

Bonnin, Gertrude Simmons. "Americanize the First American." In *Recasting the Vote: How Women of Color Transformed the Suffrage Movement*, by Cathleen D. Cahill, 184–92. Chapel Hill: University of North Carolina Press, 2020.

Brandt, Jenn. "1913 Woman Suffrage Procession." 100 Years of the Women's Vote. California State University, Dominguez Hills, Spring 2020. https://scalar.usc.edu /works/100-years-of-the-womens-vote/1913-woman-suffrage-procession-poster.

Bruyneel, Kevin. *Settler Memory: The Disavowal of Indigeneity and the Politics of Race in the United States*. Chapel Hill: University of North Carolina Press, 2021.

Cahill, Cathleen D. "Marie Louise Bottineau Baldwin: Indigenizing the Federal Indian Service." *American Indian Quarterly* 37, no. 3 (Summer 2013): 63–86.

———. "'Our Democracy and the American Indian': Citizenship, Sovereignty, and the Native Vote in the 1920s." *Journal of Women's History* 32, no. 1 (Spring 2020): 41–51.

Cahoon, Ben. "US Native American Nations." *World Statesman*, n.d. Accessed September 18, 2020. https://www.worldstatesmen.org/US_NativeAM.html.

Campbell, Ben Nighthorse. Foreword to *Diplomats in Buckskin: A History of Indian Delegations in Washington City*, by Herman J. Viola, 7–8. Bluffton, SC: Rivilo, 1995.

Cantrell, Doyne. *Western Cherokee Nation of Arkansas and Missouri: A History, a Heritage*. Morrisville, NC: Lulu, 2009.

Caro, Mario A. "The National Museum of the American Indian and the Siting of Identity." In *The National Museum of the American Indian: Critical Conversations*, ed. Amanda J. Cobb and Amy Lonetree. Lincoln: University of Nebraska Press, 2008.

Carpenter, Cari M. "Sarah Winnemucca Goes to Washington: Rhetoric and Resistance in the Capital City." *American Indian Quarterly* 40, no. 2 (Spring 2016): 87–108.

Clark, Ann. *Young Hunter of Picuris*. Washington, DC: US Department of the Interior, 1943.

Cleland, Charles E. *The Place of the Pike (Gnoozhekaaning): A History of the Bay Mills Indian Community*. Ann Arbor: University of Michigan Press, 2001.

———. *Rites of Conquest: The History and Culture of Michigan's Native Americans*. Ann Arbor: University of Michigan Press, 1992.

Cobb, Amanda J. "The National Museum of the American Indian as Cultural Sovereignty." *American Quarterly* 57, no. 2 (June 2005): 485–506.

Cobb, Amanda J., and Amy Lonetree, eds. *The National Museum of the American Indian: Critical Conversations*. Lincoln: University of Nebraska Press, 2008.

Conley, Robert J. *A Cherokee Encyclopedia*. Albuquerque: University of New Mexico Press, 2007.

Cowger, Thomas W. *The National Congress of American Indians: The Founding Years*. Lincoln: University of Nebraska Press, 1999.

Cross, Anne. *Raven and the First Men: From Conception to Completion*. Vancouver: University of British Columbia Museum of Anthropology, 1990.

Cushman, Ellen. "'We're Taking the Genius of Sequoyah into This Century': The Cherokee Syllabary, Peoplehood, and Perseverance," *Wicazo Sa Review* 26, no. 1 (Spring 2011): 67–83.

Deloria, Philip J. *Indians in Unexpected Places*. Lawrence: University of Kansas Press, 2004.

Deloria, Vine, Jr. *Custer Died for Your Sins: An Indian Manifesto*. Norman: University of Oklahoma Press, 1988.

Duffek, Karen, and Charlotte Townsend-Gault. *Bill Reid and Beyond: Expanding on Modern Native Art*. Vancouver, B.C.: Douglas & McIntyre, 2005.

Duncan, David Ewing. "The Object at Hand." *Smithsonian* 22, no. 6 (September 1991): 22.

Estes, Nick. "Fighting for Our Lives: #NoDAPL in Historical Context." *Wicazo Sa Review* 32, no. 2 (Fall 2017): 115–22.

———. *Our History Is the Future: Standing Rock Versus the Dakota Access Pipeline, and the Long Tradition of Indigenous Resistance*. London: Verso, 2019.

Fields, Gregory P. Introduction to *A Totem Pole History: The Work of Lummi Carver Joe Hillaire*, by Pauline Hillaire, xxiii–xxxvii. Lincoln: University of Nebraska Press, 2013.

Finger, John R. *The Eastern Band of Cherokees, 1819–1900*. Knoxville: University of Tennessee Press, 1984.

Foreman, Carolyn Thomas. "A Cherokee Pioneer, Ella Floora Coodey Robinson." *Chronicles of Oklahoma* 7, no. 4 (1929): 364–74.

———. "The Coodey Family of the Indian Territory." *Chronicles of Oklahoma* 25, no. 4 (Winter 1947–48): 323–41.

Fur, Gunlög. "'The Earrings': Friendship across Ethnic and Gendered Boundaries in the American West." *Women's History Review* 28, no. 1 (2019): 23–41.

———. *Painting Culture, Painting Nature: Stephen Mopope, Oscar Jacobson, and the Development of Indian Art in Oklahoma*. Norman: University of Oklahoma Press, 2019.

Goeman, Mishuana. *Mark My Words: Native Women Mapping Our Nations*. Minneapolis: University of Minnesota Press, 2013.

Grafe, Steven L. *American Indian Painting: Twentieth-Century Masters*. Goldendale, WA: Maryhill Museum of Art, 2015.

Hagel, Chuck. "Remembering Soldiers and Their Families." Speech, May 24, 2006. Arlington National Cemetery website. http://www.arlingtoncemetery.net/jrrice.htm.

Hammel, Eric. *Two Flags over Iwo Jima: Solving the Mystery of the U.S. Marine Corps' Proudest Moment*. Oxford: Casemate, 2018.

Holm, Tom. *Strong Hearts, Wounded Souls: Native American Veterans of the Vietnam War*. Austin: University of Texas Press, 1996.

———. "Strong Hearts, Wounded Souls Revisited: The Research, the Findings, and Some Observations of Recent Native Veteran Readjustment." *Wicazo Sa Review* 32, no. 1 (Spring 2017): 118–28.

Hopper, Frank. "National Native American Veterans Memorial Artist Explains His Design." *Indian Country Today*, July 23, 2019. https://indiancountrytoday.com /culture/national-native-american-veterans-memorial-artist-explains-his-design -gSMOTYz6RkaSZlXAc8ubKQ.

Humphrey, Robert L., and Mary Elizabeth Chambers. *Ancient Washington: American Indian Cultures of the Potomac Valley*. Washington, DC: George Washington University, 1977.

Jacknis, Ira. "A New Thing? The National Museum of the American Indian in Historical and Institutional Context." In *The National Museum of the American Indian: Critical Conversations*, ed. Amanda J. Cobb and Amy Lonetree. Lincoln: University of Nebraska Press, 2008.

Jennings, Vanessa Paukeigope. "Kiowa Battle Tipi." *Whispering Wind* 34, no. 6 (2004): 16–18.

Jones, Trevor M. "Pegg, Thomas." *The Encyclopedia of Oklahoma History and Culture*, accessed September 1, 2020. https://www.okhistory.org/publications/enc/entry .php?entry=PE008.

Kappler, Charles Joseph, ed. "Treaty with the Chippewa, 1837." In *Indian Affairs: Laws and Treaties*, Vol. 2, *Treaties*, 491–92. Washington, DC: Government Printing Office, 1904.

———, ed. "Treaty with the Winnebago, 1859." In *Indian Affairs: Laws and Treaties*, Vol. 2, *Treaties*, 790–92. Washington, DC: Government Printing Office, 1904.

Kotlowski, Dean J. "Burying Sergeant Rice: Racial Justice and Native American Rights in the Truman Era." *Journal of American Studies* 38, no. 2 (2004): 199–225.

Landrum, Cynthia L. "Kicking Bear, John Trudell, and Anthony Kiedis (of the Red Hot Chili Peppers): 'Show Indians' and Pop-Cultural Colonialism." *American Indian Quarterly* 36, no. 2 (Spring 2012): 182–214.

Lincecum, Gideon. *Pushmataha: A Choctaw Leader and His People*. Tuscaloosa: University of Alabama Press, 2004.

Little, John A. "Between Cultures: Sioux Warriors and the Vietnam War." *Great Plains Quarterly* 35, no. 4 (Fall 2015): 357–75.

Lomawaima, K. Tsianina. *They Called It Prairie Light: The Story of Chilocco Indian School*. Lincoln: University of Nebraska Press, 1994.

Look, David W., and Carole L. Perrault. *The Interior Building: Its Architecture and Its Art*. Washington, DC: US Department of the Interior, National Park Service, Preservation Assistance Division, 1986.

Lowery, Malinda Maynor. *Lumbee Indians in the Jim Crow South: Race, Identity, and the Making of a Nation*. Chapel Hill: University of North Carolina Press, 2010.

Maddra, Sam A. *Hostiles? The Lakota Ghost Dance and Buffalo Bill's Wild West*. Norman: University of Oklahoma Press, 2006.

Martineau, Joel. "Autoethnography and Material Culture: The Case of Bill Reid." *Biography* 24, no. 1 (Winter 2001): 242–58.

McBeth, Sally. "Memory, History, and Contested Pasts: Re-Imagining Sacagawea/Sacajawea." *American Indian Culture and Research Journal* 27, no. 1 (2003): 1–32.

McLaughlin, James. *My Friend the Indian*. Cambridge, MA: Riverside, 1910.

McLerran, Jennifer. "The History and Progress of the Navajo People: Dual Signification in Gerald Nailor's Navajo Nation Council Chambers Murals." *American Indian Art Magazine* 4, no. 37 (2012): 40–49.

———. *A New Deal for Native Art: Indian Arts and Federal Policy, 1933–1943*. Tucson: University of Arizona Press, 2009.

Minner, Ashley. "The Lumbee Community: Revisiting the Reservation of Baltimore's Fells Point." In *Baltimore Revisited: Stories of Inequality and Resistance in a US City*, ed. P. Nicole King, Kate Drabinski, and Joshua Clark Davis. New Brunswick, NJ: Rutgers University Press, 2019.

Minnesota Historical Society. *The Fox and Ojibwa War*. St. Paul: Minnesota Historical Society, 1872.

Mooney, James. "The Powhatan Confederacy, Past and Present." *American Anthropologist* 9, no. 1 (January–March 1907): 129–52.

Myers, Robert A. "Cherokee Pioneers in Arkansas: The St. Francis Years, 1785–1813." *Arkansas Historical Quarterly* 56, no. 2 (Summer 1997): 127–57.

National Congress of American Indians (NCAI). *National Congress of American Indians Annual Report*. Washington, DC: National Congress of American Indians, 2008.

———. *National Congress of American Indians Annual Report*. Washington, DC: National Congress of American Indians, 2009.

———. *National Congress of American Indians Annual Report*. Washington, DC: National Congress of American Indians, 2014.

National Museum of the American Indian (NMAI). *National Native American Veterans Memorial: Consultation Report*. Washington, DC: National Museum of the American Indian, 2018.

———. *National Native American Veterans Memorial: Honoring Native American Military Service*. Washington, DC: National Museum of the American Indian, n.d.

Neihardt, John G. *Black Elk Speaks*. Lincoln: University of Nebraska Press, 1932.

Nye, Edwin Darby. "Revisiting Washington's Forty Boundary Stones, 1972." *Records of the Columbia Historical Society* 48 (1973): 740–51.

Ostrowitz, Judith. "Concourse and Periphery: Planning the National Museum of the American Indian." In *The National Museum of the American Indian: Critical Conversations*, ed. Amanda J. Cobb and Amy Lonetree. Lincoln: University of Nebraska Press, 2008.

Pate, James P. "Pitchlynn, Peter Perkins." In *The Encyclopedia of Oklahoma History and Culture*. https://www.okhistory.org/publications/enc/entry.php?entry=PI013.

Pate, J'Nell. "Kiowa Art from Rainy Mountain: The Story of James Auchiah." *American Indian Quarterly* 1, no. 3 (1974): 193–200.

Penn Boudinot, William, ed. *Laws of the Cherokee Nation, Passed during the Years 1839–1867*. St. Louis: Missouri Democrat Print, 1868.

Phillips, Victoria F. and Ryan M. Van Olst. "The Longstanding Pro Bono Battle Challenging the Washington Football Team Trademarks." *Landslide* 8, no. 3 (January/February 2016).

Pitchlynn, Peter. "A Man between Nations: The Diary of Peter Pitchlynn." *Missouri Review* 14, no. 3 (1991): 53–92.

Presidential Advisory Council on HIV/AIDS. *AIDS: No Time to Spare: The Final Report to the President of the United States.* Washington, DC: Presidential Advisory Council on HIV/AIDS, 2000.

Prucha, Francis Paul. *The Great Father: The United States Government and the American Indians.* Lincoln: University of Nebraska Press, 1984.

Ramirez, Renya K. *Native Hubs: Culture, Community, and Belonging in Silicon Valley and Beyond.* Durham, NC: Duke University Press, 2007.

Reid, Bill. "The Spirit of Haida Gwaii." In *Solitary Raven: The Essential Writings of Bill Reid,* edited by Robert Bringhurst, 228–30. Seattle: University of Washington Press, 2000.

Rice, James D. "War and Politics: Powhatan Expansionism and the Problem of Native American Warfare." *William and Mary Quarterly* 77, no. 1 (January 2020): 3–32.

Ricky, Donald. *Indians of Louisiana.* St. Clair Shores, MI: Somerset, 1999.

Roberts, Rebecca Boggs, and Sandra K. Schmidt. *Historic Congressional Cemetery.* Charleston, SC: Arcadia, 2012.

Santoro, Miléna, and Erick Detlef Langer. *Hemispheric Indigeneities: Native Identity and Agency in Mesoamerica, the Andes, and Canada.* Lincoln: University of Nebraska Press, 2018.

Silva, Noenoe K. *Aloha Betrayed: Native Hawaiian Resistance to American Colonialism.* Durham, NC: Duke University Press, 2004.

Smith, Paul Chaat. *Everything You Know about Indians Is Wrong.* Minneapolis: University of Minnesota Press, 2009.

Smith, Paul Chaat, and Robert Allen Warrior. *Like a Hurricane: The Indian Movement from Alcatraz to Wounded Knee.* New York: New Press, 1996.

The Spirit of Missions. Burlington: J. L. Powell, 1837.

Stamm, Henry E. *People of the Wind River: The Eastern Shoshones, 1825–1900.* Norman: University of Oklahoma Press, 1999.

Stanciu, Cristina. "An Indian Woman of Many Hats: Laura Cornelius Kellogg's Embattled Search for an Indigenous Voice." *American Indian Quarterly* 37, no. 3 (Summer 2013): 87–115.

Stubben, Jerry D. *Native Americans and Political Participation: A Reference Handbook.* Santa Barbara, CA: ABC-CLIO, 2006.

Swanton, John. *Source Material for the Social and Ceremonial Life of the Choctaw Indians.* Washington, DC: Government Printing Office, 1931.

Sweeney, Edwin R., ed. *Cochise: Firsthand Accounts of the Chiricahua Apache Chief.* Norman: University of Oklahoma Press, 2014.

Tayac, Gabrielle A. *Spirits in the River: A Report on the Piscataway People.* Washington, DC: Smithsonian Institution, National Museum of the American Indian, 1999.

Valaskakis, Gail Guthrie. *Indian Country: Essays on Contemporary Native Culture.* Waterloo, ONT: Wilfrid Laurier University Press, 2005.

Velikova, Roumiana. "Will Rogers's Indian Humor." *Studies in American Indian Literatures* 19, no. 2 (Summer 2007): 83–103.

Viola, Herman J. *Diplomats in Buckskin: A History of Indian Delegations in Washington City.* Bluffton, SC: Rivilo, 1995.

Warde, Mary Jane. *When the Wolf Came: The Civil War and the Indian Territory.* Fayetteville: University of Arkansas Press, 2013.

Ware, Amy M. *The Cherokee Kid: Will Rogers, Tribal Identity, and the Making of an American Icon.* Lawrence: University of Kansas Press, 2015.

Warren, William W., ed. *History of the Ojibway People.* St. Paul: Minnesota Historical Society Press, 1984.

INDEX

Note: Figures are indicated by page numbers in *italics*.

ABOUT THE AUTHOR

Elizabeth Rule, PhD, is an enrolled citizen of the Chickasaw Nation and assistant professor of Critical Race, Gender, and Culture Studies at American University.

Rule's research on issues in her Native American community has been featured in the *Washington Post*, *Matter of Fact with Soledad O'Brien*, *Atlantic*, *Newsy*, and *NPR*. She has also released scholarly articles in *American Quarterly* and the *American Indian Culture and Research Journal*. Rule is additionally the founder of the Guide to Indigenous Lands Project, which builds mobile applications and digital maps featuring Indigenous sites on the city, state, tribal, and national levels. In 2019 she launched the Guide to Indigenous DC to highlight Indigenous influences in the nation's capital and has since developed a Guide to Indigenous Baltimore and a Guide to Indigenous Maryland, with others in progress.

Prior to joining American University, Rule served as the director of George Washington University's AT&T Center for Indigenous Politics and Policy, the District's only university-based research center dedicated to Indigenous issues.

Rule's work has received support from MIT Solve, the Ford Foundation, the Mellon Foundation, the Henry Luce Foundation, the Center for Black, Brown, and Queer Studies, and more. She has been recognized as an AT&T Women's History Month Honoree; was named among the National Center for American Indian Enterprise Development's "40 Under 40"; won the Julien Mezey Award for best dissertation from the Association for the Study of Law, Culture, and the Humanities in 2020; and received the Library Company of Philadelphia's Innovation Award. Rule received her MA and PhD in American Studies from Brown University and her BA from Yale University.